THE
PROMOTERS' CITY

BUILDING THE
INDUSTRIAL TOWN
OF MAISONNEUVE
1883-1918

PAUL-ANDRE LINTEAU
TRANSLATED BY
ROBERT CHODOS

T H E
PROMOTERS'
CITY

BUILDING THE
INDUSTRIAL TOWN
OF MAISONNEUVE
1883-1918

Originally published as *Maisonneuve, ou Comment des promoteurs fabriquent une ville, 1883-1918*

Copyright © 1981 Les Éditions du Boréal Express.

Translation copyright © 1985 by James Lorimer & Company, Publishers.

ISBN 0-88862-782-3 paper   0-88862-783-1 cloth

Cover Design: Dreadnaught
Maps: Assembly Dave Hunter
Illustrations are reproduced courtesy of:
Public Archives Canada (5, 9); Montreal Urban Community Transit Commission (51, 89, 95, 99, 101, 127, 132); Alain Laforest/Phyllis Lambert (57, 67, 83, 131, 148, 150, 152, 154, 159); Canadian Centre for Architecture/Alain Laforest (cover); *Le Devoir* (71); Gilles Rivest/Le Musée des Arts décoratifs de Montreal (160); Viau Biscuits (30); Montreal City Archives (161); Antonio Chaput; l'Atelier d'histoire Hochelaga-Maisonneuve.

Canadian Cataloguing in Publication Data

Linteau, Paul André, 1946-
   The promoters' city

Translation of: Maisonneuve ou Comment des promoteurs fabriquent une ville.
Includes index.
Bibliography

1. Maisonneuve (Montréal, Quebec) — History
2. Maisonneuve (Montréal, Quebec) — Industries
3. Urbanization — Quebec (Province) — Montréal — History.
4. Real estate development — Quebec (Province) — Montréal — History. I. Title.

FC2947.52.l5613   1985   971.4'28103   C85-098330-4
F1054.5.M8L56   1985

This translation, as well as the original book, has been published with the help of a grant from the Social Science Federation of Canada, using funds provided by the Social Sciences and Humanities Research Council of Canada.

The translation of this book was assisted by a grant from the Canada Council.

James Lorimer & Company, Publishers
Egerton Ryerson Memorial Building
35 Britain Street
Toronto, Ontario   M5A 1R7

CONTENTS

MAPS

To my parents

PREFACE

It was in 1968 that I discovered the existence of the old town of Maison-neuve. At the time, I was researching the period 1910-1929 in the Montreal newspaper *Le Devoir*, and I was struck by the advertisements and articles dealing with this Montreal suburb. The picture that emerged from this material was very different from the traditional one painted by Quebec's clerical-nationalist ideology.

There was a wide gap between the "agriculturalism" or "ruralism" of French Canada's official thinking and the reality of social and economic development in a Quebec that was rapidly becoming an urban society. While this gap had been pointed out by some writers, the reality itself remained poorly understood, and a number of questions had not been answered by historians. When, how and how fast did Quebec become urbanized and industrialized? What was the place of French Canadians in this process? Was there a basis in reality for the widespread impression that francophone businessmen were completely excluded from it? These questions led me to put aside my initial interest — the study of economic thought — to try to come to grips with the actual facts.

My goal was to understand the twofold process of industrialization and urbanization in Quebec in the early twentieth century. To do this, it seemed essential to look at the development of the Montreal region, which constituted the largest urban and industrial concentration in Quebec. Within this region, I tried to find a smaller, well-defined unit that could illustrate the wider process. The town of Maisonneuve, which grew from a small rural village into Montreal's leading industrial suburb in the space of thirty-five years, was particularly well suited to this project. The fact that the span of Maisonneuve's existence as a self-governing town completely encompassed the period of rapid economic growth which characterized the early part of the twentieth century made it even more interesting.

I decided, therefore, to devote my doctoral thesis to recounting the history of the town of Maisonneuve between 1883 and 1918. I was very fortunate because a large part of the town's archives, notably the minutes of the town council, assessment rolls and correspondence files, were preserved in the Archives of the City of Montreal. These archives were the main documentary source for my research.

This book contains the major results I presented in my thesis. My goal here is not only to describe the vicissitudes experienced by the town of Maisonneuve but also to use these events to understand a wider process. The kind of urbanization that Maisonneuve underwent was repeated — with some variation, of course — in many other Quebec towns. I especially wanted to understand how a town is "made," and to identify the actors who bring about the transformation of agricultural land into an urban area. Naturally, I focused my attention on the developers, or promoters, who are responsible for the creation of a town and who establish the broad outlines of its course. These developers represent a form of capital — land capital — that is very active in urban settings. Blithely melding their own private interests with the public interest, developers play a large role in organizing and planning space. This makes the case of Maisonneuve doubly interesting: the town's course was clearly determined by a handful of developers, of whom a majority were French Canadians.

Within the overall plan of these developers, two major stages can be identified. The first was the stage of development through industry: the developers hoped to urbanize the territory and induce large numbers of residents to settle there by attracting industrial enterprises. In the years before the First World War, however, they moved on to another stage: development through beautification. In this period, Maisonneuve was the scene of an ambitious beautification plan, involving the construction of public buildings, boulevards and parks. Implementation of this plan made it possible for the developers to put forward a new image of their town, which could now be presented not only as a major industrial centre but also as a well-planned town with a pleasant living environment.

Many people helped in the course of my research. The staffs of the Archives of the City of Montreal, the major Montreal libraries, and my department at the University of Quebec at Montreal were particularly helpful. I benefited from the stimulating comments offered by a number of colleagues with whom I discussed my research and results, especially René Durocher, Jean-Claude Robert and Normand Séguin. In addition, I received scholarships from the Canada Council and the University of Quebec at Montreal. I would like to offer my sincere thanks to all these people and institutions for their support. I would also like to thank the publisher of the original French edition Antoine Del Busso, the translator Robert Chodos and the editor of the English edition Ted Mumford for their valuable contribution in helping to revise the manuscript for publication. And finally, I would like to mention the part played by my parents, who allowed me to carry out my studies over a long period of time under favourable material conditions, in an atmosphere of complete respect for my intellectual autonomy and personal development.

Paul-André Linteau

PART I

THE CREATION OF A TOWN, 1883-1896

CHAPTER 1

THE BIRTH OF MAISONNEUVE

There was a smile on the face of Raymond Préfontaine, mayor of the small town of Hochelaga, Quebec, on the evening of November 23, 1883. The town's property owners had just voted unanimously to endorse his plan to have Hochelaga annexed to the neighbouring city of Montreal. For Préfontaine, annexation was the beginning of a new and brilliant political career. When he was no longer the town's mayor, he would represent the new Hochelaga Ward on Montreal city council, where he would find a larger arena for his ambitions. Within a short time, he would unquestionably be one of the leading figures in Montreal city politics, and his long career would culminate in his election as mayor of Montreal in 1898.

Joseph Barsalou, a businessman, and Alphonse Desjardins, his son-in-law and the federal member of Parliament for Hochelaga riding, had different reasons for being satisfied with the voters' decision on November 23, 1883. Barsalou and Desjardins were the leaders of a group of landowners with large holdings in the eastern part of Hochelaga. They had little interest in annexation, and their plan to have their lands turned into a separate municipality — what would become the town of Maisonneuve — had just been approved. For Barsalou and Desjardins, as for Préfontaine, this was the beginning of a new era.

The annexation of Hochelaga and the creation of Maisonneuve were the results of an intertwining of private and public interests that was typical of urban development in the Montreal region.

Montreal in the 1880s

In 1883 Montreal was the largest city in Canada and it was growing fast (Table 1-1). Its population had risen from 57,715 in 1851 to more than 140,000, not counting approximately 30,000 people who lived in its suburbs. By the time of the 1901 census, Montreal's population would be 267,730, or almost 325,000 if the suburbs were included. This population growth was a reflection of the substantial economic development that was taking place in Montreal, especially in the areas of communications and industrial production.

Montreal's geographical situation made it a mandatory transshipment point for river traffic. Although considerable work had to be done on the river — upstream, downstream and in Montreal harbour itself — to enable the city to benefit from its natural advantage, by 1883 these major projects were on the road to completion.[1] To facilitate water transportation to Montreal and the Great Lakes, a series of canals had been built in the 1810s and 1820s and enlarged in the 1840s and 1870s.

Meanwhile, the affairs of Montreal harbour had been taken in hand by the city's commercial bourgeoisie, on whose instigation the Harbour Commission had been formed in 1830. This was a largely autonomous body in which the Montreal Board of Trade and its affiliated organizations constituted the dominant force. The commission took charge of building facilities and managing operations in the harbour, and it pursued this task vigorously. In 1850, while constructing new facilities in the harbour, the commission also began work on a ship channel between Montreal and Quebec City to make Montreal accessible to ocean-going vessels. This channel was enlarged year

Table 1-1
**Population of Montreal,
1851-1901**

Year	City of Montreal	Montreal and Suburbs
1851	57,715	62,749
1861	90,323	100,723[1]
1871	107,225	126,314[1]
1881	140,247	170,745[1]
1891	216,650[1]	250,165[1]
1901	267,730[1]	324,880[1]

[1] Includes a larger area than the previous census.
Source: *Census of Canada*, 1851-1921.

This bird's-eye view of Montreal in 1889 gives us a good picture of the two areas in which industry was concentrated: along the Lachine Canal to the left, and in Sainte-Marie and Hochelaga to the right.

by year, and in 1888 it was 8.5 metres deep and 135 metres wide. By this time, Montreal had long since replaced Quebec City as the leading port in Canada in terms of value of goods unloaded. In the 1880s, the value of Montreal harbour's import traffic was generally between $40 and $50 million, while its export traffic varied between $25 and $30 million.[2]

In the second half of the nineteenth century, besides being the hub of Canada's river transport system, Montreal also became the pivot of its railway network. Three major lines met at Montreal. The first was the Grand Trunk, which began operations in the 1850s and stretched from Sarnia, Ontario, to Rivière-du-Loup, Quebec, with connections to Portland, Maine. The second line was the Quebec, Montreal, Ottawa and Occidental (QMO&O), completed in 1879, which ran from Quebec City to Ottawa along the north shore of the St. Lawrence and Ottawa rivers. The QMO&O, which contributed to the development of the east end of Montreal, became part of the Canadian Pacific Railway system between 1882 and 1884. The CPR, with its line stretching from Vancouver to Montreal — later extended to Saint John, New Brunswick — was the third major line.

Other important railway lines linked Montreal to large cities in the United States, especially Boston and New York. And the early twentieth century saw the arrival of another transcontinental, the Canadian Northern, which ran its rails across the east end of Montreal Island and gained access to downtown Montreal through a long tunnel under Mount Royal. It was not surprising that the large railway companies concentrated their activities in Montreal. The Grand Trunk established its maintenance shops in the city and was for a long time Montreal's largest employer. The presence of the Grand Trunk had an impact on the whole southwestern part of the city. Montreal also became the site of the Canadian Pacific's shops, as well as its head office and main terminus. The construction of the CPR's Angus Shops was largely responsible for the rapid growth of Hochelaga Ward in Montreal and the suburban municipalities of Rosemount and Maisonneuve in the early part of the twentieth century (see Map 1).

Montreal's fortunate situation as a communications centre was a powerful inducement to both commercial and manufacturing enterprises to locate there and helped the city achieve a dominant position as a metropolis for all of Canada. On Montreal Island itself, the location of the harbour and railway routes determined where industry would become concentrated.

Canada's industrial revolution really began in the 1850s, and Montreal quickly became the major centre of manufacturing production. The large wave of immigration that arrived between 1840 and 1855 substantially increased the size of Canada's domestic market and provided its embryonic industry with a cheap and plentiful — and often starving — labour force. Along with these general conditions, a technological factor also encouraged industrial growth in Montreal. The redevelopment of the Lachine Canal in the 1840s made available large quantities of hydraulic energy that could be used to operate industrial machinery. Starting in 1847, a number of factories were built along the banks of the canal and within a few years the southwestern part of Montreal had become the industrial heart of the city.[3]

The depression of 1873-1878 brought hard times to Montreal's manufacturers, but it was followed by a second stage of industrial investment. In addition to the slow but steady growth of the city's population and the expansion of the railway systems, there were two factors underlying this new stage — the protective tariff of 1879 and increasing specialization in Quebec agriculture. Specialization meant that rural Quebecers were more and more inclined to be consumers of manufactured goods, which the railway had made easily accessible.[4]

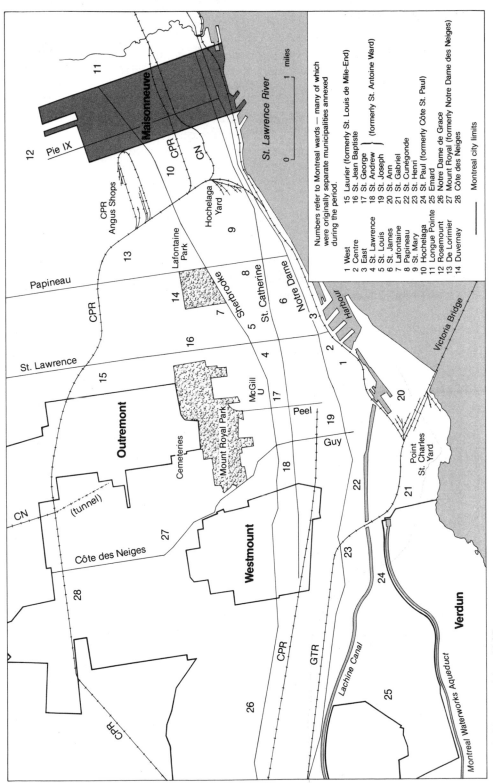

Numbers refer to Montreal wards — many of which
were originally separate municipalities annexed
during the period.

1 West
2 Centre
3 East
4 St. Lawrence
5 St. Louis
6 St. James
7 Lafontaine
8 Papineau
9 St. Mary
10 Hochelaga
11 Longue Pointe
12 Rosemount
13 De Lorimier
14 Duvernay
15 Laurier (formerly St. Louis de Mile-End)
16 St. Jean Baptiste
17 St. George
18 St. Andrew   (formerly St. Antoine Ward)
19 St. Joseph
20 St. Ann
21 St. Gabriel
22 St. Cunégonde
23 St. Henri
24 St. Paul (formerly Côte St. Paul)
25 Emard
26 Notre Dame de Grace
27 Mount Royal (formerly Notre Dame des Neiges)
28 Côte des Neiges

———— Montreal city limits

0   1 miles

Map 1: Montreal by 1915

The most conspicuous industrial groups in Montreal were the highly labour-intensive textile, clothing and shoe industries and the iron and steel industries. The first group, and especially the textile and clothing industries, really took off with the advent of the protective tariff. The textile mills were built primarily in the suburbs, southwestern Montreal and Hochelaga Ward; the clothing establishments were concentrated in Saint-Lawrence Ward; and the shoe factories were located in Saint-Antoine Ward in the west end and Sainte-Marie in the east (Map 1, page 7). Shoe manufacturing had been established in Montreal longer than the other industries and had dominated the city's industrial output until about 1871, but in the 1880s its relative importance was clearly on the wane. The iron and steel industries, meanwhile, were growing rapidly. A number of foundries and factories producing boilers, machines and assorted tools were in full operation, while the manufacturing of railway rolling stock was developing quickly and employed several thousand people in the late nineteenth century. Most of the iron and steel establishments were clustered along the Lachine Canal. Montreal's other significant industries at the time included tobacco and food. Sugar refineries and meat-curing establishments, for example, grew rapidly in the 1880s.[5]

The marketing of these products was facilitated by Montreal's location and a commercial structure that had existed well before industrialization. Nevertheless, the city's commercial activity was still closely linked to import-export business. The Canadian economy was directed towards the export of raw materials, and making Montreal a centre for this traffic had always been a goal of the city's bourgeoisie. This strategy was at the root of the efforts to develop the harbour and improve navigation. Most of the shipments from Montreal consisted of agricultural products.

Between 1850 and 1920, Montreal was a true metropolis with a dual zone of influence. On one level, it had a zone of influence immediately surrounding the city, to which it supplied a very wide variety of goods and services. This zone grew as transportation improved, thus its dimensions varied. However, it could be said to extend to the American border in the south, a little beyond the Richelieu River in the east and to the Laurentian Mountains in the north. Close relations were established between Montreal, on the one hand, and the regional subcentres and their rural regions, on the other. There were similar zones of influence around Quebec City, Trois-Rivières and Sherbrooke.[6] On another level, Montreal had a second zone of influence that included practically all of Canada, since Montreal was the nerve centre of Canada's banking and communications systems and of international trade.

As a result of all this economic activity, there was a heavy demand for manpower, which was met primarily by people moving into the area. In the 1840s and 1850s, massive immigration from the United Kingdom and espe-

View of Montreal from Mount Royal facing east, about 1880 or 1890.

cially from Ireland had swelled Montreal's population and changed its face. This transatlantic migration slowed after 1855 and, for the rest of the century, internal population shifts constituted the dominant migratory movement. One of these shifts was the flow of British immigrants to Montreal from where they had originally settled in the Quebec countryside.* But this movement was dwarfed by the huge exodus of rural French Canadians. Their numbers were too large for the available land, and many farmers' sons and daughters had to go elsewhere to find a job. There was a large migration of

*Canadian censuses of the time used the term "British" to refer to people of English, Scottish, Welsh and Irish origin. This usage has been followed here (translator).

rural French Canadians to the industrial towns of the United States — at least 150,000 Quebecers left in the 1880s. Surplus rural manpower was also available to fill the new industrial jobs that were created in Montreal.

Montreal's ethnic structure changed as well. For about forty years in the middle of the nineteenth century, Montreal had an English-speaking majority, but in the last third of the century the balance shifted heavily in favour of its French Canadian population. The dominance of the British was first recorded in 1831 and peaked in 1844, when 57 per cent of Montreal's population was of British origin. When Irish immigration slowed after 1850, the situation changed and the proportion of French Canadians began to grow. The 1871 census reported that French Canadians once again formed the city's majority.

Montreal's ethnic differences had a territorial dimension. The British were concentrated in the western part of the city, while the southwest, the east end and especially the new suburbs — such as Maisonneuve — were French-speaking.

At the time, there were clear social as well as ethnic distinctions. In the changed economic environment, a new working class was emerging in Montreal. It included labourers and former craftsmen but consisted primarily of new industrial workers who had come from the countryside. Working-class Montrealers lived and worked under very difficult conditions: working hours were long, wages were low, unemployment was common, housing conditions were unsanitary, and the death rate was high. Some groups of more highly skilled workers enjoyed better conditions and steadier employment, and the most fortunate of these workers were in a position to own newly built homes. Such workers were a minority, however, and the vast majority of working class Montrealers were tenants. Meanwhile, the Knights of Labor, a significant trade-union movement which had originated in the United States, became established in Montreal in the 1880s. A number of local assemblies of the Knights were founded. The trade-union movement contributed towards improving working conditions, but only a very small fraction of the working-class was unionized.[7]

At the opposite end of the scale, economic development in Montreal led to the growth and enrichment of the great railway and international trade tycoons and other members of the city's bourgeoise who accumulated large fortunes and built lavish homes on the slopes of Mount Royal. There were not very many of these big capitalists but they had substantial economic and political power, and their companies' operations extended from one end of Canada to the other. Their power was epitomized in the group of businessmen and financiers (George Stephen, Donald Smith and a few others) who ran the Bank of Montreal and the Canadian Pacific Railway. Another group of businessmen operated alongside this elite, but on a lower level and on a more regional scale. Their interests included real estate development as well as commerce, finance and industry, and a number of the developers who were active in Maisonneuve were part of this group.[8]

Montreal's class structure also showed up in the form of residential segregation. Starting in the mid-nineteenth century, the bourgeoisie had gradually left Old Montreal and settled in the opulent neighbourhood of Saint-Antoine, at the foot of Mount Royal. Working people tended to concentrate in such wards as Sainte-Anne along the Lachine Canal and Sainte-Marie in the east end. There were similar separations in suburban communities. A number of Montreal suburbs were working-class towns with a territorial division based on social class within the municipality.

The Extension of Montreal and the Annexation of Hochelaga

As Montreal's population increased, it was inevitable that its inhabited area would grow as well. The city limits had been fixed in 1792; included within them, in addition to the old walled city built under the French regime and its adjoining neighbourhoods, was a large agricultural area in which fruit growing predominated. Thus, Montreal had a lot of room to expand. Bit by bit, houses replaced the fields and orchards, and Montreal's agricultural area gradually became urbanized in the second half of the nineteenth century.

The city consisted of three districts, each of which was divided into three wards. The district of Montreal Centre, made up of West, Centre and East wards, was increasingly given over to business and administration. Sainte-Anne, Saint-Antoine and Saint-Lawrence wards constituted the district of Montreal West. Sainte-Anne was industrial and working-class while Saint-Antoine was a bourgeois ward; overall, Montreal West had an English-speaking majority. The district of Montreal East, on the other hand, was overwhelmingly French-speaking. It was divided into Saint-Louis, Saint-Jacques and Sainte-Marie wards; Sainte-Marie was increasingly becoming industrialized.

As soon as the territory of Montreal proper was occupied, the population spilled over into the suburbs. The move to the suburbs first became visible in the 1870s. It was a fairly complex phenomenon and overpopulation in the city core was not the only reason for it. The forces favouring suburban growth included land developers, who played an important role in planning urban space and determining its lines of development; businesses, which went to the suburbs to escape taxes and regulation; and utility companies, which had every reason to be happy with a proliferation of small administrative units.

At the time of Confederation, the area surrounding Montreal proper for the most part still consisted of large farms stretching back from the river front. The land was fertile and the farmers could market their products in the city. However, Montreal's dominance of the countryside could already be felt. Wealthy capitalists had purchased many of the most attractive sites, especially the ones right on the river. These lots were separated from the adjacent farmlands, and new houses for their urban owners were built on them. While this was the first manifestation of the city's hold over the countryside, there was also a second one whose impact was felt over a longer period. An examination of land registers of the time, and especially the first atlas of Montreal Island published by Hopkins in 1879, shows that a number of farms had been bought by businessmen.[9] These purchasers' goals had nothing to do with agriculture. Anticipating that the city would expand, they bought the land with the intention of subdividing it into urban lots. Since the time was not yet ripe, they leased the land temporarily to tenant farmers.

Within the zone where the city's dominance had begun to be felt, the first suburban municipalities were incorporated in the 1870s and 1880s. The city became ringed on three sides with small industrial towns that attracted a working-class population (Table 1-2).

Three substantial communities were founded in the southwest, along the banks of the Lachine Canal. Saint-Gabriel, Sainte-Cunégonde and Saint-Henri appeared for the first time in the 1881 census. They were already towns of a respectable size, with an aggregate population of almost 16,000; by 1901, this figure would grow to 48,063. In both years, more than 40 per cent of the total was accounted for by Saint-Henri, the largest of the three. The manufacturing sector was strong in these towns, and they represented an extension of the industrial function of the Lachine Canal waterfront beyond the city limits.

In the north, the town of Saint-Jean-Baptiste grew rapidly in the 1880s, from a population of 5,874 in 1881 to 15,423 in 1891. It was absorbed into Montreal in 1886. Finally, the suburb of Hochelaga grew up east of Montreal. Two large cotton mills and the Montreal streetcar company's shops were established in Hochelaga, and these industries stimulated the town's growth — from just over 1,000 in 1871, its population reached 4,111 in 1881 and 8,540 in 1891.

These suburbs developed chaotically in a context of competition among developers and rivalry among municipalities. And while there were many differences among the various communities, they shared one common feature: they were all offshoots of Montreal, economically integrated into the city and with no independent existence. Sooner or later, this economic reality would be reflected in the political sphere. Many political leaders of the time took it for granted that the suburbs would be joined with Montreal in a single political unit.

Similar scenarios were played out from one town to the next. Expenditures on infrastructure put the municipality into debt and, when it was no

Table 1-2
Population of Montreal Suburbs, 1851-1911

Suburb	Year Annexed to Montreal	1851	1861	1871	1881	1891	1901	1911
					Population			
Lachine		1,089	1,315	1,696	2,406	3,761	5,561	10,669
Côte-Saint-Paul	1910				142	475	241	3,421
Notre-Dame-de-Grâce	1910				1,524	2,305	2,225	5,217
Outremont					387	408	1,148	4,820
Côte-des-Neiges	1910			842	988	391	1,156	2,444
Ville Emard	1910				949	842	1,496	6,179
Verdun					278	296	1,898	11,629
Cartierville	1916							905
Bordeaux	1910						491	994
Ahuntsic	1910						366	928
Villeray	1905						509	1,164
Longue-Pointe	1910	1,014	1,055	1,011	1,114	2,445	2,519	5,531
Tétraultville	1910							1,087
Maisonneuve	1918					1,226	3,958	18,684
Hochelaga	1883			1,061	4,111	8,540	12,914	26,986
De Lorimier	1909						1,279	10,453
Petite-Côte (Rosemount)	1910						315	1,319
Saint-Jean-Baptiste	1886		2,269	4,408	5,874	15,423	26,754	21,116
Côte-Saint-Louis	1893	1,089	1,746	2,215	1,571	2,972		
Saint-Louis	1910				751	3,537	10,933	37,000
Saint-Gabriel	1887				4,506	9,986	15,959	18,961
Sainte-Cunégonde	1905				4,849	9,291	10,912	11,174
Saint-Henri	1905				6,415	13,413	21,192	30,335
Westmount	1905				884	3,076	8,856	14,579

Source: *Census of Canada*, various years.

longer able to borrow, its whole development was compromised. At this point, the town's leaders saw absorption into Montreal as a solution that would distribute the debt over a larger number of shoulders, provide the town with better services, and guarantee its continued growth. Annexationist sentiment on the part of Montreal's leaders was based on pride in the territorial growth of their city. The ethnic dimension was also a factor. Almost all the suburban municipalities had French-speaking majorities, and after 1867 the absorption of these communities helped consolidate French Canadians' majority status in Montreal. This was a significant consideration, at least in the early annexations.

It took a while for the annexation movement to gather speed. The first series of annexations, corresponding to the first stage in the growth of Montreal's suburbs, began with the absorption of Hochelaga in 1883, but twenty-one years later only three additional communities had been annexed — Saint-Jean-Baptiste in 1886, Saint-Gabriel in 1887 and Côte Saint-Louis in 1893 (see Map 5, page 110). There was nothing unusual in the way Montreal's territory evolved. In almost all large American cities at the time, the urbanized area was expanding and numerous suburban municipalities were being absorbed. Almost everywhere, municipal leaders wanted to strengthen the central city by annexing the politically autonomous communities surrounding it.[10]

Looking more closely at the case of Hochelaga, a large, still primarily agricultural area was organized into the village municipality of Hochelaga in 1870. At the time of the 1871 census, only 1,061 people lived in Hochelaga — 50 more than in the neighbouring municipality of Longue-Pointe. Ten years later, however, while Longue-Pointe's population had grown only to 1,114, Hochelaga's had reached 4,111, almost quadrupling the 1871 figure. Four large companies had recently begun operations in Hochelaga: the V. Hudon and the Sainte-Anne cotton mills, the W.C. Macdonald tobacco factory and a slaughterhouse.

Growth on this scale merited a change of status, and the village of Hochelaga became a town by an act approved on March 30, 1883.[11] Meanwhile, Hochelaga had new responsibilities and had to undertake large-scale projects — such as the construction of streets, sewers and watermains. In the summer of 1883, the mayor called a meeting of the town's property owners to discuss three options: an increase in real estate taxes, a loan, or annexation to Montreal.[12] Hochelaga Mayor Raymond Préfontaine and a majority of his council were in favour of annexation, in which they saw two advantages: Hochelaga residents would obtain more services and the required public works would be carried out by a wealthier and better-equipped government. They had little difficulty persuading the property owners.[13]

Bylaw 39, approved by the two municipal councils and the property owners of Hochelaga during the autumn of 1883, laid out the conditions of annexation. Hochelaga would become a ward of Montreal and would be represented on city council by three aldermen. The city of Montreal would install the watermains and build the sewer channels Hochelaga needed, assume Hochelaga's debt, induce the Montreal Street Railway Company to extend its lines to Hochelaga's eastern limits, and respect the tax exemptions Hochelaga had granted to six companies.[14] The ceremony officially marking the annexation was held on December 22, 1883.[15]

However, a portion of Hochelaga's territory in the easternmost part of the town was not included in this measure: instead it was separated from Hochelaga to form a new municipality. This new entity would become the town of Maisonneuve.

The Creation of the Town of Maisonneuve

The events that led to the creation of Maisonneuve began in 1882 when the plan to turn the village of Hochelaga into a town was under discussion. The act implementing this plan was adopted by the Quebec Legislative Assembly in its 1883 session. During this session, the Assembly was presented with a petition demanding the establishment of a separate municipality on a portion of Hochelaga's territory.[16] The town council was hostile to this initiative, but the act approved on March 30 provided that action would be taken on the petition if the new town of Hochelaga were annexed to Montreal.[17]

This compromise appears to have been the result of negotiations between the council and the supporters of separation. Subsequent newspaper accounts highlighted Joseph Barsalou's role in the affair. According to a 1905 article in *La Presse*, "when Hochelaga was absorbed in 1883, it was stipulated on the express demand of Mr. Joseph Barsalou that part of the old town of Hochelaga should subsequently be organized as a separate municipality."[18] A similar interpretation appeared in *La Patrie* a few years later:

> We owe a great deal to the spirit of initiative of Desjardins, Joseph Barsalou, James Morgan, Bennett, Bleau, Letourneux, Bourbonnière and Préfontaine, who had such high hopes for the future of their hamlet. Joseph Barsalou was the real father of the plan to incorporate this area as a town. With the help of the leaders mentioned above, he opened negotiations with the members of the provincial legislature, and in 1884 the whole eastern part of Hochelaga became a town under the name of the founder of Canada's largest city [Sieur de Maisonneuve].[19]

It is not known what considerations the backers of separation evoked in support of their cause, but their motives can be ascertained without too much difficulty. In Hochelaga development was taking place essentially in the western part of the town, in the area adjoining Montreal. Landowners in the east end of Hochelaga had to contribute to the costs of this growth without sharing in its immediate benefits. By establishing a separate municipality, they would be able to alleviate the tax burden while planning an appropriate form of development for their own lands.

The east-end landowners did not wait for the annexation ceremony to begin the process of creating the new town provided for in the legislation of March 1883. On December 12, they sent a petition to the Lieutenant-Governor in Council, asking that the town of Maisonneuve be established and elections held in January 1884. The petition was signed by twenty-eight people (nine of whom signed with an X). The list of signers was headed by Alphonse Desjardins and also included Bennett, Letourneux, Barsalou and Léveillé.[20]

The petition was accepted by the Quebec government and the proclamation officially creating the town of Maisonneuve was issued on December 27, 1883.[21] It established the town limits, gave the municipality the name "Town of Maisonneuve," and ordered that the election for the town's first mayor and councillors be held on January 31, 1884. The new town was to operate under the authority of the charter granted earlier to the town of Hochelaga.[22]

Maisonneuve was, of course, still a very small town, hardly more than a semi-rural village. The presence of some 50 families, comprising a total of 287 residents, was recorded in the 1884 assessment roll. It was a modest beginning, and its unassuming nature would make Maisonneuve's subsequent growth appear all the more spectacular.

The Town

Maisonneuve's development was influenced by its location and topography. Since Maisonneuve was a suburb of Montreal, it shared Montreal's advantages. The geographer Raoul Blanchard described Montreal's location as "particularly favourable; natural conditions are arranged to make it possible for a great city to be born and grow."[23] In particular, Blanchard singled out three elements of Montreal's situation. First, Montreal is near the confluence of a number of major rivers: "... the upper St. Lawrence, the Ottawa, the Richelieu, the lower St. Lawrence. There are surely few cities that can boast of a comparable concentration of mighty rivers."[24] Second, Montreal is the convergence point for a large number of land routes. Blanchard described this circumstance as "an effect of the relief system" and said that it increased the "opportunities for communication."[25] Finally, Montreal is surrounded by a large plain with especially rich soil.

The site of Maisonneuve had once been known as Côte Saint-Martin and was part of the territory organized into the village of Hochelaga in 1870. The 1883 proclamation establishing the town of Maisonneuve described the town limits.

All that extent of land, of irregular outline, situated and being in the county of Hochelaga, district of Montreal; bounded in front, to the south east, by the river Saint Lawrence, in rear, to the north west, by the limits of the municipality of the village of the Côte Visitation, as determined by proclamation dated the twenty fifth October, one thousand eight hundred and seventy, erecting the said municipality; on one side, to the south west, by the limits of the city of Montreal, or rather, by the line which divides lots numbers 18 and 22 and numbers 20 and 21, of the cadaster [land register] of the village of Hochelaga, and on another side to the west, by the parish of Longue Pointe. Such extent of territory measuring twenty five arpents in length by an average depth of fifty five arpents, and contains in area one thousand three hundred and seventy five arpents, the whole more or less.*[26]

Maisonneuve was almost rectangular in shape and occupied an area of 468 hectares. It stretched to the St. Lawrence in the south, while its western boundary was the back end of the lots fronting on the west side of Bourbonnière Street. The back end of the lots fronting on the east side of what is now Viau Street (known as 1st Avenue during the period) formed its eastern boundary. Maisonneuve's northern boundary was somewhat more jagged: in the eastern part of the town, Maisonneuve reached Côte de la Visitation Road (Rosemount Boulevard), while in the west it stretched only to where Saint-Joseph Boulevard runs now.[27] (See Map 2, which shows the town in 1916.)

Maisonneuve's most significant location advantage was clearly its frontage on the St. Lawrence, which gave it outstanding potential as a port. The development of Maisonneuve's waterfront was delayed by the fact that it was quite far from the main part of Montreal harbour, but Maisonneuve's advantage would be strengthened by the eastward extension of Montreal's harbour facilities. The distance of five or six kilometres between Maisonneuve and downtown Montreal was a slight handicap, which would be overcome by the advent of the electric streetcar in 1892.

The topography of the area is fairly simple. Two terraces extend from the

---

*The arpent is the old French Canadian unit of both length and area. The linear arpent is equal to 58 metres or 192 feet, while the square arpent is equal to about one-third of a hectare or five-sixths of an acre (translator).

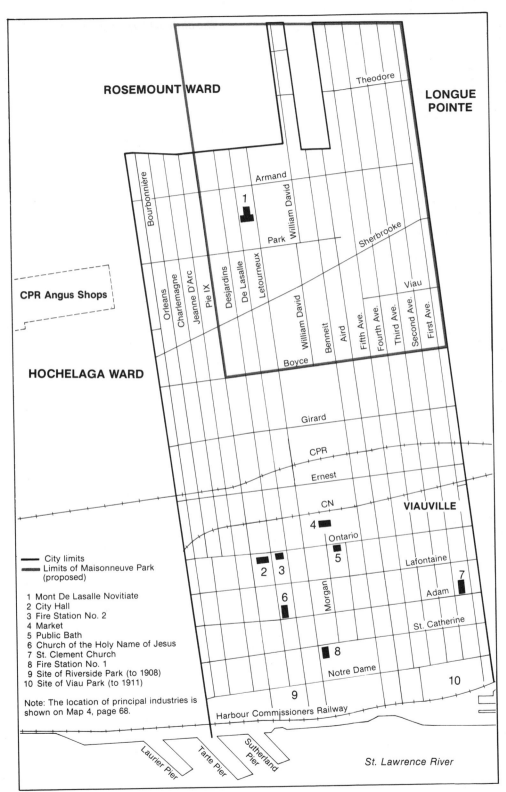

Map 2: Maisonneuve, ca. 1916

ROSEMOUNT WARD

LONGUE POINTE

Theodore

Bourbonnière

Armand

1

Park

William David

Sherbrooke

CPR Angus Shops

Orleans
Charlemagne
Jeanne D'Arc
Pie IX
Desjardins
De Lasalle
Letourneux

Viau

HOCHELAGA WARD

William David

Bennett
Aird
Fifth Ave.
Fourth Ave.
Third Ave.
Second Ave.
First Ave.

Boyce

Girard

CPR

Ernest

CN

VIAUVILLE

4

Ontario

5

Lafontaine

— City limits
Limits of Maisonneuve Park
(proposed)

2 3

7

Adam

1 Mont De Lasalle Novitiate
2 City Hall
3 Fire Station No. 2
4 Market
5 Public Bath
6 Church of the Holy Name of Jesus
7 St. Clement Church
8 Fire Station No. 1
9 Site of Riverside Park (to 1908)
10 Site of Viau Park (to 1911)

Morgan

6

St. Catherine

8

Notre Dame

10

9

Harbour Commissioners Railway

Note: The location of principal industries is
shown on Map 4, page 68.

Laurier Pier

Tarte Pier

Sutherland Pier

St. Lawrence River

eastern slope of Mount Royal to the eastern edge of Montreal Island, and the presence of these terraces is Maisonneuve's most significant topographical characteristic.[28] The lower terrace rises slowly from the St. Lawrence. Then there is a fairly steep incline — as much as fifteen metres along Pie-IX Boulevard between Pierre-de-Coubertin Street (formerly Boyce Street) and Sherbrooke Street. Sherbrooke Street runs along the southern edge of the upper terrace, straying from the grid on which all of Maisonneuve's other streets are laid out. All of Maisonneuve north of Sherbrooke Street is covered by the upper terrace, at an altitude of between forty-two and forty-six metres. These topographical features may have influenced Maisonneuve's development. The lower terrace was more easily accessible and was settled first. Although Maisonneuve's land developers tried to attract people to the upper terrace, these efforts met with little success during the period.

The most significant waterway within Maisonneuve was Migeon Creek, which ran westward across the town between Sainte-Catherine and Adam streets, and continued into Hochelaga as far as Nicolet Street, where there was a ninety-degree bend from which the creek ran down into the St. Lawrence. In 1890 the creek still flowed under open sky and was bridged by Pie-IX Boulevard, Desjardins Street and La Salle Street. Migeon Creek would later be turned into a canal, but during the period it does not appear to have either left its mark on Maisonneuve's development or influenced the lines of settlement in any way.

The site of the new town of Maisonneuve was a very attractive one but, if the town was to be developed, the site had to be structured and organized and plans had to be put into effect. In this enterprise, one group would play a key role: the large landowners who had been behind the creation of the town.

CHAPTER 2

THE DEVELOPERS

The organization of space is a basic feature of urban development and, in Quebec, primary responsibility for this spatial organization has always been left to the private sector, more specifically to large landowners. At least in the case of Maisonneuve these landowners played a determining role — a role which can be understood only by viewing it in a wider historical context.

Land Capital and Urbanization

While the entrepreneur is the dominant actor in the history of industrial corporations, a comparable figure in the history of cities is the urban developer. The developer is an entrepreneur of spatial organization, and plays a special role in capitalist economies. One writer, taking his inspiration from Marxist ideas, has suggested the following hypothesis:

> It is reasonable to think that just as there is such a thing as commercial capital or finance capital, there is a particular kind of capital whose sole function is to organize space so as to make commercial, financial and administrative activities more efficient. If it can be argued that the time and labour that capital as a whole invests in transportation makes space an important factor, then it is logical to suppose that there is a specialized form of capital whose primary role is to organize space in order to reduce the false costs of capitalist production.[1]

This specialized form of capital will be called "land capital." Its relationship with other sectors of capital is multidimensional — complementary as well as competitive. Capitalists in the land sector look out for their own interests first. They try to maximize the surplus value of land, and this affects the profits of other sectors.

Another writer, Alain Lipietz, draws a distinction between capitalists and landowners, whom he sees as two opposing groups. The legal ownership right that landowners enjoy is a legacy of the feudal mode of production. They are prepared to yield this right to capitalists in exchange for a form of land rent which Lipietz calls urban land tribute (*tribut foncier urbain*) to distinguish it from farm rent. This tribute, exacted by the landowners on the basis of their legal ownership right, is ultimately paid by the tenants, thus increasing the cost of reproduction of the labour force. Lipietz concludes: "The city is disputed territory in the primary contradiction in which the working class confronts the bourgeoisie, but it is also disputed territory in the secondary contradiction in which capitalists confront landowners and different segments of the bourgeoisie confront one another."[2]

Thus, land capital is integrated with other sectors of capital, dependent on them and, at the same time, in competition with them. The land capital sector itself does not present a unified picture, and there are rivalries among individual proprietors.

A number of categories of land ownership can be identified, and the way in which land ownership typically evolves is summarized in the following figure. Land is developed from farmland into intensively used urban land in four stages, although in actual cases some of the stages are so intertwined that it is difficult to distinguish them.[3]

During the first stage, the land is held by the original owner or his heirs, and either it is made suitable for urban use if it is a fairly large piece of farmland or, in the well-known process of urban renewal, it has already been divided into lots, urbanized and built up. Developers acquire the land, seeking to use it again as urban land, but in a new way. In the creation of a new town such as Maisonneuve, the first version of the scenario is played out.

The Evolution of Urban Land Ownership and Development

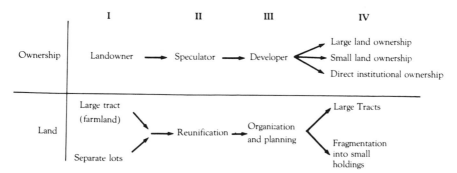

Thus, at the beginning, the landowner is a farmer himself or he allows his property to be used as farmland. He may well have acquired his ownership right by inheritance; in Quebec, the transfer of land ownership by inheritance is a significant factor which may help explain why French Canadians have played such a large role in the land sector.[4] If he is a farmer, the landowner lacks both information and capital and, with rare exceptions, has little power to transform his holding into urban land. Most landowners are content to collect the share of the land tribute they receive when they give up their ownership rights to others.

In the second stage, the speculator enters the scene. Jacques Lautman has defined the speculator as a person who can "see early on how the ways in which a particular area is used and the presence or absence of certain kinds of buildings in that area are becoming inadequate or irrational in the economic and spatial context."[5]

The speculator gambles on an eventual increase in the value of a piece of land. He buys the land at the best possible price and waits — often for several years — without making any further investment in the land beyond the purchase price (or part of the purchase price). If he has guessed right, he will later sell the land at a higher price and pocket the surplus value created in the interim in the form of profit. He is purely an intermediary who does not develop the land in any way; his profit is the result of astuteness in predicting how the land will eventually be used. He does, however, bring about one change in the organization of space: he unifies land, either by acquiring adjoining properties or by concentrating the decision-making power over a group of holdings in the hands of one owner.

After the speculator, a much more significant and dynamic actor enters the scene. He is the urban developer, land capital's central figure. Unlike the pure speculator, who stands by waiting for the value of the land to increase, the urban developer presides as headmaster over the work of transforming the land to increase its value. "Development capital" (*capital promotionnel*) is the term Lipietz uses to describe the business of the developer.[6] While the first two stages are essentially passive, this third is land capital's active phase.

The developer's work consists of developing a site. A basic factor in this process is accessibility, which is sometimes naturally available but which most often has to be created. Thus, transportation plays a crucial role: the developer needs railways, streetcars and roads for his plans to succeed. Moving a route a few kilometres or even a few blocks can make the difference between prosperity and stagnation. In these circumstances, it is not surprising that there should be close links between developers and public transporation companies.

Another aspect of development is the creation of appropriate surroundings. If the developer's plans for the site includes a wealthy residential neighbourhood, he will concentrate on the natural beauty of the area and leave room for parks, spacious avenues and the like. On the other hand, if he wants to develop a working-class neighbourhood, he will try to attract industries to the area. Creating the appropriate surroundings adds value to the land, which the developer can convert into cash in the form of land tribute.

The developer owns a large tract of land which he can organize as he wishes. He may divide it into lots of varying sizes. He may give away land to be used for building streets, churches and other amenities. These gifts are profitable investments since they make the rest of his land more accessible and attractive.

In theory, authority over the organization of space is in the hands of the municipal council, and the support of the council is important to the developer. In practice, however, municipalities in Quebec have exercised their powers in this area in a fairly relaxed fashion and have rarely done more than ratify plans drawn up by private enterprise. The developer makes sure that his interests are well represented on the council, either by becoming a member himself or by finding a councillor who will act as his loyal supporter.

But if the developer's power is primary, it is not absolute. The developer draws up plans, but these plans must take into account constraints imposed by the environment. A development is not created in the abstract, and the developer cannot succeed on his own. According to Maurice Halbwachs, "After studying the matter in depth, we came to the conclusion that the people responsible for building new roads, although they were authoritarian and may have wanted to leave their own personal stamp on the project, had to bend to the evident social needs of the city, and their actions influenced only the modalities and details of the work, but did not change or stop the play of collective forces."[7]

Halbwachs was writing about the Paris region, and it may be that the situation is very different in a country where settlement is more recent. In Quebec, developers' actions have gone beyond mere details. Collective forces, of course, exist in Quebec as well, and land development in each area has been affected by such things as the kind of economic development existing there; the rate of population growth; people's housing preferences; the price people can pay for housing, which is a function of their incomes; the major ways in which neighbouring lands are used; the area's distance from downtown; and the natural features of the environment. It must not be forgotten, however, that some of these collective forces are largely determined by the general development of capitalism, and that land capital participates in this development. In addition, a variety of forms of spatial organization are possible in the context of urban growth, and developers are left with considerable room to manoeuvre as they compete with one another.

Development and the construction of buildings are two distinct activities, although they are often related. In some cases, the construction of buildings on the developer's land is carried out by the developer himself. He will then add a profit on the sale or rental of these buildings to the land tribute. In other cases, the developer leaves the task of building to the buyer of the land parcel. Many developers follow both these strategies.

The fourth stage is the final use of the land. Here three kinds of ownership can be identified. The first is the ownership of either a large tract of land or of a number of small holdings concentrated in the hands of a single owner. In both cases ownership involves real estate development capital, which is used to organize and manage built-up space. The second kind is small residential ownership, the result of the developer's subdividing his land. The third is direct ownership by large institutions, with the final use of the land being either public (government buildings, schools, hospitals) or private (factories, railways). In this case, the developer sometimes does not even enter the scene.

In broad terms, these four stages describe the development of land ownership and organization in the urban context. In practice, these stages are often telescoped. Thus, the speculator in his pure form may not appear: in this case, the landowner and the developer share the profits from speculation. And the developer may be involved during the fourth stage as well in the business of real estate development capital. The scenario can also vary from era to era. In the last twenty years, concentration has become more pronounced in the land sector. Large real estate development companies have tended to incorporate a number of these stages, and trust companies own or administer an impressive quantity of lands and buildings. But historically, and especially in the early twentieth century, the role of each actor in the process appears to have been more clearly defined.

There are a number of other observations that are relevant to this discussion. First, it is important to distinguish between effective use and ownership. The individual who acts as the developer is not always the legal owner of the land that he develops. The owner may be his wife or another member of his family. He may act as administrator of an estate, or be the manager of a joint-stock company whose majority shareholders give him a free hand. Another consideration is the wider question of how these operations are financed at each stage. The money capital required has to be borrowed, and in the process ownership rights are mortgaged—and potentially jeopardized. The aim of the various actors who enter the picture as financiers may be to gain control of these operations.

Despite these limitations, the position of the developer is an enviable one. He makes land capital profitable and speeds up the creation of surplus value. Thus, instead of being used to describe the role of all the actors involved in the process, the term "land capital" can also be used to describe the role of the developer alone.

Finally, there is the question of the relationship between the land sector and other sectors of capital. Clearly, there is such a thing as wealth based strictly on land, accumulated from generation to generation in this sector alone. The general rule, however, is that land is gradually acquired by fortunes that have been built up in other sectors. In Montreal, by the first half of the nineteenth century, the leading merchants were already large landowners. And in the decades before the First World War, land capital did not hesitate to go into partnership with industrial or banking capital.

Maisonneuve is one example of how land capitalism operated.

Large Landowners and Developers in Maisonneuve

In Maisonneuve, some large landowners — such as the Desjardins, Letourneux and Viau families — became very dynamic developers. Others — the Bourbonnières, Bennetts and Morgans — preferred to leave development activity to specialists, but they did not play an entirely passive role. The first generation of these landowners-developers was present at the creation of Maisonneuve and did the real work of making the town a going concern. The second came on the scene a few years before the First World War, when the pace of Maisonneuve's growth was quickening, and completed the work begun by the first generation.

The names of the first generation can be found by looking at Maisonneuve's first assessment roll, drawn up in 1884. Members of the Bourbonnière family — Toussaint and Jules but chiefly the widow Olivier — held lots 18 (with 110 arpents under cultivation), 19 and 20, assessed at a total of $26,300 (see Map 3). The group led by Alphonse Desjardins held some subdivisions in lot 12 and most of lot 14, assessed at $20,025. Lina Cuvillier owned lot 11; with brick structures and greenhouse, the assessment was $11,000. The Letourneux family, and principally merchants Jean-Théophile and Charles-Henri Letourneux, owned almost all of lot 8, assessed at $27,455. The merchant James Morgan had lot 7 (73 arpents under cultivation), assessed at $12,750. The property owned by the Jesuits (lot 6, with house and out-buildings) was assessed at $10,000, as was auctioneer Joseph Barsalou's holding (lot 5, with similar facilities). Farmer William Bennett held lots 3 and 4 (164 arpents under cultivation) and part of lot 10; his property assessment was $13,600. Finally, the highest assessment — $30,900 — was reserved for the property belonging to the Bruyère estate, consisting of lots 1, 1a and 2.

In all, the town's landed property was assessed at $225,225, so that these holdings, with assessment totalling $162,030, represented 72 per cent of the overall assessed value of landed property in Maisonneuve. (The figures recorded in the assessment roll are given here only as indications; the assessed value of property was much less than its real market value, especially since large holdings that had not been subdivided were assessed as land under cultivation and not as urban lots.)

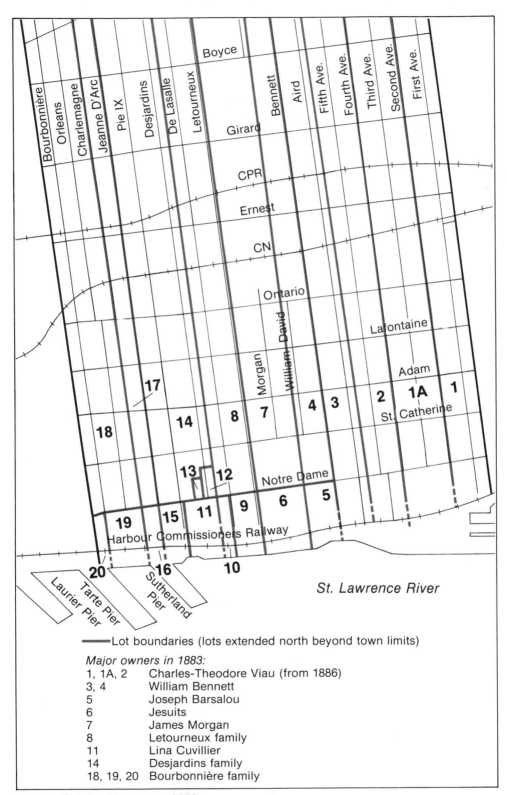

Map 3: Original Lots, ca. 1883

Boyce
Girard
CPR
Ernest
CN
Ontario
Lafontaine
Adam
St. Catherine
Notre Dame
Harbour Commissioners Railway
St. Lawrence River

Bourbonnière
Orleans
Charlemagne
Jeanne D'Arc
Pie IX
Desjardins
De Lasalle
Letourneux
Bennett
Aird
Fifth Ave.
Fourth Ave.
Third Ave.
Second Ave.
First Ave.
Morgan
William David

Laurier Pier
Tarte Pier
Sutherland Pier

17
18
14
8
7
4
3
2
1A
1
13
12
19
15
11
9
6
5
20
16
10

Lot boundaries (lots extended north beyond town limits)

Major owners in 1883:

1, 1A, 2	Charles-Theodore Viau (from 1886)
3, 4	William Bennett
5	Joseph Barsalou
6	Jesuits
7	James Morgan
8	Letourneux family
11	Lina Cuvillier
14	Desjardins family
18, 19, 20	Bourbonnière family

That the guiding spirit of this group of landowners was Joseph Barsalou was confirmed by his election as the town's first mayor in 1884. However, Barsalou dropped out of the picture in 1892 and his activities were restricted to the initial stage of the municipality's development.

Alphonse Desjardins was a more significant figure. He gained his reputation primarily in politics, although he was also a lawyer, journalist and businessman. He was born in Terrebonne, northwest of Montreal, on May 6, 1841, and died on June 4, 1912. After studying in Terrebonne and Nicolet, he became a lawyer in 1862 and practised law in Montreal for a few years before turning to journalism. He was one of the most conspicuous members of the ultramontane* group in Montreal: he was the publisher of its newspaper, *Le Nouveau Monde*, and one of the authors of its Catholic Program in 1871. Desjardins represented Hochelaga constituency in the House of Commons from 1878 until he was appointed to the Senate in 1892. After serving as a minister in the cabinets of Mackenzie Bowell and Charles Tupper, he resigned from the Senate to run for a seat in the House in the 1896 election; his defeat brought his long career in federal politics to an end. He was also active in municipal politics, and was mayor of Montreal from 1893 to 1894. At the end of his life, he was a director of the Citizens' Association, a group favouring reform of city government.

Alphonse Desjardins was also an important figure in the business world, although this career did not bring him the same prominence as his political activities. He was a good example of a type of man very common in the nineteenth century: the lawyer-businessman with his finger in a number of pies. Starting in 1874, he invested in urban development in the area that would become Maisonneuve. As an industrialist, he started a tile-making enterprise, the Montreal Terra Cotta Lumber Company, in 1887. He was also very active in the financial sector: and from 1880 to 1899 he was president of the Banque Jacques-Cartier, a bank owned by French Canadians. According to the list of shareholders published by the federal government, in 1899 — the year the Banque Jacques-Cartier closed — Alphonse Desjardins held 1,944 shares (valued at $48,600) on his own account and another 1,850 ($46,250) in trust, making him the bank's largest shareholder and giving him control over 19 per cent of its share capital. During his career, Desjardins was also president of the Crédit Foncier du Bas-Canada, vice-president of the Canada Accident Assurance Company, vice-president of the board of trustees of the Guardian Insurance Company, and a director of the Crédit Foncier Franco-Canadien, the Comptoir Mobilier du Canada and the Société d'Administration Générale. In 1899 he was elected president of the Chambre de Com-

---

*The ultramontanes were a group of conservative Catholics who favoured organizing society according to Catholic principles and giving control of its main institutions to the church.

Alphonse Desjardins: politician, financier, industrialist, and one of
Maisonneuve's leading developers.

merce du District de Montréal, indicating that he was held in fairly high
esteem by French-speaking businessmen.

As a capitalist in land, industrial and financial sectors and as a link
between business and politics, Alphonse Desjardins is an interesting example of a member of the middle bourgeoisie. In his development activities in
Maisonneuve, he was ably assisted by his son Hubert, who managed the tile
factory and served as councillor and mayor in Maisonneuve. In addition,
Alphonse Desjardins's son-in-law, L.-J.-S. Morin, was the town's counsel for
a number of years. Alphonse Desjardins was married twice, first to Virginie
Paré, the daughter of a rich Montreal merchant, and the second time to
Hortense Barsalou, the daughter of Joseph Barsalou.[8]

After Desjardins, clearly the most interesting developer was Charles-
Théodore Viau. Viau had not yet entered the picture in 1884, but in 1886

he acquired large land holdings from the Bruyère estate. Originally from the South Shore community of Longueuil, Viau was an industrialist before he was a land developer. In 1867 he founded Viau & Viger, a company specializing in the manufacture of biscuits, candy and flour (the name was changed to Viau et Frère in 1873). It quickly became one of the largest companies in the industry, and in 1894 had annual sales of $300,000. Viau was a member of the Montreal Board of Trade. Towards the end of the century, he initiated a vast development project on his Maisonneuve lands, but he died in 1898 before it was completed. The Viau estate took charge of both the manufacturing company and the Maisonneuve development. Charles-Théodore's brother-in-law, Jean-Baptiste Deguise, assumed the leadership of the Viau enterprises, with the assistance of the founder's three sons.[9]

Little is known about the Letourneux family. They were merchants who were among the first families to succeed in the development industry, and they donated large tracts of land to a religious community, the Christian Brothers.

Julie and Emilie Bourbonnière inherited a huge tract of land, lot 18, and in 1896 they sold the entire northern part of the lot, as far south as Sainte-Catherine Street.[10] The buyer was Isaïe Préfontaine, brother of the illustrious Raymond Préfontaine, mayor of Hochelaga until its annexation and then a Montreal city councillor, mayor of Montreal and finally a minister in the cabinet of Sir Wilfrid Laurier. Isaïe left politics to his brother and concentrated on business. *La Presse* wrote of him in 1910:

> Since he arrived in Montreal in 1888, he has always had substantial land interests and is currently one of the largest landowners on Montreal Island . . . . He is also president of Dominion Gold Fields of Canada, a company whose great value has recently been acknowledged; the company's board of directors is made up of presidents and directors of other powerful companies, and people who own shares in it can consider themselves fortunate. Mr. Préfontaine is also involved in a number of other public companies. The activity and energy he brings to these great enterprises make this excellent businessman one of the pillars of the French Canadian race.[11]

Isaïe Préfontaine was president of the Chambre de Commerce du District de Montréal in 1908-1909 and the Fédération des Chambres de Commerce de la Province de Québec in 1909-1910. He was president of Montreal's French-language business school, the Ecole des Hautes Etudes Commerciales, and was appointed to the board of the Ecole Technique de Montréal in 1911. He was also an elected director of the Montreal Citizens' Association in 1909.[12]

William Bennett was a farmer who tried to sell lots in the southern part

The Viauville area of Maisonneuve was named after the industrialist and developer Charles-Théodore Viau.

of his large holding. He sat on the Maisonneuve town council for a number of years, and his son Percy was also a town councillor. William Bennett died in June 1905.

Finally, James Morgan was president of the Montreal department store Henry Morgan and Co. Ltd. (now the Montreal outlet of the Hudson's Bay Company) and of the Colonial Real Estate Company. He was one of the promoters of the British Canadian Bank Note Company in 1904 and the Montreal Cement Company in 1915. He was very active in the Montreal Citizens' Association, and became its treasurer.[13] He was less interested in development than any of Maisonneuve's other large landowners, and his holding was the last to be subdivided. In 1914 he was appointed vice-president of the Maisonneuve Park Commission, but three years later the town council concluded that the commission's work was being completely paralysed by Morgan's continued absence from its sessions.[14]

These large landowners constituted Maisonneuve's first generation. The most active developers were Desjardins, Viau and Letourneux, and later Préfontaine. After the turn of the century, the second generation would breathe new life into the town's development and help speed up its pace.

The Developers' Operations: The General Framework

Maisonneuve's large landholdings were developed within the framework of a plan of organization and settlement, which was worked out and gradually implemented over the thirty-five-year lifetime of the town. In pursuing their goals, developers had the help of a political instrument, the Maisonneuve town council. Either by being directly represented on the town council or by maintaining good relations with council members, developers were able to bring the council to adopt policies favourable to its interests.

Control of the town council was important because it held substantial powers in certain areas of competence. Municipalities were creatures of the provincial government, which defined these areas of competence through municipal legislation.

When Maisonneuve was founded, municipal institutions were relatively new in Quebec. Montreal and Quebec City had been granted charters in 1833, but except for these special cases it was only under the Union regime (1841-1867) that municipal legislation took shape. Acts adopted in 1840, 1845, 1847, 1854 and 1860 gradually fleshed out an administrative system which was given its final form by the Municipal Code of 1870 and the Cities and Towns Act of 1876. With minor modifications, this system lasted for more than a century.[15]

It was necessary to have works of a local nature administered and paid for at the local level, and establishing municipalities was one way of accomplishing this. In the mid-nineteenth century, local works consisted primarily of road construction and maintenance. Very quickly, however, new responsibilities were added, especially in the most heavily populated areas: police, fire protection, public health, local regulation. In the late nineteenth and early twentieth centuries, a town such as Maisonneuve had a variety of powers, some of which directly affected land capital.[16]

The municipality was legally responsible for organizing the territory under its jurisdiction: it drew up a town plan, decided where streets would go and built them, laid out parks, provided water distribution and sewer systems. The municipality could expropriate the land it needed for these projects. It had the authority to organize the built-up area of the town, regulate construction, outlaw the use of particular materials or the building of particular kinds of factories, enact zoning bylaws, and the like. It was also responsible for a number of utilities, among them water, power, street lighting and public transportation. In addition, it had a variety of responsibilities related to the protection of the town's citizens: police and fire departments, public health, pollution control, and regulation of the sale and quality of such items as food and building materials.

To carry out these tasks, a municipality needed its own spending and financing powers. The first major revenue source was property tax, which could be either an ordinary tax, used to meet the municipality's general administrative expenses, or a special tax, earmarked for particular projects, such as sewer construction. The second was business tax, levied on individuals or groups doing business in the town. Finally, the municipality could borrow money. Loans were used to finance large projects, and they were repaid out of money raised through special taxes. Loans had to be approved by a majority of the town's property owners, on the basis of both number and total property value, and by the provincial government. In practice, this provision gave the municipality's property owners veto power over the organization of its territory. As we will see further on, municipalities also used tax policy as their main instrument for granting benefits to companies that opened factories in the area under their jurisdiction.

As the creatures of a higher authority (the provincial government), municipalities enjoyed only limited autonomy. But within this context of subordination, they had significant responsibilities in the area of local management. There was, of course, a gap between the legal situation and reality, and the fact that a particular power was attributed to a municipality did not automatically mean that it would be exercised. Especially in their early years, municipalities tended to rely on private enterprise. Often, the only role played by a municipality in organizing the territory under its jurisdiction was the ratification of plans drawn up by developers. As a town grew, however, the municipal government's actions became more forthright and direct, at least in certain areas. In the utility field, for example, municipalities had to intervene very early on, and when they decided to entrust these services to private enterprise, they did so through contracts that laid out its conditions of operation. Obviously, it was in the interests of developers to control municipal institutions, and especially the town council, which exercised the powers vested in the municipality.

Maisonneuve's town council was composed of a mayor and six councillors. At first, councillors sat on an at-large basis, but from 1898 on the town was divided into three wards, each represented by two councillors. Councillors served staggered two-year terms, with half the council (one councillor from each ward) facing re-election each year. Starting in 1909, however, the entire council was elected every two years. Only property owners were eligible to sit on the council. The mayor had to own real property worth at least $2,000 "over and above any charges or mortgages encumbering the said property"; the minimum for councillors was $1,000. Voters had to own real property worth at least $100 or be tenants or occupants of a building with a rental value of at least $20.

Hubert Desjardins, son of the developer Alphonse Desjardins, was the manager of the family's tile factory and mayor of Maisonneuve from 1894 to 1896 and 1897 to 1901.

Sitting on town council was the most effective way of influencing it. Joseph Barsalou was mayor from 1884 to 1889 and again from 1890 to 1892, while in 1889-1890 the office was occupied by Joseph Bourbonnière. Hubert Desjardins was mayor from 1894 to 1896 and 1897 to 1901, and then sat as a councillor between 1902 and 1904. Alexandre Michaud was a councillor from 1905 to 1909 and mayor from 1909 to 1915. And William Bennett was a councillor from 1885 to 1894, as was his son Percy from 1903 to 1905 and 1909 to 1911. Thus, between 1884 and 1915, there were only two years in which no large landowners sat on the town council. The names of councillors who were dependent (financially or otherwise) on the large landowners or associated with them should probably be added to this list, but it is difficult to identify these councillors. Occasionally, conflict arose between one or another of the large landowners and the council but, on the whole, relations between the two groups were excellent.

Land capital could make its influence felt in another way as well. All bylaws passed by the council had to be ratified by a majority of the town's property owners, calculated both according to the number of individual property owners and according to the value of the real estate they owned. This system was weighted in favour of the largest landowners. In addition, the property owners defined their relationship with the municipality in a series of agreements, modelled on the agreement signed between Charles-Théodore Viau and the municipality in 1892.

The general framework for all these agreements was the same. Two issues were involved: street construction and the assessment of large land holdings. To ensure the success of development projects, new streets or sections of streets had to be built quickly when the lots facing on them were sold. Normally, the town would have to buy the land needed for the streets, but it was in the interests of the landowner to speed up the process by donating the land. This gift, along with the tax concessions the landowner obtained in return, was the subject of his agreement with the town.

According to the agreement, the land was given free to the town, but ownership remained with the landowner until the streets were opened to traffic. Either party could require the opening on three months' notice. The town was responsible for grading and constructing the street, while the landowner took care of fences and sidewalks. The street would be paved and water and sewer pipes laid only when the town considered it appropriate. In exchange, assessment of the landowner's property was fixed for fifteen years. During this period, the property would be taxed as lands under cultivation except for lots already taxed by the square foot. If a lot was sold or granted, the new owner would not benefit from the tax break but, if the landowner sold all or a large part of his property, the concession would continue to apply. Later, these agreements would be confirmed by the town's charter. Even when the fifteen-year period provided for in the agreements ran out, large landowners did not face an undue tax burden, since an amendment to the charter adopted in 1909 stipulated that the tax on lands under cultivation and uncleared lands could not exceed three-eights of 1 per cent.[17]

Thus, the assessment of Charles-Théodore Viau's lands was fixed at $73,050 for fifteen years in 1892. For Julie and Emilie Bourbonnière, the assessment was established at $26,074 in 1894. The next year, the assessment of James Morgan's property was fixed at $14,219. In 1899 William Bennett reached an agreement with the town fixing his assessment at $7,950.[18] The group headed by Alphonse Desjardins had granted land for streets free of charge in 1884, and the assessment of its property was later placed on the same basis as that of the other large landowners.[19] The Letourneux family, on the other hand, sold the land for streets on its property for $2,000 in 1889.[20]

These agreements created some of the conditions for profitable development of the land. They guaranteed that taxes would remain low, that streets would be built as the lands were settled, and that the town would carry out at least a minimum level of investment. These conditions were not sufficient in themselves to ensure that the land would be developed quickly, but in conjunction with other measures they proved very effective.

One of the development instruments favoured in Maisonneuve was an industrial policy aimed at attracting companies to the town, a policy that had obvious benefits for landowners. A company entering Maisonneuve would have to buy a large tract of land; even more important, however, was that when a company came to town so would a large number of workers to whom lots could be sold or houses rented. Thus, Maisonneuve's industrial policy contributed substantially to the growth of surplus value in the land sector, and it could only be put into effect if the town council adopted the goals of the land capitalists. It is noteworthy that the town began to implement the policy when Hubert Desjardins became mayor of Maisonneuve.

On the whole, public investment helped land capital attain its goals. Although establishing an effective, well-equipped fire department was an expensive proposition for the town, it led to lower insurance rates and made building houses more attractive. The development of pleasant surroundings — boulevards, parks, public buildings — contributed towards rising land prices and rents, and the prospect of being served by high-quality utilities attracted residents. However, public investment was a double-edged sword. In the short run, it helped the town grow but, in the long run, it was a heavy burden to bear. Thus, the capitalist had to develop or sell his land fairly quickly so that this burden would fall onto other shoulders.

There were also other factors that could help the developer get rich. One of these was the town's religious infrastructure, which like other collective facilities was part of the development plan. The developers looked on churches as investments contributing towards their overall profit. Interestingly, the two most active developers, Alphonse Desjardins and Charles-Théodore Viau, contributed the most towards the construction of Maisonneuve's two parish churches. A revealing indication of the place of religion in the developers' plans appeared in *La Patrie* in 1909:

> The erection of all of Maisonneuve as a mission in 1888 contributed greatly to the town's subsequent growth. Secular development and religious development go together in Quebec, and when Maisonneuve became a town, its residents asked the diocesan authorities for their own church. The Bishop of Montreal granted their request and gave them an

administrator, and a temporary chapel was built. It was thanks to the generosity of Hon. Desjardins, the former cabinet minister, that Très-Saint-Nom-de-Jésus parish in Maisonneuve obtained the land for its church. From that time on, the population of Maisonneuve began to grow.[21]

The connection could not be stated more clearly. In the same way, Saint-Clément parish was created at Viau's instigation; like Desjardins, Viau donated the land.[22] Of course, the developers' religious convictions have to be taken into account, especially in the light of Desjardins's identification with the ultramontane group. In addition, philanthropy was a highly respected activity among rich capitalists of all religious persuasions in the late nineteenth century. Though it cannot be said that the landowners' donations were motivated purely by mercantile considerations, this gesture was undoubtedly closely related to the ambitious development plans that Desjardins and Viau had worked out.

It should be noted that we are dealing here not with spontaneous, isolated decisions but with development plans—a coherent, inexorable course based on the far-sighted logic of land capital. However, the developers' will was not the only factor in play, and the course they had set out could be changed by a number of external influences. They had to take geographical factors into account; in this area Maisonneuve, with its river frontage and its proximity to railways, was in a very fortunate position. The economic context of the Montreal region also had to be reckoned with. The economic situation was not always favourable, and the developers chomped at the bit during the first decade of Maisonneuve's existence. They would be amply rewarded, however: the lean years were followed by a period of the most vigorous economic growth that Canada had yet experienced, and their town grew along with the country. Starting in 1913, the economic tide ebbed again, and the Montreal real estate market collapsed. By this time, however, the developers had cashed in their chips: they had developed a town, pocketed the profits, and left a large debt to the thousands of workers who now lived in Maisonneuve.

Maisonneuve's industrialists had no interest in challenging this system since they benefited from the town's generous tax exemption policy. Thus, there was an alliance between industrial capital and land capital. Most closely identified with the landowners were those industrialists who not only established their factories in Maisonneuve but also came to live there. A number of manufacturers acquired houses on Pie-IX Boulevard. They became involved in real estate operations and formed a local bourgeoisie along with the large landowners. This alliance between industrial capital and land capital was epitomized in the team of Alexandre Michaud and Oscar Dufresne, which dominated the town government between 1909 and 1915. However, not all industrialists were active participants in this power-sharing scheme. The people who ran giant corporations such as St. Law-rence Sugar or Canadian Vickers did not become involved in town affairs in any way. The closest links with the developers were forged by shoe-factory owners.

In general, therefore, the town's development was directed and stimu-lated by businessmen. In this regard, Maisonneuve is not in any sense an exceptional case, for the same situation prevailed in varying degrees in all North American urban centres. A number of studies by American writers have demonstrated this fact for cities in the United States. Closer to home, Ronald Rudin, in his comparative study of Sherbrooke, Saint-Hyacinthe, Sorel and Trois-Rivières, attributes differences in their growth rates to dif-ferent levels of dynamism in their business communities.[23] In the history of Winnipeg and other western Canadian cities, Alan F.J. Artibise has spot-lighted the determining role of "boosters" — businessmen pursuing at any price a policy of urban growth, a phenomenon he calls "boosterism."[24]

While the developers as a group stood for the broad interests of land cap-ital, they did not form a permanent united front. Each developer also pur-sued his own individual interests. On occasion, a developer might feel that the town council's actions were unfair. When the council borrowed money to carry out capital improvements, each developer wanted a large portion of the money spent on his land. Therefore, the allocation of resources some-times led to bitter struggles and resentments among developers.

In 1899 the Viau estate wanted to make its holding into a separate munic-ipality because it thought the town council was not paying enough atten-tion to the development of the eastern part of Maisonneuve.[25] In 1906, it was Isaïe Préfontaine's turn to threaten to secede. This time it was the west-ern part of Maisonneuve that was involved, and Préfontaine proposed that it be annexed to Montreal because works that had been promised in the area had not been carried out. Préfontaine's complaints to the council are a good illustration of the tension between the particular interests of one developer and the general interests of land capital. He was

> . . . prepared to say that the Préfontaine farm, bordering on Montreal and the Canadian Pacific shops, has received far from its fair share of work in the past. He has already had occasion to note to the council that a sum of $29,326.97 was spent on lot no. 18 of the Hochelaga land register (the Préfontaine farm), while on the basis of the assessment of the property, $119,533 should have been spent to place this property on the same foot-ing as other lots from the point of view of the expenditure of money that has already been borrowed for improvements.[26]

Of course, the large landowners were not the only residents of Maison-neuve. As the town developed, a growing number of small property owners and tenants settled in Maisonneuve, and their interests were not the same as those of the large landowners. Thus, the controversy over the streetcar contract in 1904 and 1905 was, according to *La Presse*, a struggle between large and small property owners.[27]

Land Development

Because it is difficult to establish land values, the profitability of real estate operations is very hard to measure. The municipality, of course, assigns an assessed value to each piece of land on the basis of its location, the size and use of its buildings, and other factors. The assessed value, however, is an arbitrary measure that at best can serve as an indication of the land's real value. It is generally acknowledged that a lot's assessed value is less than its market value. However, market value is a very vague concept. The price of a lot is determined by certain conditions prevailing at the time of sale — conditions that do not necessarily apply to neighbouring lots. Halbwachs has pointed out the difficulty of evaluating the price of land at a specific time.[28]

We are faced with the question of how to compare transactions taking place at the same time but involving two different lots, or transactions involving the same lot but taking place at different times. Sales can be considered as indications of the state of the real estate market at a particular time but the price paid for a lot does not establish the value of lots that are not sold. Besides, changes in the real estate market over time are irregular and discontinuous. Prices in an area may rise quickly and substantially as a result of the opening of a traffic artery, expropriations, or a new development, but once having risen, prices may remain at their new level for several years.[29]

Thus, the profitability of real estate operations can only be determined on the basis of actual sales. To establish the income of the large landowners in the case we are studying, it would be necessary to trace all the transactions involving a large number of lots. Terms of payment and financing would have to be taken into account, as would interest rates, which varied substantially over the long period. Then, the developer's expenses would have to be subtracted — the cost of buying the property and financing the purchase, real estate taxes, closing costs and other investment and development expenses. In the following case study, a few transactions have been singled out to provide a rough overall description of what was at stake. The exact figures are less important here than the general picture of the phenomenon.

Assembling the Desjardins property was a fairly complicated process involving a large number of transactions between 1874 and 1890.[30] The land was called the Domaine Mathieu, after Major Etienne Mathieu of Lachenaie, a village on the mainland near the eastern tip of Montreal Island. Major Mathieu acquired the land in 1863 from his son-in-law, Jean-Baptiste Decary, whose family had owned it for several decades. When Mathieu died in 1872, the land passed to his daughter and Decary's wife, Josephte Rachel. At that time, the Domaine Mathieu consisted of lots 14 and 15 and a few subdivisions of lot 12, and extended from the St. Lawrence to the northern limits of Maisonneuve. It covered a narrow strip on each side of where Pie-IX Boulevard now runs, from the site of Jeanne-d'Arc Street in the west to just east of Desjardins Street (see Map 3, page 26). In 1874 Josephte Rachel Decary sold the whole property to a group of businessmen led by Senator F.-X. Anselme Trudel. The group included Alphonse Desjardins, by now an M.P.; Emmanuel Persillier-Lachapelle, a doctor; L.-J. Arthur Surveyer, a merchant; Henri Girard, a landowner; Trefflé Marsan, a court clerk; and Narcisse Paquette. These men were ultramontane Conservatives, but their goals in buying the land were not inspired by the glorification of rural life which was an important part of ultramontane ideology. According to the partnership agreement signed a few weeks later, "they bought this land with the aim of subdividing it and reselling it in lots or parcels as they find most advantageous."[31] The sale price was $125,000 — $20,000 cash, $5,000 due on May 1, 1876, and $100,000 to be paid within fifteen years at 7 per cent interest. This $100,000 balance would never be paid: it disappeared in the course of subsequent transactions. Some time later, Narcisse Paquette sold his share to a new partner, Pierre-Olivier Trudel, and Henri Girard sold his to the partners as a group, who in turn sold it to Pierre-Olivier Trudel.

Partly because of a world-wide depression which began in 1873, the partners had a difficult time paying Madame Decary. They had hoped to finance the operation through the sale of lands, but the depression dealt a severe blow to the real estate market. Thanks to his in-laws, Alphonse Desjardins was in a better position than the other partners. He turned his 20 per cent share in the partnership over to his wife Virginie Paré and her sister Zaïde. In these transactions, the sisters were represented by their husbands; Zaïde Paré's husband was none other than Alphonse Desjardins's brother Edouard. Because the other partners had not paid, Madame Decary decided to take back her lands. She said, however, that she wanted the partners to remain involved, using their experience to sell lots. Her statement confirms that land development was the aim of the enterprise from the beginning. Thus, in 1877 Madame Decary repossessed three-fifths of the Domaine Mathieu, with the Paré-Desjardins sisters continuing to hold one-fifth, while the other partners as a group held the remaining one-fifth.

In 1878 Pierre-Olivier Trudel withdrew from the partnership and received subdivisions of lot 12 in return for his share. The same year, Madame Decary turned a one-fifth share over to her partners; in exchange she became owner of most of lot 15. As a result of these transactions, the Domaine Mathieu now consisted of lot 14, a huge tract of land. Virginie Paré-Desjardins died in 1879 and her share passed to her four children; as minors they were represented by their father Alphonse Desjardins. In 1880 F.-X. Anselme Trudel, Lachapelle and Surveyer sold their shares in the partnership to Alphonse Desjardins, as trustee for his children, and Zaïde Paré-Desjardins. Thus, when Maisonneuve was created in 1883, the Desjardins group owned a majority interest (60 per cent) in the Domaine Mathieu.

On June 7, 1887, Alphonse Desjardins bought for himself part of lot 15 from Madame Decary for $12,372. This land was bounded by Pie-IX Boulevard in the east, Sainte-Marie Street (the present-day Notre-Dame Street) in the north, Jeanne-d'Arc Street in the west and the St. Lawrence in the south. Desjardins sold it on September 24 of the same year for $20,000 to the St. Lawrence Sugar Refining Company. He also bought all of what remained of the Domaine Mathieu — in other words, lot 14 — in 1890 for $70,000. Madame Decary received $21,000 of this sum and made her exit from the story of the Domaine Mathieu. The $70,000 price was considerably lower than the $125,000 she had been able to obtain for the land in 1874. In the interim, the land had been partly dismembered and some lots had been sold. Nevertheless, it can be concluded that the value of the land did not rise significantly between 1874 and 1890 and may even have fallen.

A few days after he bought the land in 1890, Alphonse Desjardins resold to his sister-in-law Zaïde Paré-Desjardins the two-fifths share she had previously owned. He also sold three-fortieths of the land to his son Joseph, and set aside equal shares for his other children (who were still minors). Ownership of the Domaine Mathieu now took the form of a family business, managed by Alphonse Desjardins, who owned only a two-fifths share. The property remained undivided until 1896, when the division of lots south of Sherbrooke Street among the four children began. This division was completed in 1899 for the three youngest children. The land north of Sherbrooke Street was still undivided.

Lot 14 extended from Notre-Dame Street to the northern limits of Maisonneuve. It included the east side of Jeanne-d'Arc Street and both sides of Pie-IX Boulevard and Desjardins Street. (Like Desjardins, each of the other large landowners had a street in Maisonneuve named after him.) A subdivision of building lots had been drawn up for the first group of developers; Desjardins had this subdivision revised in 1896. As a result, lot 14 was divided into parcels numbered from 1 to 1,197; in fact, since many of these parcels were further subdivided (in which case the number was followed by a letter), there were probably as many as 1,400 building lots.

A number of manufacturing establishments were built on the Desjardins property. First, there was the developer's own factory, the Montreal Terra Cotta Lumber Company, which was built on the northern part of his lot (see Map 4, page 68). There was also the sugar refinery involved in Desjardins's 1887 land deal. These were the first two large enterprises in Maisonneuve and, for a long time, they were the only ones. For $9,000, Desjardins also sold the land needed for the construction of the Watson, Foster and Co. wallpaper plant. The other factories on the Desjardins land were Dufresne

& Locke (shoes), Acme Can Works, National Licorice, Gilmour Bros. (confectioners), Bell Telephone and a wooden door and box factory.[32] In addition, a number of lots were devoted to uses that were neither industrial nor residential, including Maisonneuve's town hall; fire station no. 2; the Très-Saint-Nom-de-Jésus Church; the classical college; the convent; the Sisters of Providence hospice; and the St. Cyrian Church (see Map 2, page 18).

However, most of the lots were intended for residential construction. In some cases, houses were built by the developer himself. Thus, in a letter to the town council in 1887, Desjardins informed the councillors that he had built eight houses in which eight families were living and asked that they be provided with a suitable water supply.[33] It appears, however, that these cases were exceptions, and Maisonneuve's developers were interested primarily in selling lots and leaving the responsibility for construction to the buyers.

The prices at which lots were sold varied widely, generally ranging between $200 and $600. Napoléon Goyette, for example, purchased a lot in 1885 for $400.[34] In 1896 Desjardins sold five lots on Sainte-Catherine Street and two on Desjardins Street to a businessman, Alphonse Valiquette, for $2,000 (an average of $285 per lot).[35] Three years later, Alexandre Prévost, an broker, bought a 9-by-32-metre lot for $600.[36] Lots were also sometimes sold in a block to other developers. In 1902 Desjardins sold 189 lots to John Stuart Buchan and Antoine Avila Sénécal for $25,000, or an average of $132.28. Desjardins agreed to a lower average price in this case because of the large number of lots involved in the sale.[37] In 1907 a real estate agent advertised that he had numerous lots to sell on the Desjardins land at prices ranging from $240 to $560.[38]

More substantial profits were made by selling land to the municipality. In 1905 the town paid $9,656 for three lots for the fire station at the corner of Desjardins and Ontario streets purchased from Alphonse Desjardins's daughter Auréa Morin. Even higher prices were paid for lands purchased as part of the Maisonneuve Park project. Hubert Desjardins acquired fourteen lots from his father for $5,200 in 1909, and sold them to the town in 1913 along with their buildings for $29,775. In 1913 Alphonse Desjardins's estate sold 156 lots on the Domaine Mathieu to the town for $195,816. In June and July 1915, various members of the Desjardins family sold a cluster of lands to Joseph Rhéaume for $818,064. Rhéaume subsequently sold these lands to the town for a much higher price, along with others he had acquired elsewhere. On sales related to Maisonneuve Park alone, the Desjardins family received more than $1 million for portions of a piece of land for which Alphonse Desjardins had paid $70,000 twenty-five years earlier. This manna did not fall in equal measure on all members of the family. Of the $818,064 obtained in the operations of July 1915, $568,573 — 69.5 per cent of the total — went to Auréa Desjardins Morin and her husband L.-J.-S. Morin, legal counsel for the city of Maisonneuve.[40]

Even without the enormous surplus value obtained through the Maisonneuve Park lands, the Desjardins family's land development operations appear to have been very profitable. When the real estate market collapsed in 1913-1914, most of the lots in the southern part of the Desjardins property, between the St. Lawrence and the railway, had been sold and buildings constructed on them.

The other interesting case study is the Viau property. As an industrialist running his own company (Viau et Frère), Charles-Théodore Viau enjoyed a fairly substantial income, ranging between $25,000 and $50,000 a year.[41] In 1886 he bought a large property consisting of lots 1, 1a and 2, in the extreme east end of Maisonneuve, from two brothers, R.-F.-A. and J.-E.-A. Bruyère (see Map 3, page 26). The sale price was $60,000, of which $15,000 was payable on May 1, 1887, with the balance due in ten years at 5 per cent interest.[42] Viau also owned a property of comparable size in Longue-Pointe (lots 1 through 8), bordering on his Maisonneuve lands, and here he established his residence. His original goal in buying these lands appears to have been vertical integration of his biscuit enterprise.[43]

At the time, the Viau property was located in a sparsely populated area, and any plans for urban development of the area would probably have been premature. However, with the arrival of the streetcar in 1892, the eastern part of Maisonneuve was brought more firmly within the orbit of Montreal, and the possibility of selling building lots emerged. This probably explained why a contract was signed that same year between Viau and the Maisonneuve town council providing for street construction and the maintenance of taxes at a predetermined level. Nevertheless, Viau did not become actively involved in land development until 1897-1898.

His first move that year was to get the council to extend all the streets, from Notre-Dame Street as far north as Ontario Street, to his land. They were built between October 1897 and September 1898.[44] Next, Viau got the bishop to erect a new parish, Saint-Clément. He was extraordinarily generous, donating more than 9,000 square metres of land for the church and schools. For the construction of the church, he gave $5,000 outright and agreed to loan another $5,000, interest-free for ten years and at 1 to 4 per cent interest thereafter. He also agreed to provide a residence for the curé for five years and pay him an income of $800 a year; this amount would be progressively reduced as the number of parishioners increased.[45]

Viau, and his estate after his death, also undertook a form of planned development of the portion of his property located in Maisonneuve. The strip of land between the St. Lawrence and Notre-Dame Street was made into a park. An early form of zoning was imposed on residents through the sales contracts they signed. As *La Presse* reported in 1899, "In order to make the buildings as uniform as possible and establish a character of cleanliness, orderliness and extraordinary comfort, sales contracts require that houses be built ten feet from the sidewalk, two storeys in height, and with freestone facades."[46]

Developers tried to sell their lands by attracting residents to Maisonneuve. This advertisement for land in Viauville asks the reader, "Are you thinking about tomorrow?," promises him a 100 per cent return on his investment, and trumpets, "Viauville is the future!"

Viau's dream was the creation of a new municipality, Viauville. When he died in 1898, the project was taken up by the administrators of his estate, who presented a petition to the Legislative Assembly in January 1899. They asked that a new municipality be formed out of parts of Maisonneuve and Longue-Pointe, consisting of 700 arpents (230 hectares) in all, of which 660 arpents belonged to the Viau estate. In its petition, the Viau estate argued that 140 lots had already been sold and agreements — "lease with promise to sell" — had been signed for another 161 lots. It pointed to the establishment of the parish and maintained that the town of Maisonneuve had not lived up to its obligations to complete street work on the Viau property.[47]

The town council reacted vigorously, hiring two lawyers and circulating petitions asking the taxpayers to resist the separation plan.[48] The two parties held a meeting in Quebec City, and the Viau group revealed two other motives for its initiative: "Mr. Viau believed that the authorities of the town of Maisonneuve were ill disposed towards him" and "he saw that the town could not carry out improvements with its annual revenue." The representatives of the town council maintained that the council had been acting in good faith and declared that the works that were required on the Viau property would be carried out progressively as the need arose. The council also agreed to name the eastern part of Maisonneuve after Viau. After this meeting, the Viau estate agreed to withdraw its bill.[49]

Thus, the Viau property was developed as part of the town of Maison-neuve.[50] However, it retained its own character along with its own name, Viauville. Its numbered streets (1st through 5th avenues), its more homo-geneous architecture and its residential nature, all made it different from the industrial area of the town. In addition, Viauville was separated from the main part of Maisonneuve by the Bennett and Morgan farms and remained somewhat isolated until these farms were subdivided a number of years later.

The Viau development was a success. Goad's 1914 atlas shows houses closely arrayed almost everywhere on the streets of the Viau property south of Lafontaine Street. Between Lafontaine Street and the railway, there were still a substantial number of vacant lots, but quite a few buildings had been built. The area north of the railway, however, was still almost completely empty.[51]

The Viau estate succeeded in preserving the residential character of the area until 1906. In that year the Viau biscuit and candy factory in Montreal was expropriated to make way for a new Canadian Pacific Railway line, and the company moved its facilities to a new location in Maisonneuve, on 1st Avenue north of Ontario Street. A few years later two other companies, Oxford Motor Car & Foundry Ltd. and L'Air Liquide, built factories near the Viau plant. But, despite these industrial installations, Viauville remained essentially residential.

At about this time, the Viau estate appears to have all but abandoned its land development activities and passed the torch to a new generation of developers. Thus, on August 11, 1909, it sold 1,207 lots in the northern part of the property to J.-L. Clément & Cie for $350,000. These lots were sub-sequently resold to the Viauville Land Company, which tried to develop the area by offering lots for sale at $550 and up.[52] Finally, the company sold its lots to the town in 1911 as part of the Maisonneuve Park project.

Thus, the developers' involvement has to be seen as a long-term venture. The creation of a separate municipality in 1883 was only a first step, pro-viding them with a legal and political framework favourable to the devel-opment of their lands. The area covered by the municipality, however, was still poorly organized. It still had to be given a structure, institutions had to be set up, and policies had to be worked out.

CHAPTER 3

ORGANIZING THE TOWN

The first twelve years of Maisonneuve's existence were less hectic than the years that followed, but they were no less important. The town's population grew slowly and a large part of Maisonneuve was still uninhabited. The face of Maisonneuve was changing in a very subtle way. It was developing from a simple village into a town and laying the groundwork for rapid growth. During this period, town services were established and an urban development policy was worked out.

Town Government

During its first dozen years, Maisonneuve had four mayors and twenty-six councillors. There was a high turnover rate among the councillors: fourteen served a single term or less — in eleven cases, a councillor resigned or had his seat declared vacant before his term was over. Some councillors lost their seats when they moved out of the town.[1]

One of the council's first tasks was to pass bylaws to regulate various aspects of town life. During the first year, fifteen were adopted. Public hygiene bylaws regulated public enclosures and stray animals; the maintenance of pigs and waste heaps; water; horses; and public health. The other bylaws addressed bathing hours; licences for the sale of alcohol; the construction of buildings; sidewalk maintenance; house numbers and street names; and the planting of trees.

In this era, municipalities employed only a few public servants. The key person in a small municipality was the secretary-treasurer. Maisonnueve's first secretary-treasurer was the notary Adolphe Lecours. Appointed in Feb-

ruary 1886, he resigned after two months and was succeeded by the lawyer
J.-J. Beauchamp, who held the position until 1889. The council also hired
a number of employees in lower positions but at this level there were frequent firings. It is impossible to tell from the sources whether this high turnover was due to the employees' incompetence or a system of favouritism.

The conduct of Maisonneuve's police department was not particularly
professional during the early years. The police chief was the council's fac-
totum: town hall watchman, public works supervisor, building inspector, etc.
There were three police chiefs between 1884 and 1889 and complaints were
lodged against each of them. The last chief was fired in 1889 for "use of
drink" and insubordination.[2] The town advertised in the newspapers for a
replacement and recruited Thomas O'Farrell, who remained police chief
until 1903.[3] In 1891 the police department was reorganized. The council also
established a fire department in 1889; with this improvement in fire protection, the council asked the association of fire insurers for a reduction in
Maisonneuve's insurance premiums.[4]

Questions relating to road and sewer works occupy a considerable portion
of the minutes and other documents in the town archives. Road construction and maintenance is undoubtedly the oldest municipal responsibility in
Quebec.[5] In the early nineteenth century, each landowner was responsible
for maintaining the section of road bordering on his land (in Maisonneuve's
early years, this responsibility extended to sidewalk maintenance). The system did not ensure uniform quality, and people began to see that co-ordi-
nation of road works by local authorities was a necessity. But even when road
works came under the control of local authorities, the actual work was still
done by the residents under a system of statute labour. The quality of work
remained highly variable, and it became obvious that workers hired for the
job could do it more effectively, with the residents paying the cost through
a local improvement tax rather than in unpaid labour.

Aiming to provide for Maisonneuve's development and rapid population
growth, the council extended the town's network of streets and sewers as
soon as new houses were built. In its first fifteen years, almost all of Maisonneuve's street and sewer work was carried out within the quadilateral
bounded by Letourneux, Ontario and Bourbonnière streets and the St. Lawrence.

Utilities and Monopolies

Municipalities were also responsible for organizing local community services. In rural and semi-rural communities these services were limited, consisting only of providing a watermain and lighting the main street. The
situation was different in urban centres, where higher population densities

made the development of water, lighting, gas and transportation services both possible and necessary.

Development of these services was closely tied to the expansion of the urban fabric. In some cases, services were established a short time before urbanization and actually encouraged urban growth. In general, these services required substantial investment which made it necessary to resort to long-term financing. The town government would incur a considerable debt, betting that the town and its residents would be wealthy enough in the future to repay it. Establishing utilities and providing a satisfactory level of service were an important aspect of urban development, and a municipality could fulfill these responsibilities either by spending money to provide an infrastructure and operating utilities itself or by entrusting these responsibilities to private enterprise.

Municipalities already bore the costs of local government and police and fire departments. They built streets and sewers and were responsible for public buildings and parks. The question of whether they should be responsible for other services as well was a subject of widespread debate in all North American cities and towns in the second half of the nineteenth century and the early years of the twentieth. The answer varied from municipality to municipality. In many cases, the water distribution system came under municipal control but private enterprise was put in charge of transportation and lighting.[6] The Montreal metropolitan area was, in general, heavily dependent on private enterprise for water, gas, electricity and public transportation services. Westmount, which operated its own electricity service, was an exceptional case. In Maisonneuve, after a brief experiment in municipal operation of water and electricity services, private enterprise was put in charge across the board.

From the point of view of the entrepreneur, utilities differ significantly from other industries because entry into the utility sector is not open to all. The agreement of the municipality or higher authorities is necessary, and this condition limits the number of companies that can serve a given area. In addition, the very nature of utilities imposes a geographical division of labour. People would not be pleased to see competition in the form of three or four streetcar companies laying their tracks side by side on the same street. Rather than simply accepting these inherent limitations, entrepreneurs invested heavily to enter the utility sector of the economy and sought to maximize their return by obtaining a monopoly. Their instrument was the franchise, or exclusive operation agreement.

The franchise system was common to all major North American urban centres, but the actual content of franchise agreements varied widely. A franchise agreement was a contract between the municipality and the operating company, which gave the company the right to operate a given utility and, in most cases, specifying whether this right applied to a particular street, a neighbourhood, or the municipality as a whole. The contract also outlined the company's obligations, the rates it could charge, the services it had to provide, the advantages it had to accord the municipality, and the duration of the contract.[7]

In the nineteenth century, municipalities entered into these agreements without too much controversy but, with the rise of urban reform movements after the turn of the century, a strong opposition to utility franchises emerged. In some cases, the opposition demanded municipal ownership of utilities. More often, it pressed for much tighter control of the operations of private companies. The good and bad points of the franchise system were extensively discussed. Opponents of municipal ownership raised the spectre of tax increases. Because of the carelessness that marked some government services, people feared that any form of public ownership would result in lower quality service. On the other hand, the primary goal of the companies was not the welfare of the population but paying dividends to their stockholders. Because of their monopoly position, companies could provide poor service and still charge high rates. The companies' need for municipal council support to obtain, keep or change a franchise agreement invited corruption of elected officials. These problems became even more serious when, in the utility sector as in other industries, corporate concentration led to the formation of powerful trusts, which made scandalous profits, attained a high degree of control over municipal politics, and became increasingly difficult to dislodge.[8]

Though there are studies of the history of these monopolies in a number of North American cities, very few examine the situation in Quebec. It is worth looking at this situation in some detail, and the story of utility monopolies in Maisonneuve can be considered as a case study of a phenomenon that occurred in many places in Quebec.

Water Supply

Water supply was one of the earliest concerns of Maisonneuve's civic leaders. As the town grew, it needed an adequate supply of water and a quality of service comparable to Montreal's, and this was the underlying goal of the town council's water policy. In trying to attain it, however, the council ran into numerous problems.

Maisonneuve borders on a vast natural reservoir, the St. Lawrence River, but this handy source of water was unusable. Passing by Montreal, the water became so polluted that it was no longer drinkable by the time it reached Maisonneuve, downstream from the city. Maisonneuve had to look for other sources of supply, and after a fruitless attempt to use a local source, the town turned to Montreal for its water.

As the years passed, Maisonneuve's water distribution network grew and lines had to be installed in a number of streets to meet residents' demands. However, the town experienced difficulties in paying its bill to Montreal. On a number of occasions, Montreal threatened to cut off Maisonneuve's water supply if its account was not settled.[9]

Starting in 1889, Maisonneuve tried to improve the situation by having its rate reduced from forty to fifteen cents per thousand gallons. It backed up its demand with two arguments. Maisonneuve's residents had to pay very high water rates, and yet the money the town collected from them was not enough to pay its bill to Montreal. In addition, Maisonneuve's representatives maintained, Montreal had a responsibility of sorts towards its neighbour since it was the city's practice of emptying its sewers into the St. Lawrence that made it impossible for Maisonneuve to obtain its water supply from the river.[10]

Montreal's authorities refused to be moved by these arguments. They maintained that the reason for Maisonneuve's large bill was the high degree of leakage that occurred in the town. Thus, a Montreal inspector reported that on January 20, 1890, leakage within Maisonneuve accounted for 56 per cent of that day's water consumption in the town, which illustrates the management and competence problems faced by small municipalities.[11]

Finally, Maisonneuve's town council came up with what it considered a solution to these problems — the same solution that most municipalities resorted to when faced with the need to provide essential services. Instead of establishing effective structures of its own to remedy the defects of its system, the council decided to turn its powers over to a private company.

In the autumn of 1890, the council reached an agreement with the Montreal Island Water and Electric Company.[12] By virtue of this agreement, the company obtained the exclusive privilege of operating a water distribution system within Maisonneuve's town limits for twenty-five years, and a tax exemption for twenty years. In return, it promised to provide "a continuous and adequate supply of good, healthful and drinkable water to the aforesaid town and its inhabitants for public and household use."[13] The agreement also specified the time period in which construction would be carried out and the rates the company could charge. A few months later, the Montreal Island Water and Electric Company yielded its rights to the Montreal Water and Power Company. At the request of the new franchise holder, the company's exclusive privilege was extended for an additional twenty-five years.[14] Montreal Water and Power specialized in supplying water to the suburbs of Montreal and was quickly building up a small empire in this field.[15]

Entrusting its water supply to a private company, however, did not end Maisonneuve's problems. In fact, the contract of 1890-1891 was the beginning of a decade-long battle between the town council and Montreal Water and Power.

According to the agreement, construction of the water lines had to be completed within two years. The company did not meet the deadline and, while the councillors were quick to protest, they nevertheless accommodated the company by extending the deadline to May 1, 1894.[16]

Meanwhile, Maisonneuve was still battling Montreal, which was continuing to supply water until the company's system was completed. Even with the extension, Montreal Water and Power still did not fulfill its obligations. A series of legal proceedings ensued, and Maisonneuve's position was upheld, forcing the company to change its position. Afraid of losing its contract, Montreal Water and Power agreed to a bylaw negotiated with the town in 1898.[17] Thus, after seven years of legal battles, Maisonneuve's residents were finally assured of water service.

Public Transportation

In the case of Maisonneuve, public transportation has to be studied in a regional perspective, in the context of transportation between Montreal and its suburbs.

Until the middle of the nineteenth century, the typical city was relatively small, a "walking city" whose dimensions were no greater than the distance a person could cover on foot in a day.[18] A person generally lived near his workplace, and only a few wealthy individuals could afford the luxury of living in the suburbs and riding downtown each day.

Although the railway had brought the city closer to its surrounding regions, it was not suited to transportation over short distances, especially in densely populated urban areas. The streetcar changed all this. Widespread by the 1850s, early streetcars were horse-drawn vehicles running on tracks. Because a large number of workers could now be transported each morning and evening, and a person's residence could be a considerable distance from his workplace, the radius of the city increased. This new mode of transportation had a profound effect on the way land was occupied and settlement was extended.[19]

The first streetcars in Montreal began running in 1861, when the city council granted permission to the Montreal City Passenger Railway Company to operate a streetcar service. This company changed its name to the Montreal Street Railway Company in 1886, and six years later its managers took the most significant step in the company's history when they decided to electrify its system.

This technical innovation made it possible for the company to provide more frequent and more regular service. Larger streetcars could be used, geographical obstacles (especially inclines) were more manageable, and routes could easily be lengthened. Horses were very quickly replaced, and conversion to electric vehicles was completed by 1894. The benefits the horse-

A restored electric streetcar used by the Montreal Street Railway Company starting in 1892.

drawn streetcar had brought were provided even more conspicuously by the electric streetcar, and suburbs were integrated in the city at a faster pace.[20]

In the eyes of Maisonneuve's large landowners and civic leaders, it was as important to bring streetcar service to the town as it was to bring factories. Public transportation would drain a portion of Montreal's population to the suburbs, make it easier to sell lots (which would become more accessible) and build houses, and encourage industry to move to the suburbs. Factory owners locating in Maisonneuve would benefit from land that was cheaper than Montreal's, industrial incentives and other significant advantages. At the same time they could easily draw from the city's labour pool. The growth of Maisonneuve would be unquestionably linked to the quality of its communications with Montreal, and the streetcar would play an essential role.

In 1889 the Maisonneuve town council made an unsuccessful attempt to interest the Montreal Street Railway Company in extending its lines beyond the city limits.[21] Maisonneuve tried again in 1892, the year of electrification, and this time the company was interested. However, it demanded a thirty-year contract, with a tax exemption and an exclusive concession.[22] As negotiations dragged on, a new impetus appeared when a competitor, Albert J. Corriveau, offered to establish a streetcar service. The two proposals were studied in 1893. In the new context of competition, the Montreal Street Railway softened its position and reduced its demands — enough to win the contract.[23]

The company was awarded the right to establish an electric streetcar service in Maisonneuve, but the agreement covered only passenger service and did not include freight. Initially, three lines were provided for — on Notre-Dame Street starting in the summer of 1893 and on Sainte-Catherine and Ontario streets as soon as they were opened to the public. The company would also establish a line "on any other street that Council may designate in future when these streets are opened and macadamized." This clause gave the council fairly wide powers.

The company did not obtain an exclusive concession, and one clause in the agreement stated explicitly that "nothing contained in this by-law shall be construed as giving an exclusive franchise to the Company." The contract stated that the town could also grant the privilege of operating an elevated or suspended railway or award a right-of-way on streets extending from the eastern limits of Montreal to a company operating in the city. The right-of-way provision gave priority to lines and new routes built by the Montreal Street Railway Company. The contract also specified the frequency of the streetcar runs (which the council could change unilaterally), maximum speed, duration of stops, and price of tickets — fifteen cents in the daytime and eight cents at night. (Workers could get tickets at a reduced price — eight for twenty-five cents between six and eight o'clock in the morning and between five and seven o'clock in the evening.) When the contract expired in thirty years, the town could, after giving notice, acquire the company's installations "by paying a price to be determined by arbitrators plus ten per cent above the estimate."

On the whole, the agreement contained some advantageous provisions for Maisonneuve and its residents. Despite its small population, the town was now linked to Montreal. Wide powers were left in the hands of the town council and the company did not have a monopoly, at least in theory. However, subsequent events made it appear that the company had made at least some of these concessions only as a way of gaining a foothold in Maisonneuve. The company's stance after the contract was signed was aimed at obtaining a monopoly and increasing its powers at the municipality's expense.

As in the case of the Montreal Water and Power Company, problems arose when it came to implementing the agreement. The town complained that the company was putting streetcars in operation too slowly, running its cars less often than the schedule in the contract had specified, and failing to install tracks on Ontario and Sainte-Catherine streets despite repeated demands from the council. Thus, within a few months, the Montreal Street Railway had found a way of getting around several of its obligations. Its tactic was simple: pocket the money collected from passengers, carry out its commitments and improve the quality of its service as slowly as possible, and wait for protests from the town council before doing anything. Each time the council objected, the company proclaimed its good intentions and said it was doing everything in its power to provide the service required.[24]

Electricity

Like water distribution and public transportation, electricity distribution was also frequently turned over to private companies in North American cities. Maisonneuve, however, experimented with municipal operation of electricity service. The product in this case was a new one, and the market for it was expanding rapidly.

By the 1870s and 1880s, the widespread use of electricity as a source of energy for households and industries was feasible, and serious use began around the time the town of Maisonneuve was established. During the 1870s, the generators used to produce electricity were still fairly rudimentary, and the only practical application was the use of arc lamps for street lighting. In 1882 Thomas Edison opened his first electric generating station in New York. This significant technological advance made it possible to use electricity for other purposes and during the 1880s electric companies were established in various parts of North America. Edison's system had a major disadvantage: because it worked on direct current, energy could not be transported outside a one-kilometre radius without serious problems. This problem was overcome by the work of George Westinghouse and other inventors, and alternating current began to be used. Nevertheless, most generating stations remained small until 1895 with the construction of the Niagara Falls station. The first large generating station in North America, it inaugurated a new era.[25]

In Quebec construction of the Shawinigan generating station got underway soon after the Niagara station began operation. By this time, electricity had been produced in Quebec for a number of years. In Montreal several companies had been formed, but the market was dominated by the Royal Electric Company. Founded in 1884, Royal Electric obtained the City of Montreal's street lighting contract in 1889. It initally supplied direct current produced by a steam generator, and began to supply alternating current in 1890. In 1901 the company merged with two other electric companies and a gas company to form a powerful conglomerate, the Montreal Light, Heat and Power Company.[26]

Maisonneuve's civic leaders first expressed interest in this new form of energy in 1888. The municipality already had a street lighting system, and in the autumn of 1888 the town council discussed the cost of lighting its streets with electricity.[27] But the council does not appear to have pursued the matter, and the subject of electric lighting was not examined again until 1891. The town engineer, Emile Vanier, submitted an electrification plan which was studied by the council and then adopted on September 21, 1891. Under this plan, the municipality would produce its own electricity using a thermal generating station and would own the distribution system as well. The necessary facilities, however, would be built by a company specializing in electrical construction.

Among the bids submitted, two — those of the Edison General Electric Company and the Royal Electric Company — interested the council. The four French-speaking councillors favoured Edison, while the two English-speaking councillors leaned towards Royal Electric. The contract was initially awarded to Edison, but a few days later the council reconsidered the resolution and Councillor Louis Champagne changed sides, leading to a tie vote and allowing Mayor Joseph Barsalou to cast a deciding vote in favour of Royal Electric. The supporters of Edison continued to argue against this decision. They maintained that Edison's system was better than Royal's and accused Champagne of changing his vote under pressure from Royal Electric and the St. Lawrence Sugar Refining Company, and finally tried to have him barred from voting on grounds of conflict of interest.[28]

Town elections took place a few weeks later. The voters of Maisonneuve elected a new mayor, Aristide Bélair, and three new councillors who all supported Edison, and the town came back to its original choice.[29] Along with the political manoeuvring, the battle for the contract was marked by a number of lawsuits, illustrating the intensity with which companies competed to capture the electricity market in the Montreal region.

Thus, from 1892 on, the town of Maisonneuve produced its own electricity, which it used both to meet public needs and to distribute to residents. To operate this service, the town had to maintain satisfactory equipment and employ personnel with specialized skills. After a few years fraught with problems, it began to consider turning the service over to a private company.[30] Maisonneuve's secretary-treasurer, M.-G. Ecrement, later explained the situation in the following terms:

> I must also tell you that for the first two years after the system in question was placed in operation, the Council was fairly satisfied, but after that date it was impossible to obtain satisfaction from the system in question. I

believe that operation of an electric system by the town is much more costly than operation by a Company. The directors of a Company can give the system much more consistent attention than the councillors of a town who change, often every year; it is also very difficult to hire employees who have the energy needed to resist orders — most of which are erroneous — from a Lighting Committee that knows little or almost nothing about what an electric lighting system is. When we discontinued the Town lighting system, it cost us $4,400 a year to operate 28 electric arc lamps and about 200 incandescent lamps, and if we had continued we would have had to make repairs costing about two to three thousand dollars and we still would not have had a satisfactory system. My opinion is that it is much more advantageous to turn electric lighting over to a Company.[31]

The story of Maisonneuve's muncipal electricity service is an illustration of a wider problem: in the late nineteenth century, especially in small towns such as Maisonneuve, a strong, competent municipal civil service did not exist, and elected officials intervened constantly in all aspects of administration.

In the first years of Maisonneuve's existence, the town council's top priority was the establishment of a number of utilities, which were undoubtedly essential if the council wanted to attract residents in significant numbers. Maisonneuve experienced some difficulties in establishing these utilities, but by 1896 the town had water, electricity and public transportation services that could be said to meet its needs. But this was not enough to generate rapid growth, and Maisonneuve's elected officials devoted their attention to encouraging the creation of economic activities that would help the town grow.

Development through Industry

In Montreal in the 1880s, industry was the principal motive behind urban growth. Suburban municipalities had only to look at the example of the two periods of rapid industrial growth experienced by the city of Montreal in the mid-nineteenth century and again in the 1880s. The suburbs could offer manufacturing companies large tracts of land which were usually cheaper than lots available in the city. Some kinds of industries, notably those especially inclined to pollute the environment, could be attracted by the suburbs' more accommodating regulatory structures. And the tax exemptions or other advantages offered by the suburbs could be an additional incentive.

Of course, not all suburban municipalities were in the same position, and some of them offered a more attractive location. With its river frontage, Maisonneuve had clear advantages over other municipalities on Montreal

Island. However, these potential assets would only operate to Maisonneuve's advantage if circumstances were favourable. At the time Maisonneuve was created, it was still quite far from the main city core. In addition,
industrial growth was slow in Montreal starting in the mid-1880s, and the
early 1890s were marked by a general slowdown in economic activity. Maisonneuve's time had clearly not yet come, and it was not until the economic
recovery of 1896 that industries began to be established in Maisonneuve.
Even with these unfavourable circumstances, Maisonneuve's developers and
civic leaders tried to attract industries to the town, but they devoted only
limited resources to this endeavour.

The first measure undertaken by the Maisonneuve town council was a tax
exemption policy, which stood to deprive the town of future revenues but
had the advantage of involving no immediate cost. Barely a year after it was
set up, the town council passed a resolution "that the Secretary be authorized to offer any factory that wishes to become established in Maisonneuve
a tax exemption for twenty-five years, and that an advertisement to this effect
be placed in the *Star*, *La Minerve* and *La Patrie* for six months."[32] Interestingly, only three months earlier Maisonneuve's civic leaders had refused to
grant the Jesuits a tax exemption on their land "in the light of the poverty
of the town."[33] This double-edged attitude shows that the councillors were
acutely aware of their economic interests. They clearly didn't expect many
economic benefits from the Jesuits' ownership of a large tract of land.

Maisonneuve got its first opportunity in the summer of 1887. The St.
Lawrence Sugar Refining Company wanted to establish a refinery in Maisonneuve and the town council, by a simple resolution, granted it a twenty-
year tax exemption and a right-of-way for a railway line.[34] Thus, St. Lawrence Sugar, which had refined sugar in Montreal since 1878, moved to Maisonneuve in 1887 and established its refinery in a large quadrilateral bounded
by the river, Bourbonnière Street, Notre-Dame Street and Pie-IX Boulevard
(Map 4, page 68). To meet the needs of the sugar refinery, in 1889 the
Montreal Harbour Commission began building Maisonneuve's first pier:
Sutherland Pier was completed in 1891.

Meanwhile, the Montreal Terra Cotta Lumber Company obtained a
twenty-year tax exemption in 1888. This was Alphonse Desjardins's company, and the factory was established on his land. It specialized in the manufacture of a fireproof porous tile used in the construction of large buildings.
The raw material for the tile was clay extracted on the northern part of the
Desjardins property (north of Sherbrooke Street), and it was processed in the
company's factory at the foot of the Sherbrooke Street hill.[35]

These early successes were followed by a series of lean years in which no
new companies were established in Maisonneuve. Despite repeated efforts
by town councillors to attract new industries, no new projects appeared until
late 1894. Meanwhile, the town had time to organize its industrial assist-

The St. Lawrence Sugar refinery was the first large industrial establishment in Maisonneuve. The oldest part of the refinery can be easily distinguished from newer construction.

ance programs more effectively. In the early years, the conditions it imposed in exchange for tax exemptions were highly variable; sometimes there were no conditions at all. This ad hoc way of proceeding was later replaced by a more systematic policy.

Organization and Settlement of the Town

During the initial period, while Maisonneuve's administrative structures were being established, the territory of the municipality was being organized as well. The grid formed by the town's streets gradually took shape. The rectangular layout adopted by Maisonneuve both followed Montreal's example and conformed to the way the territory had been divided when it was a rural area made up of long rectangular farms stretching back from the St. Lawrence. The east-west streets were planned as extensions of the equivalent streets in Montreal and were sometimes given the same names.

The initial grid was a result of plans drawn up by the large landowners, who provided for space for streets when they subdivided their lands into building lots. These plans were approved by the town council and then confirmed by the Superior Court. The council had expropriation rights that allowed it to change the lots proposed by the landowners, but on the whole this question does not seem to have raised any serious problems. There were fourteen east-west streets between the St. Lawrence and Maisonneuve's northern limits, and seventeen north-south streets perpendicular to these (see Table 3-1 and Map 2, page 18). Because of its contracts with the large landowners, the town was responsible for building these streets, and did so progressively as lots were sold and residents moved in.

The territory was organized in another way as well. It was divided into wards which served as the basis for representation on the town council, with each ward electing two councillors. This administrative division was also used in drawing up Maisonneuve's assessment roll. The council passed a bylaw in 1890 dividing the town into three wards.[36] Christened West, Centre and East wards, they followed the old agricultural division of the land, forming three long parallel strips stretching from the St. Lawrence to Maisonneuve's northern limits. West Ward consisted of Bourbonnière, Orléans, Charlemagne and Jeanne-d'Arc streets and the west side of Pie-IX Boulevard. Centre Ward, about the same size as West Ward, extended from the east side of Pie-IX past Desjardins and De La Salle streets to the west side of Letourneux Street. By far the largest, East Ward covered a larger area than the other two combined since the eastern part of Maisonneuve was much more sparsely populated in 1890 than areas closer to Montreal, which had developed more quickly. The east side of Letourneux Street was the western boundary of East Ward, which stretched to the back of 1st Avenue. The ward boundaries established in 1890 remained unchanged until annexation in 1918.

In terms of religious organization, Maisonneuve was initially part of Nativité-de-la-Très-Sainte-Vierge parish of Hochelaga. In August 1888, following a request from Maisonneuve's freeholders, the archdiocese of Montreal agreed to establish a separate parish. Called Très-Saint-Nom-de-Jésus de Maisonneuve, the new parish, whose boundaries coincided with the town limits, was at first administered as a mission by Hochelaga, but it became a full-fledged parish in 1892.[37]

During this early period, Maisonneuve's urbanized area was small and concentrated in the southwestern part of the town. The atlas published in 1890 by Charles Edward Goad shows that a large majority of Maisonneuve's

Table 3-1
The Streets of Maisonneuve

Old Name	Name in 1883-1918	Present Name
East-West Streets		
Sainte-Marie	Notre-Dame	Notre-Dame
	Sainte-Catherine	Sainte-Catherine
Gustave; Logan	Adam	Adam
	Lafontaine	Lafontaine
	Ontario	Ontario
	Ernest	Rouen
	Girard	Hochelaga
	Boyce	Pierre-de-Coubertin
	Viau	Ray Murphy
	Sherbrooke	Sherbrooke
	Nolan	Rachel
	Du Parc	Mount Royal
	Armand	Saint-Joseph
	Théodore	Masson
North-South Streets		
	Bourbonnière	Bourbonnière
	Orléans	Orléans
	Charlemagne	Charlemagne
	Jeanne-d'Arc	Jeanne-d'Arc
	Pie-IX	Pie-IX
Decary; Maisonneuve	Desjardins	Desjardins
Charles Henry	De La Salle	De La Salle
Lecours	Letourneux	Letourneux
Oneida	Morgan	Morgana
	William David	William David
	Bennett	Bennett
	Aird	Aird
	5th Avenue	Sicard
	4th Avenue	Leclaire
	3rd Avenue	Théodore
	2nd Avenue	Saint-Clément
	1st Avenue	Viau

buildings stood along Notre-Dame Street, forming a line parallel to the river. On the streets perpendicular to the river, growth was beginning towards the north but it did not go very far. Only De La Salle Street was open as far as Maisonneuve's northern limits, probably to give access to the Christian Brothers' property in the northern part of the town. Only short sections of the other north-south streets were open, and they did not extend past Adam Street. There were a few scattered buildings on Orléans, Jeanne-d'Arc, Pie-IX, Desjardins and De La Salle streets. Notre-Dame Street was not only the major access route between Maisonneuve and Montreal, but also the town's communications link towards the east, with the neighbouring municipality of Longue-Pointe and, further afield, with the rest of Quebec. Notre-Dame Street was one of the oldest streets in the Montreal area and formed part of the Chemin du Roi, which had linked Montreal with Quebec City since the French regime.

Maisonneuve's population grew slowly during the period. The year Maisonneuve was established, it was estimated at 350. The 1891 census, which constituted the first relatively accurate measurement of Maisonneuve's population, reported it as 1,226. In 1896, at the end of the initial settlement period, Maisonneuve's population can be estimated at about 2,000. While the population of 1883 was still largely rural, in 1896 a large majority of Maisonneuve's people could clearly be classified as urban.

Between 1883 and 1896, in a period when economic conditions were difficult and agriculture reigned supreme in theory if not in practice, Maisonneuve clearly established an authentic urban development policy. Utilities were set up and could be extended to meet demand. The town council systematically encouraged companies to build factories and people to live in Maisonneuve. The conditions for the rapid growth of the town and the development desired by its large landowners were all in place.

PART II

"THE PITTSBURGH OF CANADA": DEVELOPMENT THROUGH INDUSTRY, 1896-1910

CHAPTER 4

INDUSTRIAL DEVELOPMENT

The year 1896 was a turning point in the history of Maisonneuve. The town was now taking off, and the efforts of the previous thirteen years began showing results. Maisonneuve's population doubled in five years to almost 4,000 in 1901 and grew even more rapidly in the next decade, reaching more than 18,000 in 1911. Maisonneuve's growth coincided with the establishment of a large number of manufacturing companies, attracted as much by the town's location advantages as by its industrial development policy. Within a few years, it became a highly industrialized town, with a majority working-class population. The town council, happy with the situation it had helped create, dubbed Maisonneuve the "Pittsburgh of Canada."

The Context of Industrialization

The period 1896-1914 was marked by rapid economic growth in Canada as a whole. It was western Canada's great era of development, as hundreds of thousands of immigrants transformed the vast prairies into wheat farms. Its was also a period of heavy investment in infrastructure, particularly railways. The railway network previously dominated by the Canadian Pacific and the Grand Trunk was now substantially extended with the addition of two new transcontinentals. All these developments stimulated manufacturing production in the large cities of eastern Canada, and especially in Montreal.[1]

Montreal, which had experienced two previous great waves of industrialization in the 1850s and 1880s, was swept by a third wave during this period. Many companies enlarged their facilities, new factories were built, and tens of thousands of new residents were attracted to the city. Some of these new Montrealers came from the Quebec countryside; others came from Europe, not only from the British Isles as in previous periods of heavy immigration but from eastern Europe as well. Montreal's population grew from 267,730 in 1901 to a 1911 figure of 467,886 — more than 500,000 if the suburbs are counted. This rate of growth has been matched in few other periods in Montreal's history.

Many industrialists faced an important decision. With demand rapidly rising, they had to increase their production substantially either by modernizing their equipment or by enlarging their facilities. Frequently, physical constraints made it impossible for a company to enlarge its facilities in its existing location. Looking for new sites, some industrialists decided to build in the suburbs rather than in Montreal, and a number of these settled in Maisonneuve.

In general, all peripheral municipalities had the disadvantage of being far from the commercial and financial heart of the city, but they had advantages as well. Sites were cheaper in the suburbs than downtown, and their large size gave companies room to expand. In addition, suburban taxes were lower. Not all suburbs, however, could take advantage of these general factors to the same extent. Other factors entered into the equation, and some of these help explain the success of Maisonneuve.

One significant element was advertising. Montreal had several dozen suburbs, and those most successful in promoting themselves found it easier to attract manufacturing companies. On this front, the Maisonneuve town council was very active — at least partly because of pressure from the town's developers. The council authorized a major publicity campaign and it produced tangible results: Maisonneuve became far better known than such communities as Ahuntsic, Montreal North and Rosemount. Advertising had limitations. It had to be used effectively and it had to be backed up by real advantages. Callow, credulous individuals might be induced to buy near-worthless lands through clever advertising, but this strategy would be less likely to work with manufacturers. It was precisely because Maisonneuve did have significant advantages that it was able to launch a successful advertising campaign aimed at attracting industries.

Among these advantages were tax concessions and grants, which clearly helped make the town attractive to industrialists seeking to maximize their profits. A small town such as Maisonneuve could pursue this sort of policy much more easily than a large city such as Montreal, but it faced vigorous competition from other suburban municipalities with similar policies. A town could afford to spurn the industrialists' advances only if — like Outremont — it sought to attract a wealthier population.[2] Competition among suburbs waned after a number were annexed by Montreal between 1905 and

1910. By this time, however, quite a few companies had already established themselves in Maisonneuve.

While Maisonneuve's industrial policy had an impact on factory location, it was not the only significant variable. In Maisonneuve's case, the presence of both the harbour and railways appears to have been especially important.

Montreal harbour and the Lachine Canal had played a major role in the growth of industry in the city since the mid-nineteenth century.[3] Although the banks of the Lachine Canal were the real birthplace of industry in Montreal, in the late nineteenth century Montreal's harbour facilities proved insufficient to meet the needs of an economy entering a major expansion phase. Thus, in the twenty years preceding the First World War, a considerable effort was put into modernizing and expanding these facilities. But there were competing interests involved, which resulted in considerable conflict. At the end of the nineteenth century, controversy arose over the developments of the eastern part of the harbour — an issue that directly affected Maisonneuve. The Harbour Commission, dominated by Montreal's anglophone bourgeoisie, planned to concentrate on developing the western part of the harbour, near the entrance to the Lachine Canal. However, the francophone bourgeoisie argued that construction was needed farther east.

The commission had in its files a plan called the "Eastern Basin," involving the construction of an island basin in Hochelaga Ward, and for several years a number of francophone organizations had been demanding some action of this project. Among these organizations was the Maisonneuve town council, which had repeatedly made representations to the federal government and local M.P.s.[4] Despite the pressure, the project was getting nowhere.

The controversy was rekindled when the 1896 federal election brought the Liberals to power. The new minister of public works, whose portfolio included responsibility for the Harbour Commission, was J.-Israël Tarte. Tarte argued that some of the federal government loan to the Harbour Commission should be devoted to construction in the east end to give the residents of the area a measure of justice.[5] The council of the Montreal Board of Trade, acting as the voice of the anglophone bourgeoisie, maintained that the Harbour Commission and not the minister should decide which projects to carry out and that development of the eastern part of the harbour was not urgent.[6] The Chambre de Commerce du District de Montréal, representing the francophone bourgeoisie, also entered the debate. While the Chambre de Commerce shared many interests with the Board of Trade, it took a different position on this question, arguing that construction in the east end was needed.[7]

Underlying the ethnic division in this debate were divergent economic interests. The French Canadian bourgeoisie was based in the east end of Montreal, and especially in the land sector. Investment in the harbour was sure to result in rising land prices. It is noteworthy that the movement's leaders included Alphonse Desjardins, who was president of the Chambre de Commerce at the time as well as a large Maisonneuve landowner and father of the town's mayor. Another of these large landowners was Isaïe Préfontaine, future president of the Chambre de Commerce and brother of Raymond Préfontaine, the federal M.P. for Hochelaga, mayor of Montreal, a member of the Harbour Commission and an ardent supporter of developing the eastern part of Montreal harbour.

Partly as a result of the pressure from Maisonneuve's land capitalists, development of the east end of the harbour was eventually carried out. The "Eastern Basin" project was abandoned, but construction began on other facilities. Initially, Tarte had his own department build a large pier off Maisonneuve, later named Tarte Pier. In subsequent years, the east end of Montreal developed rapidly. This changed the attitude of the harbour commissioners and led them to invest in that part of the island.

Even before the controversy reached significant proportions, some construction had already been carried out in the east end. When Maisonneuve was founded, there were no wharves on its waterfront. The Harbour Commission undertook its first project in Maisonneuve in 1889. Completed in 1891, the Sutherland Pier at the foot of Jeanne-d'Arc Street was built essentially to meet the needs of the St. Lawrence Sugar refinery.[8] A second wharf, Laurier Pier, was built between 1894 and 1896 in Hochelaga, right near Maisonneuve.[9] And finally, there was the construction of Tarte Pier. Begun in 1900, it took eight years to complete for a total cost of more than a million dollars.[10] A few years later, the Harbour Commissioners added four large merchandise sheds.[11]

These three sawtooth-shaped piers became the heart of the east end of Montreal harbour. Manufacturers in Maisonneuve now had access to major harbour facilities and to piers farther west through the network of railway lines which the Harbour Commission had built on its territory. Meanwhile, the eastern part of Maisonneuve's waterfront was developed with the establishment of the Canadian Vickers plant in 1910 and the construction of a floating dry dock, opened in 1912.[12]

The large landowners regarded the presence of the harbour as a determining factor in Maisonneuve's growth, which accounts for its prominence in the town's promotional material. Three substantial companies built their factories in the area immediately adjoining the harbour — St. Lawrence Sugar, Canadian Spool Cotton and Canadian Vickers. These industries were particularly dependent on water transportation, but other factories built farther north also benefited from having harbour facilities nearby.

Railways were another asset. A major railway line, built by the Chateaug-

The Canadian Spool Cotton factory, built in 1907 at the corner of Pie-IX Boulevard and Notre-Dame Street, bordering on the harbour.

uay and Northern Railway Company, crossed Maisonneuve from west to east. In 1896 the town council granted the company permission to cross Maisonneuve's streets.[13] It followed the same route as the Montreal Terminal Railway crossing town between Ontario and Ernest streets. A large concentration of factories grew up along the line, and the larger ones — Watson Foster & Co., Warden King & Son, and Viau et Frère — had spur lines connecting them to the main trunk (see Map 4). In 1903 the Chateauguay and Northern became part of the Canadian Northern Railway system, linking Maisonneuve with a vast network that would stretch from Lake St. John to Vancouver. When railway traffic in Maisonneuve grew to fairly substantial proportions, the town council appealed to the company to build a local station and a freight yard, and its petition was supported by an order

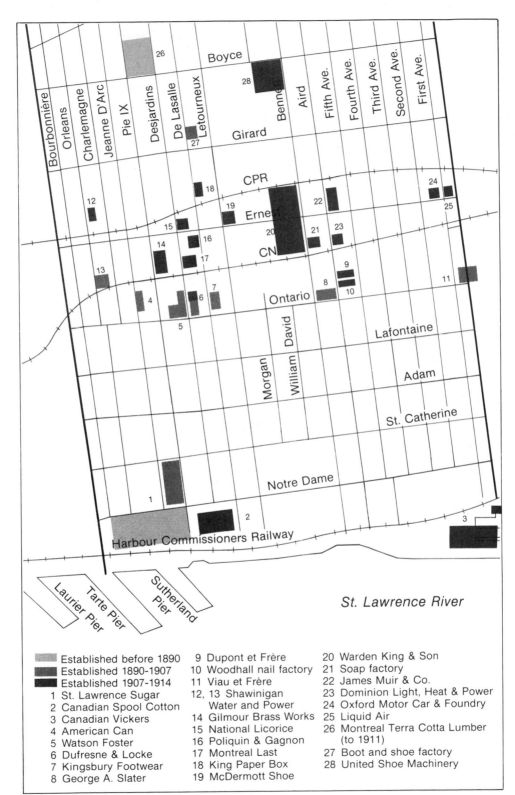

Map 4: Location of Industries, 1890-1914

Legend:
- Established before 1890
- Established 1890-1907
- Established 1907-1914

1 St. Lawrence Sugar
2 Canadian Spool Cotton
3 Canadian Vickers
4 American Can
5 Watson Foster
6 Dufresne & Locke
7 Kingsbury Footwear
8 George A. Slater
9 Dupont et Frère
10 Woodhall nail factory
11 Viau et Frère
12, 13 Shawinigan Water and Power
14 Gilmour Brass Works
15 National Licorice
16 Poliquin & Gagnon
17 Montreal Last
18 King Paper Box
19 McDermott Shoe
20 Warden King & Son
21 Soap factory
22 James Muir & Co.
23 Dominion Light, Heat & Power
24 Oxford Motor Car & Foundry
25 Liquid Air
26 Montreal Terra Cotta Lumber (to 1911)
27 Boot and shoe factory
28 United Shoe Machinery

from the Railway Commission.[14] The municipality also authorized the Canadian Pacific to establish a branch line on Jeanne-d'Arc Street to link the sugar refinery with its Montreal network.[15]

Before the First World War, car and truck transportation was still in its infancy and a high-quality road system capable of carrying goods rapidly and efficiently did not yet exist. It was the railway that supplied industries with raw materials and shipped their manufactured products. By the 1920s, the truck would be able to compete effectively with the train but, in the age of the horse-drawn carriage, rail transportation clearly had the upper hand.

The harbour and the railway were clearly important location factors for industries on Montreal Island (at least before the First World War), and the presence of both these factors in Maisonneuve explains why companies decided to build their plants there rather than in other suburbs such as Rosemount or Montreal North. With a few exceptions, they chose locations either along the river or in a double line north of Ontario Street, on either side of the railway. But Maisonneuve had other advantages. The fact that it was linked with the Montreal streetcar system at an early date was a significant asset: the streetcar provided fast communication with downtown Montreal and its large financial and commercial institutions and facilitated the transportation of workers to Maisonneuve's factories. And finally, the presence of large vacant lots, especially north of Ontario Street, made it possible to build large factories and ensured that there would be enough space for expansion.

Industrial Policy

The goal of Maisonneuve's industrial policy was defined very early on and remained unchanged until annexation. The details of the policy, however, were worked out over time, and the means used to implement it varied somewhat over the years. Among the many different forms the policy took, two are especially noteworthy. First, Maisonneuve conducted publicity campaigns aimed at industrialists and, second, it granted a variety of concessions to make the town an attractive location for industry.

Maisonneuve promoted its advantages primarily through newspapers. This kind of promotion was sporadic at first, but the newspaper advertising campaign Maisonneuve conducted between 1907 and 1915 was systematic and intensive. The municipality placed advertisements in two kinds of publications — general circulation Montreal newspapers and specialized newspapers and magazines. In the first category, Maisonneuve advertised in most of Montreal's dailies: the *Herald*, the *Star*, *La Presse*, *La Patrie*, *Le Pays*, *Le Devoir*. The second group consisted of a wide range of business publications, such as *La Chambre de commerce du district de Montréal*, *Le Prix courant*, *Le*

Moniteur de commerce and the *Commercial Monthly Magazine*. Maisonneuve even bought two pages of advertising in *Montréal et le congrès eucharistique*, a brochure published when the international Eucharistic Congress was held in Montreal in 1910. Since the goals of the congress were primarily spiritual, the headline of Maisonneuve's advertisement was not without irony: "Everybody who is seeking success and fortune, come visit Maisonneuve and share in the great prosperity that prevails there."[16]

Some large Montreal newspapers published special sections devoted to Maisonneuve (in *La Patrie* on June 26, 1909; in *La Presse* on June 12, 1912; and again in *La Patrie* on December 4, 1915), which were extensively illustrated and full of information about the town's life and its public services. Many advertisements were purchased by manufacturers, testifying to Maisonneuve's industrial vocation and providing an incentive to other companies.

Newspapers were not the only medium used in Maisonneuve's publicity campaign. In 1911 the town council published a thirty-nine-page pamphlet called *La ville de Maisonneuve ... Le principal faubourg industriel de Montréal* (The Town of Maisonneuve ... Montreal's Leading Industrial Suburb).[17] It contained a detailed account of the town's services and a description of its industries, both copiously illustrated with photographs. The town also aimed its publicity directly at individuals and companies. When Maisonneuve's civic leaders learned of a new company looking for a location or an existing one wanting to move its factory, they quickly wrote to its owners to exalt the advantages of Maisonneuve.[18]

While the words might differ from one advertisement to another, the arguments remained essentially the same. Primary emphasis was placed on the quality of Maisonneuve's communications network, and especially on the harbour facilities: "Maisonneuve has huge wharves where the largest ocean-going ships come to load or unload their cargoes."[19] Railways and streetcars were also highlighted: "Maisonneuve, with its three national railways, its electric line for freight transportation, operating under a special franchise across town streets and linked with the railways, and its superb water facilities that have no rival in the entire Dominion, Maisonneuve, from the point of view of shipping, is unique in its class."[20]

Besides also pointing out the quality of Maisonneuve's public services (water, gas, electricity, sewers, paved streets), advertisements noted that there had never been a strike in Maisonneuve, which was attributed to the fact that many workers owned their homes.[21] And, of course, Maisonneuve's town council was described as "active, progressive so that it is worth locating in the municipality" or "progressive, intelligent, ready and willing to have factories."[22] That many companies were already established in Maisonneuve was a good argument to attract others. Industrial production statistics placing Maisonneuve among the leading cities in Canada were widely

An example of Maisonneuve's advertising aimed at manufacturers. This advertisement notes that a factory in Maisonneuve would have "docks in front and a railway in the rear."

quoted and led the municipality to don the mantle of "the Pittsburg [sic] of Canada."[23] The high-sounding phrases, the vainglorious arguments and the optimistic tone contributed to the image Maisonneuve created for itself through the media — an image of a place where there was spectacular progress, room for everybody, and a fortune to be made.

The cornerstone of Maisonneuve's industrial policy, however, was the granting of advantages to companies in the form of tax concessions or cash. This aspect of the policy was not a new invention: municipal governments had been using such measures for a long time.

The municipal bonus system dated back to the early periods of railway fever, from the 1830s to the 1860s.[24] Later, with the coming of the industrial revolution, the establishment of a manufacturing firm also became an important factor in urban growth, and the material support that municipal governments had given railway companies was redirected to the manufacturing sector. In both cases, the interests of land capital were involved. In the late nineteenth century, the system of cash grants or tax concessions was widespread, and the Maisonneuve town council caught the prevailing wind. Maisonneuve differed from other municipalities, however, in the systematic nature of its bonus policy and in the number and size of the companies to which it granted favours.

While the provincial government authorized the bonus system, it also established some standards aimed at avoiding massive debt, which a number of towns had experienced in the railway era, and aimed also at limiting the ruinous consequences of excessively zealous competition among municipalities. On the whole, however, the legislation was fairly lax. Municipalities could participate in the financing not only of public enterprises (such as bridges and roads) but also of manufacturing companies. Municipal governments could exercise these options by passing bylaws:

> To aid in the construction of any bridge, causeway, pier, wharf, slide, macadamized road, railroad, or other public works, or any manufacturing establishments situated in whole or in part within the municipality or in its vicinity, undertaken and built by any incorporated company, or by the Provincial Government:
>
> 1. By taking and subscribing for shares in any company formed for such purpose;
>
> 2. By giving or lending money to such company or to the Provincial Government;
>
> 3. By guaranteeing by endorsation or otherwise any sum of money borrowed by such company;
>
> 4. By exempting from the payment or municipal taxes, assessments and dues according to the provisions of section sixth of chapter second of this title.[25]

When a town council passed a bylaw under this legislation, it had to be approved by the municipality's property owners.[26] To constrain the generosity of town councils, the legislation set a maximum time period for tax exemptions. Ten years was the maximum period specified for manufacturing companies; however, the legislation also established a limit of twenty years for tax exemptions in general.[27] In practice, a municipality such as Maisonneuve was guided by the longest period allowed — twenty years.

Under normal circumstances, the companies granted tax exemptions would be new firms. But the legislation allowed an exception in the case of

MAISONNEUVE

"LE PITTSBURG DU CANADA"

La Ville la plus Progressive du Dominion du Canada

Population de 1911 (recensement), 18,000. Population en 1913 (d'après Lovell), 32,000

Maisonneuve's industrial vocation was a source of pride. Here Maisonneuve is characterized as the "Pittsburg of Canada" and "the most progressive town in the Dominion of Canada."

a company threatened by the establishment of a new tax-exempt competitor in the same municipality. The town council could then restore the balance by granting a tax exemption to the existing company as well.[28] In the case of cash grants, the legislation was even clearer in providing for existing companies in the same industry: "No municipality shall grant a bonus to any manufacturer who proposes to establish, within its limits, an industry of a nature similar to one already established in such municipality without having received a bonus."[29]

Provisions which came into effect in 1901 eliminated the abuse of municipal grants to attract companies already established elsewhere in Quebec: "No subsidy shall be granted by any municipality to attract within its limits an industrial establishment already established in this Province; and every subsidy granted contrary to this section on or after the 28th day of July, 1901, is and shall be absolutely null."[30] This provision directly affected Maisonneuve, which attracted industries from Montreal. However, the restriction applied only to cash grants and it was still legal to grant tax exemptions to companies moving from other Quebec municipalities.

Within the framework of Quebec's regulations governing municipal bonusing, Maisonneuve's charter allowed the municipality quite a lot of room to manoeuvre. Under amendments passed in 1893, the town council was empowered to make arrangements with property owners by a simple resolution that would establish how a particular property would be assessed and taxed or that would determine the level of its assessment and taxes for a given period.[31] Amendments adopted in 1897 further extended the town council's powers, providing for bonuses in the ostensible form of land grants:

> Notwithstanding article 4404 of the Revised Statutes [the provincial legislation governing municipal bonuses], and in the spirit of the said article, permission is hereby granted to the town to grant aid to any railway, manufactory, brewery, distillery or other industrial or commercial establishment now established or which may wish to establish themselves within the limits of the town, by giving or undertaking to give them land for their buildings and operations, provided such bonus to any one company shall not exceed ten thousand dollars. The town may acquire such land or lands either for cash or on credit.[32]

Three years later, new provisions were added that specified and at the same time extended the ways in which Maisonneuve could intervene. Under these provisions, it could exercise its powers "in the form of a sale, loan, gift, exchange, lease, subscription, security, endorsation, exemption from taxation or in any other way it may deem expedient."[33] However, exemptions from special taxes were outlawed, and future exemptions could only be awarded on "the ordinary and yearly taxes levied on immoveables."[34]

In the early years, Maisonneuve town council used tax exemptions to attract industries. A new policy of cash grants began in 1894 and reached its height between 1896 and 1900.

While there were slight variations from case to case, the general framework of all these grants was the same. The municipality granted the company a cash bonus for purchasing land and buildings. The details of payment varied, but usually an initial sum was paid when the factory began production and the other payments were staggered over several years. In most cases, these subsequent payments were a function of the amount the company paid in wages to Maisonneuve residents. At first, a twenty-year tax exemption went along with the bonus, but this generous provision was not included in contracts with companies signed after 1896.

In exchange, a number of conditions were imposed on the company. It had to build its factory within a certain time period (often a few months) and operate it for a minimum number of years (usually ten). The agreement covered the type of building that could be constructed, and specified the minimum number of employees, the proportion (80 per cent) who had to be residents of Maisonneuve, and the minimum annual wages. The municipality also had the power to inspect the company's books to ensure that conditions were really being fulfilled. The interests of land capital are clearly visible here: in order to respect the conditions of the contract, companies would encourage their employees to live in Maisonneuve. To protect its investment, the town held the company's first mortgage on the land, buildings and machinery for the amount of the grant. It also obtained fire insurance for the same amount.

In less than six years, between 1894 and 1900, Maisonneuve granted a total of $83,500 to ten companies. Two companies went bankrupt, but their municipal grants of $6,500 were only 7.8 per cent of the total. The other eight companies — six shoe factories, a wallpaper mill and a can factory — were well established.

As the twentieth century began, Maisonneuve had a substantial manufacturing sector, based mainly on the shoe industry. Since other factors were involved, it is hard to say whether this situation was due primarily to the town council's industrial policy. Were cash grants more effective than tax exemptions? According to two industrialists, manufacturers preferred cash grants. The cash grant system was also better from the point of view of Maisonneuve's civic leaders, whose ultimate goal was to increase the town's population. Under this system, they could periodically check where a company's employees lived and, with the factory owners as intermediaries, encourage workers to make their home in Maisonneuve.

Nevertheless, the town council suspended the cash grant system. After 1900 it returned to tax measures, which had been used to attract small companies even in the cash grant era. Between 1901 and 1905 only one company established a factory in Maisonneuve. Warden King & Son, a manufacturer of furnaces and other cast iron products, obtained a twenty-year tax break under which it paid yearly municipal taxes of only $200. The company agreed to hire an initial workforce of some forty employees, pay them $20,000 a year in wages, and build facilities costing $15,000.[35]

But while new companies were rare, old ones were active. The gains of the previous period were consolidated in these years. Manufacturers fulfilled the conditions specified in their agreements with the town, their output increased, and the municipality paid them the money it had promised. However, with the stimulative effects of the grants now having partly worn off, companies sought new advantages from the town council. Those companies that had received grants but no tax concessions formed the Association des manufacturiers de Maisonneuve (Maisonneuve Manufacturers' Association) to obtain tax advantages comparable to those granted to other companies, and demanded that the assessment of their property be limited to a fixed amount.[36] The town council turned down this request but, when the manufacturers threatened to take legal action, it yielded to their pressure and fixed the assessment of six companies.[37] A few years later, the council confirmed these exemptions in a contract and extended them for twenty years.[38] In addition, two of these companies obtained tax advantages to enlarge their facilities.

Starting in 1906, companies once again began to move into Maisonneuve. The town council continued to be generous, although its largesse was now limited to tax exemptions and the time period was reduced to ten years, except in the case of very large companies where twenty-year exemptions were still granted. As before, a company had to meet certain conditions: it had to build a factory of a size agreed upon by the two parties, and hire a minimum number of employees. Between 1906 and 1915, the council granted tax exemptions to eighteen companies. Four of the exemptions were limited to twenty years, another twelve, to ten years and another two, to five years.[39] These new companies included a number of large employers whose presence added considerably to Maisonneuve's industrial capacity: the Viau et Frère biscuit factory, the Canadian Spool Cotton textile mill, the United Shoe Machinery factory and the Canadian Vickers shipyard. This third wave of industrialization in Maisonneuve came to an end with the outbreak of the First World War.

The Maisonneuve town council's industrial policy went through three major stages corresponding to the three waves of industrialization in the municipality. During the first stage, between 1887 and 1889, the council used tax exemptions to attract companies; during the second, between 1894 and 1900, cash grants were the major enticement; and during the third, between 1906 and 1915, the council went back to using tax concessions. If the objective of this industrial policy was to attract industries, the council's ultimate goal was to have these companies' employees live in Maisonneuve. Thus, it is not surprising to see the town council supervising the composition of a company's workforce — especially its employees' place of residence — and carefully checking manufacturers' reports. Companies had specific obligations and fulfilled them to the council's satisfaction.[40]

The town council's measures in support of industry were not limited to cash grants and tax exemptions. To attract manufacturers further municipal action was necessary, such as providing a new fire station. The police and fire station was originally located at the corner of Notre-Dame and Letourneux streets, four blocks south of the railway line where a number of factories were clustered. Although this was not a long distance for firemen to travel, the industrialists were not satisfied. So the town council decided in 1905 to build a second fire station at the corner of Ontario and Desjardins streets, only four blocks from the the first one (Map 2, page 18).[41] Many contemporaries considered this decision indefensible, and the only reason for locating two fire halls so close together was the council's desire to please the industrialists.[42] The burden of paying for the new fire station would, of course, fall on the shoulders of property owners and tenants, since manufacturers were exempt from municipal taxes.

The council acted in the same co-operative spirit on a number of other occasions. It asked the Department of Customs to deliver imported articles directly to Maisonneuve so that companies would not have to send employees to Montreal to pick them up.[43] It was quick to act whenever manufacturers complained about the services provided by the utility companies, especially in the case of streetcar and water services. And it granted streetcar companies the right to transport freight through the streets of Maisonneuve — a measure that benefited only the manufacturers and created traffic congestion for Maisonneuve residents generally.

These few instances illustrate the close co-operation that existed between civic leaders and representatives of industry. They were elements in a coherent industrial policy worked out fairly early in Maisonneuve's history. Its components — advertising, bonuses to companies, and other forms of support — fit together in a consistent pattern. This policy can be seen as part of the logic of urban development and, in particular, of its two driving forces: land capital and industrial capital. But the actual effect of these measures should not be exaggerated. An entrepreneur does not decide where to locate his business primarily on the basis of the tax burden. Access to markets and availability of manpower are the primary location factors. The second phase of making the decision consists of choosing among various sites, and it is at this stage that the advantages offered by a municipality can have an effect.

Maisonneuve's Industrial Structure

In 1890 there were only eight industrial establishments in Maisonneuve, and this figure would be even smaller if craftsmen's shops and other small businesses with fewer than five employees were excluded (see Table 4-1). Total output was only slightly higher than $3.6 million. By 1900 it had grown by 64 per cent; between 1900 and 1910 it jumped by 246 per cent. The increase in the number of workers was just as spectacular — 593 per cent between

Table 4-1
Manufacturing Statistics,
Town of Maisonneuve,
1890-1910

	1890	1900[1]	1910
Factories	8	12	20
Capital	$546,708	$4,147,533	$7,919,080
Employees	394	2,729	9,112
Salaries and wages	$158,668	$912,789	$4,856,496
Cost of materials	$3,299,960	$4,366,893	$14,040,953
Value of products	$3,653,584	$6,008,780	$20,813,774

[1] Starting in 1900, only factories with five or more paid employees are counted.
Source: *Census of Canada*, 1890-1910.

1890 and 1900 and 234 per cent between 1900 and 1910.[44] The impressive nature of the results achieved by Maisonneuve showed up clearly in the 1911 census: in 1910, Maisonneuve was fifth among Canadian cities in terms of value of manufactured products and second among cities in Quebec, and accounted for almost 6 per cent of Quebec's total production.[45]

What were the components of Maisonneuve's industrial structure? The food products industry was the first to attain prominence, with the construction of the St. Lawrence Sugar refinery on the Maisonneuve waterfront in 1887. One of the town's largest employers, it had between 400 and 500 workers on its payroll during the first decade of the twentieth century. It was also one of the largest sugar refineries in Canada: by comparing Maisonneuve statistics with the 1911 census, it can be estimated that St. Lawrence Sugar accounted for between 20 and 25 per cent of Canadian sugar output.

This industrial group was later augmented by the arrival of the Viau et Frère, a major biscuit concern. Founded in 1867 by Charles-Théodore Viau, the major landowner in the Viauville section of Maisonneuve, its factory had been located on Notre-Dame Street in Montreal. In 1907, when the Canadian Pacific Railway needed the factory's land, the Viau family decided to move its manufacturing establishment to its Maisonneuve property. When it opened in 1907, the new factory employed 200 people. By 1913 its workforce had grown to 350 and the value of its output was almost $1 million a year. Other companies in the food products group were much smaller: a small biscuit factory belonging to Georges N. Pichet and a confectionery established in 1907 as a subsidiary of the National Licorice Company of Brooklyn, New York.[46]

Also represented in Maisonneuve was the iron and steel industry. In Quebec this group was concentrated primarily in the Montreal region, and since iron and steel plants required considerable space, they were often built in the suburbs. The first of several plants that located in Maisonneuve was the Commiré foundry; established in 1897, it went bankrupt two years later. More stable was Warden King & Son, which had been in business for fifty years when it decided to build a new foundry in Maisonneuve in 1903. Behind the company's move were expansion plans involving an increase in its workforce of between forty and one hundred people. However, its business grew so rapidly that it employed 350 to 400 workers by 1909 and 550 by 1913. It occupied a very large tract of land north of the railway line and, in the space of a few years, the Warden King foundry became one of Maisonneuve's industrial giants. There were also two small nail mills and a small company that manufactured gas stoves.

Maisonneuve was home to another giant — the United Shoe Machinery Company of Canada, a subsidiary of an American company which had established a virtual trust in the manufacture of machines used in the shoe industry. The company profited from the rapid growth of this industry in the early twentieth century, and its Montreal plant soon proved inadequate. Looking for a new site, it chose Maisonneuve, where the shoe industry was already well established.[47] Its plant was built in 1911 on Boyce (Pierre-de-Coubertin) Street, and it employed between 300 and 350 workers.

The wood and construction materials industry was made up of three subgroups. The first was wood for construction, which as a general rule consisted of small plants employing no more than ten or twenty people. There were several such plants in Maisonneuve, like the Hamel & Bleau plant or the enterprise owned by Hubert Prévost, one of Maisonneuve's first industrialists. The second was the last-making industry, which was solidly established in Maisonneuve. According to the 1911 census, there were only five last factories in Quebec in 1910 and only eight in all of Canada. Four were located in Maisonneuve: the Montreal Last Company, the Dominion Die Company, Montreal Box Toe, and the United Last Company (a subsidiary of the United Shoe Machinery Company). Montreal Box Toe appears to have been the largest, with seventy-five employees in 1913.

In the third subgroup — construction materials other than wood — Maisonneuve had a number of small establishments and one more substantial one, the Montreal Terra Cotta Lumber Company. Owned by Alphonse Desjardins, it was one of the first to locate in Maisonneuve; as of 1906, it employed only about sixty people and operated only six months of the year. In 1911 Montreal Terra Cotta moved to Pointe-Claire in the western part of Montreal Island. According to one explanation for this move, the clay deposits had been exhausted; according to another, expropriation for Maisonneuve Park forced the company to relocate.[48] Whatever the reason, Montreal Terra Cotta was one of the few industries in Maisonneuve for which the proximity of raw materials was a decisive location factor.

Maisonneuve's leading industrial activity was undoubtedly the shoe industry (Table 4-2). Solidly established in Montreal for a very long time, it was one of the first industries to evolve from craft production to large-scale mechanized industry, a transformation that occurred around the middle of the nineteenth century. The industry was characterized by cheap and plentiful labour and a large number of competing companies.[49] The United Shoe Machinery Company's policy of leasing rather than selling equipment made it relatively easy for a businessman to enter the shoe industry or enlarge his existing facilities. Since not much capital was required, small French Canadian industrialists were able to begin operations in the shoe industry towards the end of the nineteenth century. The early twentieth century was a period of rapid growth for the industry in Quebec. Between 1900 and 1910, the value of annual production in Quebec grew from $14 million to $22.6 million.

In the late nineteenth and early twentieth centuries, many Montreal shoe companies moved to new locations. As demand increased, companies that

Table 4-2
The Shoe Industry in Maisonneuve, 1901-1913

Company	Years in Maisonneuve	1901-1902 Annual Wages ($000)	1906 Employees	1906 Annual Wages	1911 Employees[1]	1911 Annual Wages ($000)	1913 Employees	1913 Value of Products ($000)
Laniel & Co.	1898-1908	39	200	75	—	—	—	—
Rideau Shoe	1908-1913	—	—	—	200(150)	60	225	500
Kingsbury Footwear[2]	1900-	50	375	125	500(n/d)	n/d	800-900	1,250
Dufresne & Locke	1900-	11	200-225	120	395(500)	300	400	800
Geo. A. Slater	1900	52	250	125	275(300)	155-180	300-400	1,000
Royal Shoe	1901-1904	50	—	—	—	—	—	—
McDermott Shoe	1909-	—	—	—	125(100)	55	110	215
Poliquin & Gagnon	1909-	—	—	—	50(nd)	n/d	80	150
Dupont & Frère	1910-	—	—	150(150)	70	160	300	—
J.P. Coté	—	—	—	13(n/d)	n/d	20	12	—
Total		202	1,025-1,050	445	1,708(1,200)[3]	665[3]	2,095-2,295	4,227

Note: Except for 1901-1902 data, all figures are estimates.

[1] According to the assessment roll. The figures in parentheses come from the pamphlet *La ville de Maisonneuve*.

[2] Data appear inconsistent—either number of employees was exaggerated or wages and production were underestimated.

[3] Incomplete data.

Sources: Archives of the City of Montreal, Maisonneuve, file; *Le Canada*, July 28, 1906; Town of Maisonneuve assessment roll, 1911-1912; *La ville de Maisonneuve*, 1911; Municipal statistics, 1913.

were already cramped for space in their antiquated buildings in old sections of Montreal looked for new sites where expansion was possible. Several of them chose Maisonneuve, where large sites were available at reasonable prices and the town council was inclined to be generous. Between 1898 and 1913, twelve shoe companies — all but one of which obtained cash grants or tax exemptions — located in Maisonneuve.

The migration of the shoe industry to Maisonneuve began with the arrival of Laniel & Co. in 1898, and four years later a total of five were operating in the town. On the whole, however, the shoe industry in Maisonneuve was still fairly small. By 1906, although one of the companies had closed, the others had taken off and total wages had more than doubled. By 1911 these companies had expanded and been joined by several smaller ones between 1908 and 1910. In 1913 more than 2,000 people made their living in the shoe industry in Maisonneuve, and total production totalled more than $4 million. This was the peak: a year later the First World War would seriously disrupt the industry.

Kingsbury Footwear Company, one of the three largest, had been based in Montreal and managed by E.-H. Lanthier and Napoléon Dufresne. The company decided to move to Maisonneuve in the autumn of 1899 and obtained a grant of $8,000. Its new factory opened in the spring of 1900 and, during that first year, it recorded sales of $110,845. By 1909 it was producing 18,000 pairs of shoes a week; by 1912 its sales had increased tenfold.[50]

Another major company was Pellerin & Dufresne, which was founded in 1891 and changed its name to Dufresne & Locke in 1901. It was controlled by Thomas Dufresne and Ralph Locke and its manager was Thomas Dufresne's son Oscar, a future Maisonneuve town councillor. Dufresne and Locke received a $10,000 grant and their new factory began operation on August 22, 1900. The business grew rapidly. Tests conducted in Cairo and Alexandria demonstrated the viability of exporting shoes to Egypt, and in 1904 the company decided to add a new building to produce for this market. The town council granted a twenty-year tax exemption for the new building. The same year Dufresne & Locke bought out one of its competitors, the Royal Shoe Company of Maisonneuve. The company's weekly output was estimated at 12,500 pairs in 1909. Dufresne and Locke also owned a tannery and a factory in Acton Vale in the Eastern Townships which produced footwear for farmers.[51] Their Maisonneuve plant was located at the corner of Desjardins and Ontario streets and the company's property was assessed at more than $60,000 in 1911.[52]

The last of Maisonneuve's three leading shoe companies was Geo. A. Slater. George Slater had twenty years' experience in the shoe industry in 1900 when he decided to start his own company in Maisonneuve. He too received a $10,000 grant and his factory began operation on May 20, 1901. Like the other two companies, it began as a relatively small enterprise but grew rapidly. It had to enlarge its plant in 1903 and again in 1904. It produced more than 6,000 pairs of shoes a week in 1911, and two years later, its production was estimated at $1 million. The plant was on Ontario Street and its value was estimated at $42,000 in 1911.[53]

In a sense, the shoe industry was all-pervasive in Maisonneuve. Its scope can be seen in production figures: in 1911 it was estimated that 3.5 million pairs of shoes were made each year, and the town boasted that "Maisonneuve is the largest shoe manufacturing centre on Montreal Island."[54] The industry's omnipresence is even more evident when industries that supplied the shoe factories with lasts, boxes and machinery are considered. The shoe industry had a considerable impact on employment (see Chapter 6), and the effects of its concentration in Maisonneuve were felt in another way as well — a number of shoe manufacturers came to live in Maisonneuve and became part of the local bourgeoisie. They made their presence felt in town, school and parish institutions and their dynamism contributed to Maisonneuve's feverish growth.

The place of the textile industry in Quebec's industrial structure was extremely important. It fuelled the growth of many small towns in the late nineteenth and early twentieth centuries. In a number of places, the textile mill was the dominant industry, and the rate of urban growth varied with increases or decreases in textile production. In Maisonneuve, however, the textile industry did not carry much weight. Only one textile mill came to Maisonneuve, and it was not established until 1909, when the town's industrialization was already well underway. The Canadian Spool Cotton Company, which manufactured thread and silk, was undoubtedly a major industry and employed 400 people in 1913. But its position was not a dominant one in the light of Maisonneuve's diversified industrial structure.

The paper and printing industry was also present in Maisonneuve. Watson Foster & Co., a wallpaper manufacturer, was a fairly old Montreal firm. Founded in 1880, it was located in the west end of the city, in the heart of the "City below the Hill" described by Herbert Ames in 1897.[55] At the time Ames's book was published, Watson Foster was preparing to leave its old neighbourhood and relocate in the suburbs. The company began considering the move in 1896, and the Maisonneuve town council quickly formed a special committee to meet with its representatives.[56] Much was at stake: the company had ninety-six employees, a $40,000 annual payroll, and plans to increase production.[57] The civic leaders, with the support of Maisonneuve's property owners, were generous, providing the company with a $9,000 cash grant and a twenty-year tax exemption.[58]

Watson Foster built a factory on Ontario Street in 1897, which was evaluated fifteen years later at $155,000. In its first year of operation in Maisonneuve, the company employed about a hundred people.[59] By 1906 this figure had doubled and annual wages had reached $150,000.[60] In 1909 the com-

The Watson, Foster & Co. wallpaper factory on Ontario Street.

pany produced 60,000 rolls of wallpaper per day, and two years later it had a workforce of 250.[61] Thus, for about ten years, Watson Foster was the second largest company in Maisonneuve, after St. Lawrence Sugar. The rise of the shoe industry and the arrival of other large employers starting in 1907 pushed it back to a lower rank, but it remained one of the town's major enterprises. In the same industrial group was the King Paper Box Co. Ltd., a Montreal company that located in Maisonneuve in 1908 and specialized in making shoe boxes.

Among Maisonneuve's other industrial establishments, two are worth singling out. The first is the Acme Can Works which in 1900, after more than twenty-two years of operation, needed to enlarge its facilities and approached the Maisonneuve town council. Its new factory began operation in 1901. Seven years later, the American Can Company, based in the U.S., bought the can works and made the Maisonneuve plant its main Canadian facility. American Can enlarged the factory and modernized its equipment. In 1913 the can works employed 175 people, and four years later it was again enlarged substantially.

The other noteworthy plant was the Canadian Vickers Ltd. shipyard. Canadian Vickers was set up as a subsidiary of a British firm, Vickers, Sons and Maxim, which began exploring the possibilities of a plant in Maisonneuve in 1907. Its plans came to fruition three years later, and a shipyard was built between Notre-Dame Street and the river. In addition, a floating dock — one of the largest in the world at the time — was opened in 1912. With the establishment of Canadian Vickers, the Montreal region became one of Canada's leading shipbuilding centres. Some of the facilities were built in Maisonneuve, some in Longue-Pointe (which was by now part of Montreal) and some on Harbour Commission property. Maisonneuve's civic leaders expected that Canadian Vickers's presence in the town would have substantial economic repercussions. In 1914 the cost of building the facilities was calculated at $3 million.[62]

Completing this overall picture of Maisonneuve's industrial structure were industries located near Maisonneuve that employed some of its residents. Probably the most significant was Canadian Pacific Railway, which built its Angus Shops in Rosemount on land bordering Maisonneuve.

Thus, just before the First World War, Maisonneuve had a varied and substantial industrial structure. The town had become industrialized in three distinct stages. The first took place during the expansion phase of a short economic cycle in 1887-1888. At that time, there were only two noteworthy industrial establishments and their impact on the settlement of Maisonneuve was still relatively weak. Between 1888 and 1896, Quebec went through two depressions, and the time was not ripe for the establishment of new industries. In addition, integration into the economy of Montreal had not proceeded far enough for industries moving from old quarters in the city to locate in Maisonneuve. Streetcar service was not established until 1892, and the railway did not arrive until 1896. At this time, neither general economic conditions nor the specific situation of Maisonneuve was favourable to large-scale development.

In 1896 significant changes began to appear, as the Quebec economy entered a long-term expansion phase. The population increased, and new markets developed in western Canada. Between 1896 and 1914, in both Quebec and Canada, industrial output increased substantially and the economy grew at a pace that had not been seen since the flush times of the 1850s. Manufacturers could proceed with expansion plans and modernize their equipment.

The opening year of this boom, 1896, also saw the beginning of a second stage of industrialization in Maisonneuve, which lasted until 1901. The town now benefited from its advantages — greater integration into the Montreal economy and more adequate railway and harbour facilities. The new industrial establishments, and especially the shoe factories, were labour-intensive, and population growth was stimulated as a result.

By the end of 1901, Maisonneuve's industrial structure was already fairly diversified. There were four dominant industries: sugar refining, wallpaper, shoes and, to a lesser extent, canning. In the next five years, this base was consolidated, as production and employment increased. The only new company, a foundry, added to Maisonneuve's industrial diversity.

The third stage of industrialization lasted from 1907 to 1911 and was marked by both increased variety and increased specialization. Maisonneuve's specialization was in a single industry, shoe manufacturing, which was represented by a number of different plants. There were two developments in this industry between 1907 and 1911. One was the arrival of a new wave of shoe factories, which heightened the concentration of the industry in Maisonneuve. The second was the arrival of related industries attracted by this concentration.

Along with this specialization, Maisonneuve's industrial structure also became more diversified as new industries were established; the most significant were textile, biscuit and confectionery and shipbuilding industries. With this marked diversity and the presence of a number of fairly large companies in the town, it was impossible to describe any one firm as Maisonneuve's dominant company. In 1913 there were ten firms in Maisonneuve with more than 200 employees, and eight of these had 350 or more.

Clearly, the factors that led to the industrialization of Maisonneuve extended beyond the town limits. Production was growing in Montreal, causing industry to spill over into the suburbs. And in this context, Maisonneuve's location was particularly advantageous. Although these general conditions have to be taken into account, they don't explain everything. In a number of cases, Maisonneuve's industrial development policy appears to have been a determining factor in a company's decision to locate in Maisonneuve rather than in another suburban municipality.

This is where the logic and plans of land capital enter the picture. Very early in Maisonneuve's history the large developers, who were amply represented on the Maisonneuve town council, devised a strategy which they hoped would create favourable conditions for the development of their lands. It consisted of attracting industries by granting them advantageous terms; in turn, the industries would attract large numbers of workers, each seeking a residence near his workplace. While the impact on the market for industrial sites cannot be ignored, it was overshadowed by the effect of the arrival of workers. This policy was a clear success: Maisonneuve's population increased substantially, the developers sold their lands, and the town enjoyed rapid growth.

CHAPTER 5

THE POWER OF UTILITY MONOPOLIES

In the late nineteenth century, the utility sector in the Montreal region had evolved to the point where each industry within the sector was dominated by a single company. These powerful private monopolies were owned by leading financiers and, in a climate of rapid expansion of the region's urbanized territory and growing demand for the services they offered, they reaped substantial profits. A financier with an interest in a large utility company was concerned primarily with protecting his monopoly by eliminating any hint of competition. Another goal was to maximize profits by reducing expenses — in other words, to maintain the highest possible rates while keeping service to a minimum.

Small towns such as Maisonneuve were no match for these financial giants. Aiming to achieve rapid development, town councils were inclined to offer these companies highly advantageous conditions. But if they ventured to hold the company to its promise of adequate service, they encountered serious obstacles.

It was not only Maisonneuve that found itself in this situation: all of Montreal's other suburbs and many small towns elsewhere in Quebec and in other parts of North America faced similar problems. A close look at what happened in Maisonneuve reveals the intricate and troubled relationship between municipal governments and utility monopolies. As a beginning, the case of public transportation shows how monopolies grew more powerful at the expense of local public authorities.

The Public Transportation Trust

In 1893 Maisonneuve entrusted streetcar service to the Montreal Street Railway Company and, according to the contract, the company was obligated to run streetcar lines on Ontario and Sainte-Catherine streets as soon as the town government opened these arteries. However, when the town opened Ontario Street in 1894, the company refused to fulfil its responsibilities. Following legal action and long and laborious negotiations, a new agreement was reached in 1897. For the town, it constituted a step backwards from the 1893 contract.[1]

The company was no longer required to include the whole length of Ontario and Sainte-Catherine streets in its system. Streetcars would run on the two thoroughfares only as far as Letourneux Street, and then go down Letourneux as far as Notre-Dame Street. This mean that the eastern part of the municipality, representing a large portion of its territory, was left without service; Maisonneuve would require the extension of these two lines within five years only if there was an increase in the number of buildings constructed in that part of the town. Cars would run at ten-minute intervals on Sainte-Catherine Street, but on Ontario Street they would run at ten-minute intervals only during rush hours; at other times, the interval would be twenty minutes. This too was a reduction of the service anticipated in 1893.

In the next few years, there were frequent complaints about the service provided, especially on Ontario Street where a number of industries were located. For these enterprises, efficient transportation for their workers and quick communication with the commercial and financial centre of Montreal were essential. Most common were complaints that there were not enough streetcars and that motormen did not complete their routes and made passengers get off before reaching the end of the line. The company always replied that it was respecting its contract and delays that might occur were due to causes beyond its control.[2]

But while the Montreal Street Railway Company slowly extended its network outwards from the centre of Montreal to the periphery, other companies established during the 1890s specialized in suburban passenger transportation. One of these companies, the Park and Island Railway, served a number of localities in the northern and western part of the island, while another, the Montreal Island Belt Line, was concentrated in the east, from Maisonneuve to the end of the island.

These systems had a dual role. First, they facilitated the settlement of new suburban areas — to the great satisfaction of land developers. Second, they fulfilled a recreational function, allowing Montrealers to escape the city, especially on weekends. Their streetcars provided access to waterfront areas, which were more inviting than the cement walls of the harbour, and carried passengers to the region's amusement centres, Belmont Park and Dominion Park.[3]

The outward growth of the city towards the suburbs resulted in competition between these enterprises and the Montreal Street Railway Company with its ever-growing appetite. In a pattern that was common at the time, this competitive struggle ended with the victory of the strongest firm, which absorbed the smaller companies and became a powerful trust.

The scenario that unfolded in Maisonneuve, in this case involving the Montreal Island Belt Line, was consistent with the general pattern. In 1894 Maisonneuve's council granted the Belt Line the right to build a railway across the town; the company, however, apparently ran into difficulties and was not revived until 1896. Meanwhile, its plans had changed, and it now intended to put electric trains into service rather than a steam railway. In 1896 the Belt Line signed a new contract with Maisonneuve. Very similar to the town's existing contract with the Montreal Street Railway, it provided for the construction of a main line north of and parallel to Ontario Street. By 1900 the company had built its line but, in that year, it was reorganized again and renamed the Montreal Terminal Railway. Its relations with the council appear to have been better than those of the Montreal Street Railway, even if there were occasional complaints.

After a few years of operation, the Montreal Terminal Railway wanted to extend its system in the eastern suburbs of Montreal and signed a new contract with Maisonneuve in 1904. This contract authorized the company to build two new electric streetcar lines, one along Ernest and Adam streets and the other along Orléans and Sherbrooke streets. It also contained a large number of clauses fairly similar to those governing relations with the Montreal Street Railway. The town council retained substantial powers, especially over the scheduling of cars. Through this contract, Maisonneuve encouraged the development of a competing streetcar company and made it possible for service to reach a wider area, especially towards the north of the municipality.[4]

The 1893 contract with the Montreal Street Railway was not an exclusive one and the town was quite justified in granting a licence to another company. However, it is not surprising that the Montreal Street Railway would react to the growth of a competitor which might make life difficult in the east end and threaten its near-monopoly. This reaction was not long in coming.

Since it had begun to electrify its lines in 1892, the Montreal Street Railway had undergone considerable expansion. Its share capital had increased almost eightfold, from $900,000 in 1892 to $7 million in 1904. In 1892 the company had 8 electric streetcars in service; in 1904 it had about 300. This twelve-year period also saw an extension of the territory the Montreal Street Railway covered and an increase in the number of its lines. In 1901 the com-

A streetcar company crew at the corner of Notre-Dame and de La Salle streets, September 26, 1912.

pany gained control of the Montreal Park and Island Railway Co. During the same year, it extended its suburban network by obtaining operating concessions from the towns of Saint-Louis to north of Montreal and Saint-Paul to the southwest. In 1904 the village of De Lorimier in the east was added while the duration of the company's contract with Westmount was extended. In addition, a subsidiary, the Suburban Tramway and Power Co., obtained the right to operate in Longue-Pointe and Beaurivage in 1904.[5]

Thus, in 1904 the Montreal Street Railway had a near-monopoly. Suburban municipalities were subject to considerable pressure from the company and had virtually nowhere else to turn. Reform groups took up the public transportation issue, but their struggles were fruitless. The trust used a variety of tactics to reach its goals. Although its 1893 contract with Maisonneuve still had several years to run, it tried to obtain a new one along with more advantages.

The pretext for this new assault was the question of the Ontario and Sainte-Catherine street lines. The company had refused to run its lines over the full length of the two streets; in 1897 it had forced the town to retreat and agree to a five-year moratorium. This period ended in 1902, and the question was once more placed on the agenda. On November 19,1902, the owner of an Ontario Street shoe factory, George Slater, sent the town council a letter accompanied by a petition demanding that the streetcar line be extended that autumn. Slater advocated an eastward extension along Ontario Street as far as 1st Avenue and then onto 1st Avenue to provide service to the Slater factory and to the new houses nearby.[6] A lack of results forced him to take up the cause again the following year. The company initially refused to extend its lines and, when Maisonneuve's secretary-treasurer pointed to its contract obligations, it used delaying tactics. Sensing that it was in a powerful position, the Montreal Street Railway used the question of the Ontario and Sainte-Catherine street lines to get the town to grant it a new and more favourable contract. A lengthy exchange of letters, lasting from December 7, 1903, to September 9, 1904, shows how the company reached its ends.

On December 7, 1903, the town's lawyer presented a statement to L.-J. Forget, President of the Montreal Street Railway, demanding that the company improve streetcar service. In particular, the statement called for the same frequency of service as in Montreal, an extension of the Ontario Street line to the town's eastern boundary, streetcar service for the Slater factory during rush hours and, finally, an extension to Maisonneuve of the new Montreal line running "from Davidson Street to the CPR shops."[7] The company did not reply until March 18,1904, when its managing director, W. G. Ross, stated that he was ready to discuss extending lines or service if the town was ready to consider a new contract or an extension of the existing one.[8] Ross's next move came on April 25. Writing in less than perfect French, he demanded an exclusive franchise — the first time this demand had been made officially:

> With reference to your letter of March 8, in which you ask us to extend our streetcar lines in your municipality and increase service, we are writing to inform you that we have studied this question very seriously and we are prepared to satisfy your council's request if we can reach an agreement that will be approved by both parties.
>
> We would like to help as much as possible in the development of your municipality, but since the new lines and increased service you are

requesting will involve a considerable expenditure of capital, which is not likely to yield any profit to our company for several years, we will have to obtain preferential terms from your municipality, with no competition, so that the interests of our operation can be protected for the duration of the mandate on which we will be able to agree.[9]

The town council issued a spirited reply:

A decision has been made to tell you that before going further or entering into new negotiations, your company must extend its streetcar line along the portions of Sainte-Catherine and Ontario streets lying between Letourneux Street and the eastern limits of this town, within one month from this date. If the company fails to do this, the Town of Maisonneuve will consider it a refusal on your part to use these portions of Ontario and Sainte-Catherine streets for the operation of your system of streetcars in the future.[10]

Faced with this position, the company yielded and, on June 2, its managing director announced that it intended to extend the two lines.[11] But in mid-July work had not begun, and the company once again took a hard line, this time raising the issue of the contract the town had recently signed with the Montreal Terminal Railway.[12] This move left Montreal Street Railway standing on shaky ground. It was the responsibility of the courts to determine whether the town had broken its contract, and the Montreal Street Railway was careful not to take legal action because the council had not violated the contract when it issued an operating permit to another company.

The final attack was launched on September 7, 1904, when W.G. Ross wrote to Maisonneuve council members:

The difficulties that have recently arisen between us regarding our mutual obligations by virtue of the contract that links us, the tiresome and fruitless legal complications that could result from them, and the rapid growth of your town have persuaded us that passage of a new bylaw to govern relations between your town and the Company is urgently required by all the interested parties.

You have asked us to complete the Ontario and Sainte-Catherine street lines this autumn and build new lines next spring along Letourneux, Ontario, Pie IX and Sherbrooke streets to connect with the Canadian Pacific shops in Montreal via Nolan Street.

If you agree to grant us a new franchise as soon as possible, we will, for our part, commit ourselves to completing the Ontario and Sainte-Catherine street lines this autumn and beginning work next May on lines along Letourneux, Ontario, Pie IX and Sherbrooke streets to connect with the

Canadian Pacific shops in Montreal via Nolan Street, with operation to start in July. The franchise you grant us will have to include all streets in the Town on which routes could be established in the future, as the development of your Town requires them and after the interested parties have agreed.

Naturally, it will be impossible for us to finish work on Ontario and Sainte-Catherine streets this autumn unless a new franchise is granted us in early October, and as we understand that no bylaw can be passed without thirty days' notice having been given, we request that you be so kind as to come to an immediate decision on the advisability of giving such notice so as to proceed with all possible dispatch.

For our part, we will be prepared at any time to enter into immediate negotiations with you to decide on the terms of the by-law to be passed.[13]

The new contract the Montreal Street Railway wanted required a bylaw, passed first by the council and then approved by a majority of Maisonneuve's property owners (on the basis of both number and total property value). Bylaw 107 was presented for first reading at the town council meeting of October 10, 1904. According to the testimony of the mayor, the bylaw had not been drawn up by representatives of the town but had been submitted by the company in the exact form in which it was brought before the council.[14] Under the new contract, the council would lose a number of its powers, while the company would get an exclusive franchise for thirty years on all the town's streets and the right to carry freight.

A vigorous opposition to the bylaw was organized. On October 10, the Montreal newspaper *La Presse* sounded the alarm:

It will be in the interests of the citizens of Maisonneuve to attend the meeting of their Town Council that will take place tonight. There they will hear the most astonishing bylaw that has ever been read before a town council. In effect, the bylaw gives the Montreal Street Railway Company a perpetual exclusive franchise on all of Maisonneuve's streets without any return to the town. It is a twin to the De Lorimier bylaw. The bylaw is all the more curious in that the Company's current franchise still has eighteen years to run, and the Company has failed to live up to the terms of its contract by refusing to extend its system on Ontario and Sainte-Catherine streets.[15]

The next day, the newspaper carried the headline : "Exclusive franchise — The Street Railway demands a monopoly on Maisonneuve's streets — Draconian bylaw — a number of citizens resist the invasion of certain streets by the Tramways Company."[16] Not surprisingly, among the resisters was the Montreal Terminal Railway. Three months earlier, the council had authorized it to build lines on certain streets, and now it appeared to be giving the Montreal Street Railway the right to build competing lines on the same streets. The company's managing director, a Mr. Mullarkey, expressed his indignation to the council.

The council meeting of October 12, 1904, was the scene of a confrontation between the two companies. But with the Montreal Street Railway threatening to "withdraw its offer" if it could not run its lines on the same streets as its competitors, the council passed bylaw 107.[17] In the meantime a citizens' committee, formed under the leadership of Mayor Trefflé Bleau, Alderman Walter Reed and the lawyer Adolphe Desilets, worked to convince Maisonneuve's property owners to reject the bylaw — which they did by a large majority on October 27.[18]

The Montreal Street Railway refused to admit defeat, and it did not hesitate to resort to intimidation. Its first effort consisted of substantially reducing service on Notre-Dame, Sainte-Catherine and Ontario streets to show citizens that opposing the company wishes could have serious costs.[19] Protests from the town council were futile. Another tactic was to lay tracks across Ernest Street to delay construction of its rival's line.[20] The town had to get involved and the council asked the federal Railway Commissioners to allow the Montreal Terminal Railway's line to cross the Montreal Street Railway's.[21] The company's campaign also included a petition, dated November 29 and signed by about 400 people. Obviously instigated by supporters of the Montreal Street Railway, it stated that the slowdown in service had caused considerable harm and that the legal action the town was thinking of bringing against the company "could not yield any useful results for the town's citizens." Therefore, it suggested that the council "should make one last attempt to open negotiations with the company, discuss the question in a dispassionate manner and in the general interest and, if possible, obtain satisfaction."[22] It was because of these pressures that early in 1905 the town council passed bylaw 110 — a new and only slightly changed version of the bylaw rejected a few months earlier by Maisonneuve's property owners.[23]

It was a very different bylaw than the one the town had adopted in 1893. While the 1893 contract had been explicitly non-exclusive (thus making it possible for the town to grant a franchise to the Montreal Terminal Railway), the Montreal Street Railway was now given the privilege of exclusive operation, which would extend for thirty years on all the city's streets except 3rd Avenue and the portion of Pie-IX Boulevard between Notre-Dame and Ontario. Obviously, in the case of streets already being served by another company, the Montreal Street Railway's exclusive rights would not take effect until existing contracts expired. In the meantime, however, it obtained a concurrent right-of-way on these streets. While the 1893 agreement was limited to passenger transportation, this time the right to carry freight was added. The company also obtained a twenty-year tax exemption on all its installations. Only one new route was provided for in the agreement, in addition to the three outlined in 1893. Fares remained the same as before; schedules were fixed in the new agreement and the council lost the right it had enjoyed under the 1893 contract to change them. When the thirty-year contract expired, if the town refused to renew it for ten more years, the company could force the town to buy its system and installations in Maisonneuve at 10 per cent above a cost to be determined by arbitration. A ridiculously low fine of ten dollars a day could be imposed on the company if it failed to live up to any of its obligations under the contract.

On the whole, the new contract represented a clear reduction in the power of the town council to control public transportation, without granting any significant advantages for citizens and streetcar users. The town was caught in a vise. Not only had it cut off the possibility of creating new competition in the future, but it had undercut the effectiveness of the existing competitor, the Montreal Terminal Railway. By building lines on the same streets and thus draining off a large portion of its clientele, the Montreal Street Railway could easily wipe out its rival.

The town council passed bylaw 110 on final reading on February 22, 1905. The property owners would have their say on March 9 and, in anticipation of the vote, the battle that had raged the year before was resumed with undiminished fury. On one side was the "Progress Committee" favourable to the Montreal Street Railway. Its leaders were aldermen Riendeau, Trudel and Percy Bennett and former mayor Hubert Desjardins.[24] The opposition formed around a citizens' committee, again lead by Adolphe Desilets and Walter Reed; the Montreal Terminal Railways's lawyer, N.-K Laflamme, was also very active. The opposition mounted a slate to contest the municipal elections scheduled for March with Walter Reed as a candidate for mayor and Desilets and Alexandre Michaud and a Mr. Fafard for positions on the council.

La Presse, still involved in the fight against the trust, attacked the company's tactics of organizing petitions in favour of the bylaw. It criticized the majority group on the council for having "manouvered for the company's profit," and "conspirators working for the 'Street' " for "persisting in falsely representing bylaw 110." In particular, it charged, these conspirators had told the citizens of Maisonneuve that under the 1893 contract the company did not have to run streetcars more frequently than once every twenty minutes and that the company would reduce service if bylaw 110 was not passed.[25]

Opponents of the bylaw argued that the town and its citizens were much better protected by the 1893 contract and that service could be improved and the system expanded under its provisions. They attacked the exclusive privileges granted the Montreal Street Railway and denounced the town council's increasing powerlessness and the company's omnipotence.[26]

Letourneux Street, October 31, 1908.

However, the citizens' committee was unable to repeat the previous year's triumph of defeating the tramway trust and on March 9, 1905, Maisonneuve's property owners upheld bylaw 110 by a narrow margin of twenty-two votes (216 to 194).[27]

Credit for this reversal must be given to the effectiveness of the Montreal Street Railway's action. In the first round, in the autumn of 1904, the company tried to have bylaw 107 passed quickly, perhaps hoping that the opposition would not have time to organize. But when it returned to the fray after its initial defeat, it took the time to solidify its position and exert considerable pressure on the citizens, and it succeeded in convincing a majority of the property owners. It was not so successful, however, with the wide electorate: Walter Reed and his slate were elected by a large majority on March 20, 1905.[28] But this change came too late to overturn the bylaw. The new mayor hesitated, but finally decided to sign the measure on May 25, 1905.[29]

Contemporary observers interpreted this controversy as a battle between large and small property owners. According to this view, the large property owners supported the trust while the small property owners leaned towards the rival company.[30] The presence of representatives of the Bennett and Desjardins families on the "Progress Committee" tends to support this view. The Montreal Street Railway provided access to the entire Montreal region, while the Terminal's lines were limited to its eastern section. This would likely have been an important consideration for the large property owners, who hoped to create better conditions for Maisonneuve's population growth by supporting the trust. On the other hand, the small property owners living in Maisonneuve would have been more concerned with the improved service that competition would bring.

After the controversy ended, the Montreal Terminal Railway was no longer an important factor in Maisonneuve's history, and soon afterward was absorbed by the Montreal Street Railway. Negotiations were undertaken in 1906, and agreement was reached on the sale the following year; from then on, the tramway trust's mastery of public transportation on Montreal Island was unchallenged.[31] Its only competitors were the large railway companies which, for the most part, served the far suburbs and thus had a different clientele.

The story of Maisonneuve's streetcar system is only one episode in the history of public transportation in the Montreal region, but it is a good illustration of the methods by which monopolies were formed in the utility sector. The Montreal Street Railway's initial goal in Maisonneuve was to establish a position for itself by obtaining a contract; it was well aware that with a foothold of this sort it would be hard to dislodge. To get this first contract it was prepared to make concessions, especially since a competitor had appeared on the scene. Thus, it agreed to operate without an exclusive franchise and allowed the town council to retain significant powers.

Once it had reached this initial goal, it did not rest until it had obtained an exclusive franchise and had severely reduced the town council's powers. It went about its business as it wished, unconcerned about the many ways in which it was deviating from its commitments. Forced on the defensive, the town council issued repeated protests and notices of default. The company, however, was in no apparent hurry to comply with the town's demands, and employed the astonishing tactic of using the non-fulfillment of its obligations as an instrument of negotiation. Only if the town granted it new privileges would it agree to respect its previous commitments. The town authorities were not able to withstand blackmail of this sort.

Electricity

Maisonneuve also tried to promote competition among suppliers of electrical power. Here, too, the struggle was an unequal one, although the result was not as unsatisfactory as in the case of public transportation.

Before 1896 the electricity Maisonneuve needed for street lighting and residential consumption was produced by the municipality itself. However, Maisonneuve's civic leaders concluded that this system was unsatisfactory, and decided in 1897 to entrust electricity service to private enterprise. The Royal Electric Company, at the time the dominant electricity supplier in the Montreal region, was awarded the contract.[32] The agreement covered a ten-year period and did not give the company an exclusive franchise.

The contract established the rates to be charged and specified that, if rates were reduced in the city of Montreal, they would be lowered for Maisonneuve electricity users as well. The company was also given the responsibility of providing arc lamps for street lighting, for which the town would pay the same prices as Montreal: $124.10 for the first year, $120.45 per light for the next three years and $116.80 per light for the remaining six years of the contract.[33] Finally, the company would provide twenty-four lights to illuminate the town's municipal buildings free of charge. If the company did not respect the provisions of the agreement, it could be charged a fine of $10 per day and the contract could be cancelled.[34]

Royal Electric thus succeeded both in expanding its market in the metropolitan region and in gaining a foothold in Maisonneuve. This was clearly only a first step towards its ultimate objective of obtaining a monopoly. And to reach it, the company did not wait until the ten-year contract expired. An opportunity arose in 1899, when the town council asked the company to reduce its rates.[35] Royal Electric took advantage of this request to have the 1897 contract cancelled. Negotiations produced a new contract, more favourable to the company and covering a twenty-year period, which was signed on January 20, 1900. In its most significant new feature, it gave Royal Electric an exclusive franchise in the town of Maisonneuve.[36]

In the meantime, there was a very clear trend towards monopoly in the metropolitan region as a whole. In 1901 Royal Electric merged with two other electricity companies and the Montreal Gas Company to form a powerful electricity and gas trust. The merged enterprise, which took the name of the Montreal Light, Heat and Power Company, entered into a struggle with another conglomerate, the Lachine Rapids Hydraulics and Land Co. Ltd., which it ultimately purchased in 1903. These mergers gave Montreal Light, Heat and Power unchallenged control of Montreal's energy market.[37]

In Maisonneuve, the company tried to protect and extend its monopoly. Thus, in the autumn of 1905, it offered to change the street lighting system and reduce the annual rate from $115 to $80 per light on the condition that the town extend its exclusive privileges for a twenty-five-year period. The town council, however, wanted a larger rate reduction, and no agreement was reached.[38]

With one hand, the company protected its monopoly; with the other hand, it exploited the market. This exploitation was obvious in the high price the company charged for street lighting — $115 — when, as became clear in 1905, it could get along with much less. It also showed up in the quality of the service the company provided. The street lighting proved unsatisfactory, and the lights frequently failed, a consequence of the company's out-of-date lighting system.[39] The town collected a voluminous file on exploitation, even going so far as asking policemen to prepare reports on defective lights. But there was no response to the council's complaints.[40] As a result, the town council tried to free itself from Montreal Light, Heat and Power's control.

A new circumstance made its task easier. In the years following the formation of the Montreal electricity trust, new companies tried to capture a share of the rich urban market. One of these was the Dominion Light, Heat and Power Company.[41]

Among this corporation's five principals, the names of Ralph Locke, Raoul Lanthier and Marious Dufresne stand out. Locke and Lanthier owned shoe factories in Maisonneuve, while Marious Dufresne was the brother of Maisonneuve councillor Oscar Dufresne and would be appointed town engineer in 1910. In addition, the company planned to build its electric generating plants in Maisonneuve. The town council's eagerness to deal with Dominion Light, Heat and Power was therefore entirely understandable.

A few months after the new company was established, the town of Maisonneuve took a first step towards freeing itself from the contract with Royal Electric, now a subsidiary of Montreal Light, Heat and Power. It placed the company in default, complaining of bad lighting; more specifically, the notice of default alleged that a number of street lights were off all night and lighting for private customers was defective. It therefore demanded that the company provide a steady supply of power in the quantity required by the town. The penalty for non-compliance was a fine provided for in the agreement and, after fifteen days, cancellation of the contract.[42]

In the meantime, Dominion Light, Heat and Power began operation. Its charter authorized it to manufacture gas and electricity, distribute them on Montreal Island, and install pipes, poles and wires on and under the island's streets, roads and lanes. Thus, the company notified Maisonneuve that it planned to erect poles in the town and asked the council for help in determining their location.[43] It established its first generating plant in Maisonneuve and expected to build another in downtown Montreal. In 1910 it

The urban landscape reflected the spread of electricity: poles and wires in 1912.

began to distribute electricity, with a system of wires covering Maisonneuve, east-end Montreal, and Sainte-Catherine Street as far as Guy Street in the west-central part of the city. In an advertisement, it emphatically declared its intention of fighting the monopoly: "The Dominion Light, Heat & Power Company has begun operations in Montreal on a solid financial basis and intends to have its share of the city's customers.... Therefore, we appeal to the taxpayers of the City of Montreal to do everything in their power to combat any street lighting monopoly."[44] To attract customers, it advertised that its rates were lower than those of its rival.

Montreal Light, Heat and Power reacted quickly to its competitor's entry into the market. As early as 1909, it requested an injunction to prevent

Dominion Light, Heat, and Power from installing poles and wires on the streets of Maisonneuve, stating that this would violate the exclusive powers granted Royal Electric in 1900. The municipality replied to the company's action by arguing that the 1900 contract was invalid and even took direct measures towards having the agreement cancelled.[45] According to the town's argument, the contract was *ultra vires* because it had been approved by a simple resolution of the town council rather than a bylaw. The town also maintained that in failing to provide the required power and service the company had not lived up to its obligations, and that the price charged for street lighting was far too high.[46] This action was the opening round in a legal battle that would last two years.

Convinced that the Royal Electric contract was null and void, the town council decided in the autumn of 1910 to award Dominion Light, Heat and Power a contract to light Maisonneuve's streets for a ten-year period starting in January 1, 1911, during which it was granted exclusive privileges by the town. The price would be $80 per arc light per year, a saving of more than $25 over what had been charged previously.[47]

Not surprisingly, Montreal Light, Heat and Power responded by initiating a new round of legal proceedings.[48] These dragged on and, in 1912, Montreal Light, Heat and Power suggested that its differences with Maisonneuve be settled by arbitration.[49] With Maisonneuve's own lawyer advising that its allegations against the company were turning out to be hard to prove, the town accepted this proposal.[50]

The two parties quickly reached an agreement. The town would rescind the contract it had awarded Dominion Light, Heat and Power and reaffirm the 1900 contract with Royal Electric. It would also accept an additional one with Montreal Light, Heat and Power, covering the ten years after the twenty-year period provided for in the Royal Electric contract had run out. Montreal Light, Heat and Power would install better quality street lights and would charge only $62.50 per light per year. The parties would withdraw their legal actions, with each paying its own legal costs. Moreover, Dominion Light, Heat and Power would acknowledge the exclusive franchise granted Royal Electric and Montreal Light, Heat and Power and, in return, Montreal Light, Heat and Power would allow Dominion to carry on its operations in Maisonneuve in areas other than the lighting of streets and public places throughout the period of the franchise. Finally, the town would compensate Dominion for rescinding its 1910 contract by paying it an amount equal to the difference between the price it had been charging ($80 per light) and Montreal Light, Heat and Power's new price for 200 lights over the remainder of its contract period. It would also compensate Dominion for its legal fees.[51]

Thus, the attempt to break Montreal Light, Heat and Power's monopoly was aborted, and the electricity trust was solidly re-established in Maisonneuve. But the introduction of competition had not been in vain: in the end,

Ontario Street at de La Salle Street, looking west.

it had produced a drastic reduction in the cost of street lighting and a clear improvement in the system. In addition, while Dominion Light, Heat and Power was shut out of lighting streets and public buildings, it was still a factor in the residential consumption market, where it provided an alternative to the trust.

Because of where its plant was and who its principals were, Dominion Light, Heat and Power was regarded as a Maisonneuve company. However, it soon lost this designation by becoming part of a conglomerate, the Public Service Corporation.[52] The 1912 agreement appears to have straightened out Montreal Light, Heat and Power's relations with the municipality, as the council found no further cause for complaint.

Water Distribution

In the area of water distribution, there were two issues that brought the town and the Montreal Water and Power Company into conflict in the years following 1896: extension of the aqueduct system and water quality. Although a number of towns attempted concerted action on the water quality issue, they did not get very far.

In an agreement reached in 1895, the municipality had committed itself to installing at its own expense the new water pipes that would be needed as Maisonneuve's inhabited area expanded and new residents arrived. The company undertook to buy these links in the aqueduct system when the return on the town's investment reached 10 per cent. A problem arose in 1901 when the company refused to buy the sections of the line the town had built. At issue in the litigation was the amount to be paid, since the company considered the town's construction costs too high. After a two-year dispute, the parties reached a compromise, ending further friction between the town council and the company over the construction of water lines.[53] A possible explanation for the company's flexible attitude is the fact that Maisonneuve was entering an era of rapid growth, which made it profitable to invest in the town with new expenditures justified by increasing revenues.

The quality of the water distributed was as much of a matter of concern as its quantity. Montreal Water and Power was required to provide clean, drinkable water. Its supply, however, was drawn — unfiltered — from the St. Lawrence. According to the Provincial Board of Health, in a opinion expressed in February 1904, the company was delivering polluted water to its suburban customers, at least at certain times of the year, a practice that heightened the risk of a typhoid epidemic.[54]

One consequence of this situation was concerted action by a number of municipalities, a rare phenomenon in the political annals of Montreal's suburbs. The idea was first put forward by the town council of Saint-Henri, which called a meeting for April 15, 1904, to discuss water quality and its effect on health. Delegates from Saint-Henri, Sainte-Cunégonde, Maisonneuve, Côte-Saint-Paul, De Lorimier and Outremont attended this meeting, and heard the mayor of Saint-Henri say: "In unity there is strength, and it is my conviction that if we unite we will succeed in reaching our common goal of having drinkable water all year round."[55]

The delegates agreed that it was necessary to discuss the question with representatives of Montreal Water and Power, but they differed on what attitude to take towards the company. A meeting was set for April 26 and, on this occasion, Westmount and Saint-Louis were represented in addition to the other towns. The president of the company, George E. Drummond, told the delegates that the cost of establishing a filtration system would have to be borne by the municipalities. The delegates responded with a cry of protest and reminded Drummond that the company's contracts required it to provide drinkable water. The company president asked for a few weeks to draw up plans and a cost estimate.[56]

A few weeks later Montreal Water and Power presented its terms in writing. The company said that it was willing to provide filtered water under certain conditions.[57] No longer was it demanding financial compensation alone; instead, it was asking for an overall revision of its contracts with the municipalities. It had general demands that applied to all the municipalities and particular ones applying to each one. To make conditions uniform, it demanded that the three towns (Westmount, Sainte-Cunégonde and Saint-Louis du Mile-End) that had not given the company fifty-year contracts extend the period in their agreements. In some towns, rates would have to be changed.

In the case of Maisonneuve, Montreal Water and Power demanded a number of changes in the company's favour. It wanted extra payment when water was shut off to install fire hydrants on factory grounds, as well as a twenty-five-year municipal tax exemption. On the question of rates, its position was that "the rates currently charged residents of Maisonneuve will remain in force until the fifty years of the franchise have run out, and any clauses to the contrary in the existing contract will be abrogated as a result." To justify its demands the company maintained that, even if these new agreements were reached, it would be impossible for it "to pay any interest or dividend in the next few years on all the capital invested in the enterprise."[58]

Intermunicipal co-operation did not bring the hoped-for results. The towns did not succeed in forming a true common front that could force the company to moderate its demands. Maisonneuve's town council rejected the company's proposal, but this did not solve the problem.[59] The question of water quality was raised again by the Board of Health three years after its initial warning:

> The Executive Committee reaffirms the opinion expressed by the Board of Health in February 1904 to the effect that the water provided by the Montreal Water and Power Company's distribution system is polluted, at least at certain times of the year, and hence does not hesitate to attribute to that water the typhoid epidemic that, again this year, has struck the suburbs of Montreal supplied by this company; this epidemic was predicted, as there had been no improvement in the conditions of the distribution system.[60]

The company replied by blaming polluted water on the town of Verdun's sewer.[61]

The filtration question was finally settled in 1911. Having first signed a contract to supply filtered water to the town of Westmount, the company agreed to extend this service to Maisonneuve. In return, article 19 of the 1891 contract, which provided for a rate change if Maisonneuve were annexed, was quashed, so that rates would remain the same until the contract expired. This was a less onerous condition than the one the company had demanded in 1904.

How can this change in the company's attitude be explained? Since 1904, the number of public health advocates had grown considerably, and citizens were clearly more aware of the problems of unfiltered water. But the determining factor in the affair was undoubtedly the special situation of the town of Westmount, which was also served by Montreal Water and Power. Westmount was the home of the richest members of Montreal's bourgeoisie. These big businessmen were primarily English-speaking and some of them controlled large Canadian corporations. They were in a position to exert strong pressure to get clean, filtered water on favourable terms. Once Montreal Water and Power had agreed to make this committment to Westmount, it could hardly refuse it to the other municipalities it served.

Water distribution is another illustration of the weakness of a small suburban town in its relation with private utility companies. Because water service in the city of Montreal was under municipal ownership, Montreal Water and Power specialized in serving the suburbs, and the small, separate municipalities it dealt with had little power to offer effective resistance.

CHAPTER 6

A WORKING-CLASS TOWN

To encourage their town's growth, Maisonneuve's developers and town council pursued a policy of providing for adequate utility service and stimulating industrialization. The policy was a success and, between 1896 and 1910, Maisonneuve underwent rapid development. As the population increased, its character changed — Maisonneuve's new population was very heavily working-class and led by a local bourgeoisie.

Population Growth

Once again, the way in which Maisonneuve developed can best be understood by placing it in a wider context. For Montreal, the first decade of the twentieth century was a period of intense growth. Its average annual rate of population growth during the period was 5.74 per cent, and the 1911 census recorded that Montreal and its close suburbs had a total population of more than half a million. In ten years, the population of the city of Montreal itself grew from 267,730 to 467,986. New residents, however, were not the only component of this increase; part of the jump was due to the numerous annexations Montreal carried out during the period. Urbanization has to be examined as a total phenomenon, with the city and its suburbs taken together. From a figure of 324,880 in 1901, their population grew in ten years to 528,397 and reached 689,753 in 1921.

Migration played a substantial role in this growth. In the early twentieth century, a large and steady stream of rural French Canadians came to settle in the city, which now offered them an alternative to emigration to the

United States. Newcomers also arrived from outside Canada, as immigration increased again, following a slowdown towards the end of the nineteenth century. However, the wave of immigration early in the twentieth century had some different features from its mid-nineteenth-century predecessor. Immigrants from the British Isles continued to arrive in large numbers, but an increasing proportion of them were English and the relative number of Irish in the city was declining. This era also saw the appearance of an entirely new stream of immigration from the European continent and especially from eastern Europe. Immigrants of Jewish origin, coming primarily from Poland and various parts of the Russian empire, arrived in Montreal by the thousands. They began to settle in Montreal in the 1890s and, by 1911, they represented about 6 per cent of the city's population. Far behind in terms of numbers were a few thousand Italians and other immigrants of diverse origins. Montreal, until then an overwhelmingly British and French city, became much more cosmopolitan. Since the city core was already a systematically inhabited zone before the influx of newcomers, the new immigration led to a substantial expansion of Montreal's populated area. As was often the case in North American cities, some immigrants settled in the old parts of Montreal, in cheap, dilapidated houses. Thus, Jews and Italians formed virtual colonies within the city's territory, while the former residents of these neighbourhoods headed for other sections of the metropolitan area and mostly for the suburbs.

Among the largest of the suburban municipalities that grew up around Montreal in the 1870s and 1880s were Saint-Henri, Sainte-Cunégonde and Saint-Gabriel in the west end, Saint-Jean-Baptiste to the north and Hochelaga in the east. Montreal annexed some of these in the late nineteenth century. The suburbs then underwent a second stage of development in the twenty years preceding the First World War, substantially extending the limits of the urbanized area surrounding Montreal. The dividing line between these two periods of development is not a clear one. Some suburbs that grew rapidly in the nineteenth century, such as Saint-Henri and Hochelaga, continued to develop in the early part of the twentieth. Saint-Gabriel and Sainte-Cunégonde, on the other hand, became fully inhabited in the nineteenth century and their populations remained almost constant in subsequent years. Some suburbs were founded in the nineteenth century but experienced the bulk of their growth later on.

The second stage of expansion was closely linked to the growth of industrial production in Montreal. The city's large manufacturing plants, employing hundreds and sometimes thousands of people and requiring huge tracts of land, date from this era. As Canada's population became larger and more urban, Montreal increasingly took on the character of a metropolis, which entailed the development of the commercial and service sectors and, consequently, created an increased demand for manpower. Unlike the first suburbs which hugged the edges of the city, the new municipalities were large consumers of space and considerably extended the frontiers of urban settlement. This geographical expansion was stimulated by the arrival of the electric streetcar. Diversity was another feature of this stage — primarily residential communities like Outremont and Rosemount grew up alongside industrial towns like Maisonneuve and Lachine. In addition, housing was organized on the basis of an increasingly clear social hierarchy: there were working-class suburbs like De Lorimier and Rosemount and upper-class ones like Westmount and Outremont. Thus, each municipality increasingly acquired a specialized role within the metropolitan area and all of them interacted with one another more and more closely.

The suburbs of Montreal were now exploding in all directions. In the southwest, Côte-Saint-Paul, Ville Emard and Verdun, which together had a population of only 3,635 in 1901, had grown to a total of 21,229 ten years later — an increase of 486 per cent. Farther afield, the old municipality of Lachine almost doubled its population in the same period. West of the city was Westmount, the fiefdom of English Canada's big capitalists, which grew rapidly from the late nineteenth century on. The neighbouring towns of Notre-Dame-de-Grâce, Notre-Dame-de-Neiges and Côte-des-Neiges also registered population increases. But they were too far from the city to experience the full effect of this wave of growth, and their populations remained small.

The tentacles of suburban Montreal stretched far to the north, reaching the Rivière des Prairies (Back River). But, despite the extent of the territory covered, population density in this area remained fairly small. Only two northern suburbs, Saint-Louis and De Lorimier, grew substantially, while Outremont was also a rising community even though its population was smaller. The other municipalities north of Montreal — Villeray, Ahuntsic, Sault-au-Recollet, Cartierville and Bordeaux — were hardly more than large villages at the beginning of the First World War. This part of the island was also the site of an interesting example of a planned community: the Town of Mount Royal was built at the northern portal of the tunnel under the mountain. However, it did not begin to become settled until the 1920s.

The urban web also extended to the east, where the major centre was Maisonneuve. There were plans to develop Maisonneuve's northern neighbour Rosemount, but its population was still small in 1914. East of Maisonneuve, Longue-Pointe occupied a huge expanse, but along with its enclaves of Tétraultville and Beaurivage it still had fewer than 10,000 people in 1911. There were, however, some new industrial developments, indicating that the process of urbanization had begun.

The development of the new territories was often anarchic, and political consolidation came to be seen as a necessity. The large sums of money spent on infrastructure led to a high level of debt and, after a few years, annexation

appeared to be an attractive solution, especially for munici-
ere growth had slowed down or reached a plateau. Only four
ities were annexed in the nineteenth century but, at the begin-
e twentieth, the annexation movement snowballed with 1905 and
ing especially active years (Table 6-1, Map 5). In 1883 the first
annexation — of Hochelaga — had led to the creation of Maisonneuve; now,
thirty-five years later, the absorption of Maisonneuve brought the second
wave of annexations to a close. Twenty-three municipalities were annexed
during the thirty-five-year period, along with a few pieces of land that were
not legally constituted. When the process was completed, the area covered
by the city of Montreal had increased.

For Maisonneuve, population figures are difficult of pin down, since there

Table 6-1
Municipalities Annexed by Montreal, 1883-1918

Year	Municipality
1883	Town of Hochelaga
1886	Town of Saint-Jean-Baptiste
1887	Village of Saint-Gabriel
1893	Town of Côte-Saint-Louis
1905	Town of Sainte-Cunégonde
1905	Town of Saint-Henri
1905	Village of Villeray
1908	Town of Notre-Dame-des-Neiges
1909	Village of De Lorimier
1910	Ville Emard
1910	Ville Saint-Paul
1910	Town of Saint-Louis
1910	Town of Côte-des-Neiges
1910	Town of Notre-Dame-de-Grâce
1910	Village of Rosemount
1910	Village of Tétraultville
1910	Village of Beaurivage-de-la-Longue-Pointe
1910	Village of Ahuntsic
1910	Town of Bordeaux
1910	Town of Longue-Pointe
1916	Town of Cartierville
1916	Town of Sault-au-Recollet
1918	Town of Maisonneuve

Source: City of Montreal, Service d'urbanisme (City Planning Department),
    Toponymie.

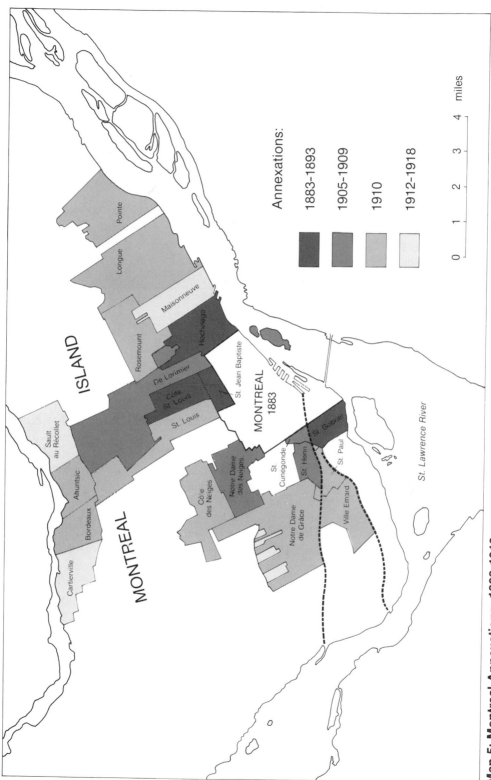

Map 5: Montreal Annexations, 1883-1918

Annexations:

1883-1893

1905-1909

1910

1912-1918

0 1 2 3 4

miles

ISLAND

MONTREAL

MONTRÉAL

Cartierville

Bordeaux

Ahuntsic

Sault
au Récollet

Côte
des Neiges

Notre Dame
des Neiges

Notre Dame
de Grâce

Ville Emard

St. Cunégonde

St. Henri

St. Paul

St. Gabriel

St. Louis

Côte
St. Louis

De Lorimier

Rosemount

Longue

Pointe

Maisonneuve

Hochelaga

St. Jean Baptiste

MONTREAL
1883

St. Lawrence River

are significant discrepancies in the available sources (Table 6-2). The more reliable figures are provided by the federal census, though the results of the 1911 census were the subject of vigorous debate in Maisonneuve:

> Municipal authorities refuse to accept the figure of 18,674 given by the census as being the population of the town. Mayor Michaud and Secretary Ecrement believe that they are in a position to establish that Maisonneuve is home to a population of 26,000 souls. Nor is the town of Maisonneuve the only one that is protesting.[1]

Privately, the secretary-treasurer wrote to a correspondent that "the Canadian census of 1911-1912 does not show the exact population of the Town of Maisonneuve; whole streets were forgotten."[2] At a town council meeting in September 1911, the mayor protested against the federal census and said that reports from curés confirmed the figure of 26,035 residents obtained by town assessors; he demanded that the federal government record what he regarded as the real population of Maisonneuve.[3] A careful examination of the assessment roll, from which the mayor's figures were taken, shows a great number of double counts and indicates that the census figures were probably quite accurate.[4]

The dispute surrounding the 1911 census is an indication of the extent to which administrators regarded population growth as an essential feature of Maisonneuve's reputation as a bustling, industrial town. But this was not the only reason they insisted on a high population figure. If the population were inflated, per capita debt could be reduced significantly. This was an extremely important consideration when they went to the financial markets trying to borrow substantial sums of money — which is precisely what they were doing in the years just before and after 1911. Maisonneuve needed large amounts for infrastructure projects, such as streets, sewers and watermains, and even more to carry out the ambitious beautification program it inaugurated in 1910. Thus, population inflation appears to have resulted much more from a cleverly planned strategy than from administrative incompetence. However, even if the figures recorded in the census were not as prodigious as those calculated by the town, the administrators had nothing to complain about. According to the census figures, Maisonneuve grew by 372 percent in the ten years between 1901 and 1911, for an annual average of 16.8 per cent. With the exception of Verdun, no other city of town in Quebec had a higher rate of growth.

A very rough estimate of the share of Maisonneuve's population growth between 1901 and 1911 attributable to natural increase can be calculated. There were 3,575 Catholics in Maisonneuve in 1901 and 16,277 in 1911, for an increase of 12,702. In this ten-year period, the births of 4,335 Catholics were registered. There was a total of 2,408 deaths in Maisonneuve dur-

Table 6-2
Calculations of Population of Town Maisonneuve, 1884-1917

Year	Lovell's Directory	Assessment Roll	Census
1884	350		
1885	350		
1886	500		
1887	500		
1888	800		
1889	800		
1890	1,350		
1891	1,350	1,037	1,226
1892	1,350	1,360	
1893	2,000	1,567	
1894	2,000	1,408	
1895	2,000	1,896	
1896	2,000	2,100	
1897	2,000	2,387	
1898	2,000	2,816	
1899	2,500	3,116	
1900	4,000	5,084	
1901	4,000	5,807	3,958
1902	5,807	6,081	
1903	6,081	7,022	
1904	7,022	8,643	
1905	10,500	10,481	
1906	10,500	10,481	
1907	14,394	16,197	
1908	18,197	18,172	
1909	20,904	19,369	
1910	22,500	23,570	
1911	30,000	26,035	18,684
1912	30,000	31,854	
1913	32,000	36,507	
1914	36,607	39,770	
1915	39,070	34,856	
1916	34,856	33,000	
1917	34,856	37,247	

ing the period. Since 90 per cent of the population of Maisonneuve in 1901 was Catholic, it can be assumed that 90 per cent of these deaths were of Catholics, for a total 2,167. This leaves a net increase of 2,168 which represents only 17.1 percent of the increase in the Catholic population during the period.[5] Despite the approximate nature of the estimate, it gives a clear picture of the basically secondary role of natural increase in Maisonneuve's population growth. Its growth can be explained, first and foremost, by the arrival of thousands of workers and their families, who were attracted by the establishment of industries and the jobs they offered.

Were these new residents French Canadians leaving the countryside for the city? Or were they part of the vast tide of immigrants that flowed into Canada in the early twentieth century?

A preliminary answer to the question can be obtained by looking at the ethnic origin of Maisonneuve's residents. A breakdown of the town's population by ethnic origin for 1901 and 1911 is shown in Table 6-3. At first glance, it is clear that Maisonneuve was a francophone town, as more than four-fifths of its population was of French origin. The proportion of French Canadians in Maisonneuve was slightly higher than in Quebec as a whole and considerably higher than in the city of Montreal. This is not surprising, since Maisonneuve was located in the east end of Montreal Island which had long been considered a francophone stronghold.

With 15 per cent of the population, the British (including Irish) also constituted a significant group. A number of Maisonneuve's manufacturing companies employed specialized workers and executives of British origin, and this probably accounts for the presence of a substantial British population in the town. Everett C. Hughes described a similar phenomenon in his study of Drummondville, although the case of Maisonneuve was different since employees of British origin would also have had the option of living in another municipality in the Montreal region.[6]

Only a limited number of residents belonged to other ethnic groups. The proportion represented by these groups grew slightly between 1901 and 1911, but not nearly as much as it did in the city of Montreal in the same period. This can be explained by the tendency of immigrants to settle in well-defined areas. In Montreal, non-British immigrants became concentrated primarily in the old parts of the city and especially in St. Lawrence and Saint-Louis wards. Only a few of them went to the suburbs.

Of course, not all people of other ethnic origins were immigrants, and it is necessary to look at another variable — place of birth. This information is provided by the 1911 census. In all, less than 3 per cent of the population was born in non-Anglo-Saxon countries. If people born in France are eliminated, this figure is reduced to 2 per cent — quite close to the figure for residents of other ethnic origins.

Table 6-4 shows that 12.5 per cent of Maisonneuve's population was born

Table 6-3
**Population of Maisonneuve by
Ethnic Origin, 1901 and 1911**

| | 1901 | | 1911 | |
Origin	no.	%	no	%
British	627	15.8	2,889	15.5
English	350	8.8	2,062	11.0
Irish	216	5.5	418	2.2
Scottish	61	1.5	406	2.2
Other			3	
French	3,245	82.0	15,203	81.3
Other	85	2.1	477	2.6
German	13	0.3	50	0.3
Austro-Hungarian			9	
Belgian	37	0.9	164	0.9
Chinese	5	0.1	25	0.1
Dutch	1		23	0.1
Greek			43	0.2
Italian	27	0.7	120	0.6
Jewish			8	
Polish			7	
Russian			14	0.1
Scandinavian	2		10	0.1
Swiss			4	
Not specified	1		115	0.6

Source: *Census of Canada*, 1901 and 1911

Table 6-4
**Population of Maisonneuve by
Place of Birth, 1911**

Place of Birth	no.	%
Quebec	156,983	85.5
Rest of Canada	354	1.9
British Isles	1,236	6.6
Continental Europe	389	2.6
United States	540	2.9
Other Countries	74	0.4

Source: *Census of Canada*, 1911

outside Canada. More than half of this group came from the British Isles. Overall, foreigners were a minority in Maisonneuve and most of the town's residents came from Quebec.

A pattern of settlement existed for foreign immigrants. Was there a comparable pattern for migrants from Quebec? Writing in 1925, the journalist Emile Benoist maintained that there was:

> It should not be thought that neighbourhoods outside the centre of Montreal were formed by the natural growth of the central core. The main source of population for these neighbourhoods has been rural centres — nearby rural centres at first, and then others farther away. Thus, Saint-Henri, Sainte-Cunégonde, St. Joseph and Point-Saint-Charles wards were settled mostly by people coming from rural areas on the South Shore — Laprairie, Saint-Rémi, Saint-Constant, Saint-Isidore, Chateauguay, etc. — and also from rural areas on Montreal Island between Lachine and Sainte-Anne-de-Bellevue.... The newcomers stopped at the gates of the city. The same phenomenon, we have been told, can be observed in Maisonneuve where a large part of the population came from the rural areas of l'Assomption, Joliette, Saint-Paul-l'Ermite and surrounding regions.[7]

It is difficult to verify this statement from available sources. However since many of Maisonneuve's manufacturing companies had plants in Montreal before moving to their new suburban location, it can be assumed that workers moved with the companies. If this were the case, the number of Montrealers who moved to Maisonneuve would be fairly large.

Settlement of Maisonneuve's Territory

Where in Maisonneuve did the newcomers settle? There was plenty of space; in the early 1890s, only the part of Maisonneuve near the river and along Notre-Dame Street was populated. This was the situation described in the Goad atlas of 1890. Two later atlases — one published by Pinsonneault about 1907 and the second by the Goad company in 1914 — give a precise picture of how settlement progressed from this point (see Map 6). Each of these atlases shows how settlement expanded over Maisonneuve's territory, where it was concentrated, and how space was divided among different activities.

The Pinsonneault atlas was published after Maisonneuve experienced its first two stages of industrialization.[8] By this time, according to the atlas, Maisonneuve's waterfront had begun to change. There were still a few large residential properties, belonging to the Bourbonnières, the Jesuits and Joseph Barsalou. Two large recreation areas had been established — Viau Park, which was run by the town, and Riverside Park, an amusement play-

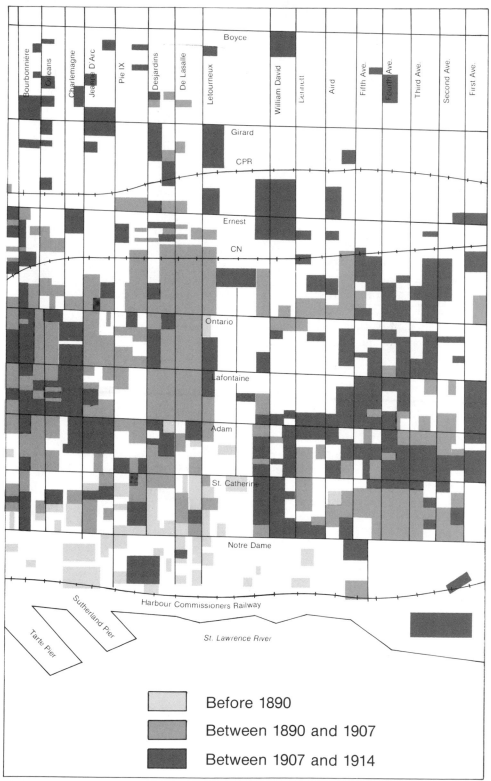

Map 6: Built-up Area, 1914

Before 1890

Between 1890 and 1907

Between 1907 and 1914

ground. There was still only one industry on the waterfront, but it was a major one — the sugar refinery. And, finally, there were two piers on the river — Sutherland and Tarte.

In West and Centre wards, the area between Notre-Dame Street and the railway tracks was covered with buildings. Industries were concentrated on the two sides of the railway tracks, between Ernest and Ontario streets. The rest of the area, between Notre-Dame and Ontario streets, was basically residential, with an educational and religious cluster occupying a fairly central position in the quadrilateral bounded by Desjardins, Adam, Letourneux and Lafontaine streets.

In East Ward, there was still only scattered settlement south of the railway tracks. The Morgan property (lot 7; see Map 3) was still untouched and it constituted a kind of barrier, breaking the continuity of settlement. East of the barrier, the wave of suburban growth weakened. Residential housing in the east — primarily in Viauville — was concentrated along Notre-Dame and Adam streets and on the cross streets between them. Except for the Viau biscuit factory, the railway had not attracted any industry to this area. (The Viau family had long been opposed to the location of industrial corporations on its property.) Also in this area, the "Le National" lacrosse club's stadium on Ontario Street was an important gathering place.

The northern part of Maisonneuve, from Ernest Street to the town limits, was almost empty in all three wards. Right in the middle of this area, lots 3, 4 and 7 were not even subdivided. The Viau family's lands were subdivided, but no buildings had been constructed on them. There were only two significant establishments: the Christian Brothers' headquarters, the "Mont De La Salle," on lot 8, and the Montreal Terra Cotta Lumber Company's tile factory on lot 14.

Thus, in 1907 southwestern Maisonneuve was quite thickly settled, the southeastern part of the town was populated, and the north end was almost empty. This was the situation just before the great period of expansion from 1909 to 1913. The Goad atlas of 1914 indicates the extent of the growth that took place in this period.

The major features that characterized Maisonneuve in 1907 could be seen even more clearly in 1914.[9] The increasingly industrial character of the waterfront was conspicuous. St. Lawrence Sugar Refining had spread its tentacles to the other side of Notre-Dame Street and had been joined by the Canadian Spool Cotton Company, which now occupied the old site of Riverside Park, and Canadian Vickers Ltd., whose facilities were in the far east end of Maisonneuve and extended into Longue-Pointe (see Map 4, page 68, for location of factories). The Harbour Commission and railway tracks ran along the entire waterfront. Between Pie-IX and Bennett streets the river bank was not yet built up, but Goad indicated the outline of a proposed pier

Greystone façades are typical of houses in Viauville.

in the area. Thus, the recreational role of the waterfront was gradually being sacrificed to the needs of large-scale industry.

(Overleaf) This drawing provides a good overall view of Maisonneuve at the beginning of the First World War, although some of the features on the northern edges of the city — like Maisonneuve Park — were never completed. On the left, the main artery going straight north, is Pie-IX Boulevard. The residential area lies between the town industrial zones. Conspicuous there, near Pie-IX, are the twin towers of the Roman Catholic church. Immediately to the right is Morgan Boulevard, leading to the imposing public market. The drawing also shows industrial sites located outside Maisonneuve: in the upper left corner, the CPR Angus Shops; on the right, a steel foundry located in Longue-Pointe.

BAIN PUBLIC & GYMNASE.

HOTEL DE VILLE

MAISO

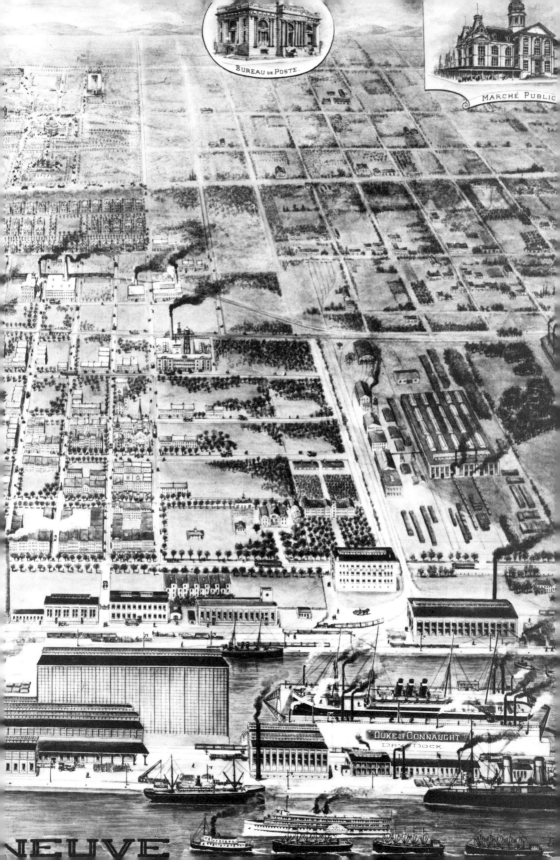

BUREAU DE POSTE.

MARCHÉ PUBLIC.

DUKE OF CONNAUGHT DRY DOCK.

NEUVE

The area immediately to the north, between Notre-Dame and Ontario streets, was, as we have seen, basically residential. This area was much more densely settled than it had been in 1907, and a large majority of its lots were covered with buildings. The Morgan and Bennett lands, which had been divided into lots later than the others, were an exception. The Morgan property (lot 7) remained unoccupied, while there were still many vacant lots north of Adam Street on the Bennett property (lots 3 and 4). On the whole, however, the map reflected the arrival of new residents in massive numbers since 1907. In the middle of this residential zone, along Lafontaine and Adam streets, there was a concentration of educational institutions (eight) and churches (four).

North of the residential zone along the railway tracks was Maisonneuve's main industrial area, where a number of new factories had been built since 1907. The most substantial of these, based on the large amount of space it occupied, was the Warden King foundry.

The industrial zone seemed somehow to contain Maisonneuve's population within the southern part of the town. The occupied area of Maisonneuve barely extended beyond Ernest Street. There were a few scattered buildings between Ernest and Boyce streets but, except for these buildings, the whole northern part of Maisonneuve consisted of vacant lots. Most of this area would later be included in Maisonneuve Park.

Thus, settlement of the southern part of Maisonneuve had almost reached its maximum level in 1914. This represented remarkable progress, which can be easily seen by comparing the 1914 Goad atlas with its predecessor of 1890. The urban developers' projects had been a success, and their task had been made easier by some of the characteristics of the site of Maisonneuve. The town's growth had been based in part on its topography, the presence of the river, the proximity of Montreal, and the existence of a good communications network. In the late nineteenth century, Maisonneuve had been a small centre on the edge of Montreal Island's urbanized area; just before the First World War, it had grown to a major suburban municipality with both a residential and an industrial function.

However, Maisonneuve's growth did not have enough force to break through to the northern part of the town. Topography was a problem: the Sherbrooke terrace represented a kind of natural barrier. More important, however, was this area's relative isolation, including poor communications with the rest of Montreal Island. For this reason, it did not attract many industries or residents. The developers had to find a new function for this area in order to make land development in Maisonneuve a complete success.

A Population of Workers

Little is known about the geographical origins of Maisonneuve's newcomers and even less about their social origins. How many were workers from Montreal transplanted to the suburbs? How many were farmers who decided to try urban life? Available sources do not offer precise answers to these questions, but we are better informed about what happened to these people once they got to Maisonneuve — about what work the newcomers did and what place they occupied in Maisonneuve society. The census and assessment roll of 1911 provide a snapshot of the effects of industrialization and of the town's social fabric.

The 1911 census table covers the "male and female population 10 years of age and over who are employed in gainful occupations." While a number of individual occupations are mentioned in the table, some data are provided only for intermediate aggregates.

In Table 6-5, the working population is broken down according to sex, age and place of birth (Canada or elsewhere). The working population was 35.1 per cent of the total population. For immigrants, the proportion was much higher — 50.2 per cent of immigrants were employed (a large number of the immigrants who came to Maisonneuve were adult workers). Looking at it another way, immigrants represented 17.3 per cent of Maisonneuve's working population but only 12.1 per cent of its total population. For native-born Canadians, the proportion of working population to total population was 33.0 per cent.

In terms of age, Table 6-5 shows, first of all, that child labour was not wide-

Table 6-5
Population Employed in Gainful Occupations, Town of Maisonneuve, 1911

	Men	*Women*	*Total*
All Workers	5,387	1,127	6,514
By Place of Birth:			
Born in Canada	4,392	998	5,390
Immigrants	995	129	1,124
By Age Group:			
10-14	88	63	151
15-24	1,515	727	2,242
25-64	3,663	328	3,991
65 years and over	121	9	130

Source: *Census of Canada*, 1911, vol. 6, table 6.

spread. Only 151 workers, or 2.3 per cent of the total, were between the ages of ten and fourteen. This age group may have been underreported since parents were reluctant to admit that their young children were in the labour market. The group between the ages of fifteen and twenty-four was very large, making up 34.4 per cent of the total. Even larger was the group of workers between twenty-five and sixty-four years, with 61.3 per cent of the total. People aged sixty-five and over were almost completely absent from the workforce, with 2 per cent of the total.

The breakdown by sex was cross-tabulated with the two other variables in the census. First, it should be noted that men were slightly overrepresented in Maisonneuve, with 51.4 per cent of the town's overall population, yielding a sex ratio (number of males per 100 females) of 105:58. This was a little different from the situation prevailing in the city of Montreal, where there were proportionally fewer men — the sex ratio was 99:81.[10]

The breakdown of the working population, however, was very different. Women represented only 17.3 per cent of the working population of Maisonneuve, while the comparable figure for the city of Montreal was 21.6 per cent.[11] An initial distinction can be made according to place of birth, as women represented only 11.5 per cent of immigrant workers as compared with 18.5 per cent of workers born in Canada. The age structure tells us a little more about the pattern of female work, which was fundamentally different from the pattern of male work. Of the female workers, 64.5 per cent were between the ages of fifteen and twenty-four, while 29.1 per cent were between the ages of twenty-five and sixty-four. For male workers, these proportions were reversed: 28.1 per cent between fifteen and twenty-four, 68.0 per cent between twenty-five and sixty-four. There was a large contingent of young women in the labour force — a third of all workers in the fifteen-to-twenty-four age group — but they dropped out of the labour force as soon as they were married. The same situation prevailed in Montreal.[12] The breakdown by occupational sector of the female workforce was also different from that of the male workforce; we will come back to this question further on.

According to these limited data for Maisonneuve's working population in 1911, immigrants were overrepresented, there were many young workers and, more specifically, many young women between the ages of fifteen and twenty-four were in the workforce. The labour force was clearly dominated by men, but the presence of women was not insignificant, especially in the younger age groups.

In addition to these demographic features of the workforce, it is also necessary to look at an economic variable — the breakdown by occupational sector. The 1911 census grouped occupations into eleven major sectors based more on technical than on social characteristics. Table 6-6 shows the breakdown into these major groups and picks out some of the more significant subgroups.

Table 6-6

Population 10 Years of Age and Over Employed in Gainful Occupations, By Occupational Sector, Town of Maisonneuve, 1911

Occupational Sector	Men		Women		Total	
	no.	%¹	no.	%²	no.	%
Agriculture	25	0.5	2	0.2	27	0.4
Building trades	850	15.8			850	13.0
Domestic and personal service	420	7.8	159	14.1	335	5.1
Municipal and government employees	176	3.3	4	0.4	424	6.5
—Municipal	383	7.1	2	0.2	385	5.9
Hunting and fishing						
Forest industries						
Manufactures and mechanical industries	2,439	45.3	745	66.1	3,184	48.9
—Iron and steel	443	8.2	3	0.3	480	7.4
—Leather and rubber goods	518	9.6	240	21.3	789	12.1
—Manufacturing day-labourers	479	8.9			479	7.4
Mining industry: metalliferous ores, fuels, salt and stone	9	0.2			9	0.1
Professions	290	5.4	94	8.3	384	5.9
Commerce	774	14.4	116	10.3	890	13.7
—Proprietors, managers, foremen	223	4.1	12	1.1	235	3.6
—Sales clerks	335	6.2	71	6.3	406	6.2
Transportation	404	7.5	7	0.6	411	6.3
Total	5,387	100.0	1,127	100.00	6,514	100.0

¹ Men working in the sector as a percentage of male workers in all sectors.

² Women working in the sector as a percentage of female workers in all sectors.

Source: *Census of Canada*, 1911, vol. 6, table 6.

The manufacturing and mechanical industries sector was clearly the dominant one, accounting for almost half the workforce, confirming that Maisonneuve was essentially an industrial town and that factory workers accounted for a large part of the population. Female workers had an important place in this sector, representing 23.4 per cent of all workers. Manufacturing represented 66.1 per cent of all jobs held by women, as compared with only 45.3 per cent of all jobs held by men.

Within this sector, the dominant subgroup was the leather and shoe industry. It accounted for a quarter of all jobs in the manufacturing sector, and a third of all jobs in the sector held by women. Indeed, 21 per cent of all women workers in Maisonneuve made shoes. The second largest industry was iron and steel, with 15 per cent of manufacturing jobs and 7.4 per cent of all jobs. The clothing industry was next, with 8 per cent of manufacturing jobs. The rest of the workers in the sector were scattered among a number of industries. Those for whom precise information was unavailable would not have been classified by the census-takers.

The 51.1 per cent of the working population that was not employed in manufacturing production was divided among eight major sectors. The largest was the commercial sector, with 13.7 per cent of the working population. This sector included a large number of small merchants serving the local population. Another 13.0 per cent worked in the various construction trades, where the largest group was "builders and contractors" (3 per cent). Thus, three-quarters of Maisonneuve's working population was employed in manufacturing, construction and commerce. None of the other sectors employed more than 6.5 per cent of the working population. In the domestic and personal service sector (5.1 per cent of the total), almost half the workers were women; 14 per cent of all working women were employed in this sector. With 383 employees, of whom 301 were day-labourers, municipal government dominated the government employees sector (6.5 per cent); there were almost no women in this sector. More than half the professional sector consisted of teachers, many of whom were women. Finally, 6.3 per cent of the workforce was employed in the transportation sector, primarily in the railways and the streetcar system.

On the basis of the census, it can be concluded that Maisonneuve's population was essentially working-class and made up primarily of factory workers. Unskilled labour made up an important part of the population, and there were 1,111 day-labourers, representing 17.1 per cent of the working population, divided among the different occupational sectors.

Unlike the census, the assessment roll gives data only for heads of household, which means that some workers — wives, roomers, young people living with their parents — were not included in the roll. We know the name, age and occupation of each head of household (except that age is not given if the head of household was a woman), whether he or she was a property owner or a tenant, the ward in which his or her residence was located, the

Table 6-7
**Most Common Occupations of Heads of
Household, Town of Maisonneuve, 1911**

Occupation	no.	%
Day-labourer	545	14.2
Carpenter	283	7.4
Shoemaker	225	5.8
Machinist	210	5.5
Foreman	126	3.3
Clerk	109	2.8
Carter	103	2.7
Engineer	94	2.4
Painter	80	2.1
Grocer	79	2.1
Merchant	76	2.0
Butcher	74	1.9
Smith	69	1.8
Accountant	60	1.6
Rentier	59	1.5
Moulder	57	1.5
Agent	57	1.5
Electrician	50	1.3
Travelling salesman	43	1.1
Operator	42	1.1
Bricklayer	38	1.0
Conductor	38	1.0
Businessman	38	1.0
Plumber	36	0.9
Total of above	2,585	69.5
Total: Heads of Households	3,850	100.0

Source: Town of Maisonneuve assessment roll, 1911.

street and number, the assessment of the property, the yearly value of the rent, and finally the number of residents.

In the assessment roll, unlike in the census, individual occupations are identified (Table 6-7). Twenty-four occupations appear thirty-six times or more, and they account for more than two-thirds (67.3 per cent) of all heads of household. The five most common occupations alone represent 36.1 per cent of the total.

The breakdown of heads of household into sectors of economic activity is slightly different from that of the working population as a whole. There is a disproportionately large number of heads of household in the group of managers and senior executives and in the group of merchants, and a disproportionately small number among office and service workers. On the whole, however, the picture that emerged from the general data of the census table is confirmed by the assessment roll. We are dealing with a population in which manual workers were by far the largest group. The population also included a small number of bourgeois families and a larger number of service workers. Because of the differences in the data, it is not possible to do a rigorous comparison of the two sources, but the same trend emerges from both of them.

On the basis of the assessment roll, it is possible to look at the spatial distribution of these occupations. If there were significant residential concentrations within Maisonneuve, they might show up in an occupational breakdown by ward. The data compiled on distribution by ward shows that all occupations were represented to some extent in all wards and that there was no residential segregation. There were, however, some concentrations of occupations, and the presence of these concentrations could lead to aggregation and segregation, but these effects are hard to identify.

Day-labourers and construction workers were overrepresented in West Ward. Day-labourers accounted for 17.0 per cent of the heads of household in the ward, while another 16.4 per cent were carpenters, painters, bricklayers and electricians. Centre Ward appears to have been the stronghold of Maisonneuve's factory workers, as it had an overrepresentation of shoemakers, leather cutters and operators (12.3 per cent of the total). Unskilled workers — day-labourers and carters — were also numerous in this ward (19.9 per cent). In addition, there was a certain concentration of merchants, grocers and butchers (7.1 per cent). Finally, East Ward had more of a petit bourgeois character. There were concentrations of specialized workers (machinists and engineers, 11.5 per cent), white-collar workers (clerks and accountants, 7.4 per cent), agents and travelling salesmen (3.4 per cent), and rentiers and manufacturers (3.2 per cent).

Though each ward had characteristic features that distinguished it from the others, hasty conclusions should not be drawn from these differences. Only between 25 and 40 per cent of the heads of household in each ward are accounted for by these groups, so that these concentrations do not exclude the possibility of a degree of residential diversity. Precise information on where individuals worked would no doubt shed further light on these concentrations. For example, two-thirds of the twenty-two policemen living in Maisonneuve were concentrated in Centre Ward near the police stations. Unfortunately, adequate information of this sort is not available.

The proportion of white-collar workers was higher in East Ward (Viauville) than in other parts of Maisonneuve.

A Population of Tenants

The assessment roll helps in answering another important question: Did Maisonneuve's working-class population have easy access to homeownership? The roll does not provide detailed information on all owners of lands and buildings, identifying non-resident owners only by their names. Thus, the population for this study consists of residents. This population will be divided into homeowners and tenants and a relationship will be established between this information and other socio-economic variables. If the head of a family lives in a house belonging to his wife, he will be considered a homeowner.

To place this study in context, it is worth noting that Montreal had long been a city of tenants. As early as 1825, only 31 per cent of heads of household in the city owned their homes.[13] Historian Terry Copp has written of the period 1867-1929: "Over 80 per cent of the population rented their dwellings and absentee landlords were the norm in Montreal."[14]

In J.I. Cooper's view, there was a higher proportion of homeowners in the suburbs than in the city of Montreal, at least in the 1880s.[15] In Maisonneuve, civic leaders maintained that the percentage of resident homeowners was very high, as the following passage from a 1911 publicity pamphlet indicates:

> The great majority of Maisonneuve's residents live in their own houses, and since most of them are craftsmen it follows that that town has a very intelligent class of workers, a fact that cannot help but please future manufacturers. Many of these craftsmen own property in the town and are as interested in the growth and development of the town as the businessman and the manufacturer.[16]

A few years later an advertisement invited readers to "come to the town of Maisonneuve, a town of workers governed by the workers for the workers."[17]

A glance at the 1911-1912 assessment roll yields a picture that is quite different from the image created by Maisonneuve's advertising. Of the 3,850 heads of families living in the town, 3,461 were tenants and only 387 were listed as owning their own houses. Thus, 89.9 per cent of heads of household were tenants, and this exceptionally high percentage can be explained in large part by Maisonneuve's occupational structure.

A quarter of all resident homeowners were carpenters (8.3 per cent), rentiers (8.0 per cent) or day-labourers (7.5 per cent). However, rentiers accounted for only 1.5 per cent of all heads of household, while day-labourers accounted for 14.2 per cent. Thus, rentiers were overrepresented among homeowners (+6.5) while day-labourers were underrepresented (−6.7). This measure indicates which groups were most likely to be homeowners. Businessmen, of course, were among these groups: entrepreneurs (+3.3), merchants (+2.7), grocers (+2.8), butchers (+2.5), milk dealers (+1.2), manufacturers (+1.1), innkeepers (+0.8), contractors (+0.8). So were specialized construction workers such as carpenters (+0.9) and plasterers (+0.7). Other overrepresented groups included rentiers (+6.5), doctors (+0.8), civil servants (+0.6), inspectors (+0.5), conductors (+1.1) and foremen (+0.3). By contrast, factory workers, clerks and unskilled labourers had a less than average likelihood of becoming homeowners: day-labourers

(−6.7), shoemakers (−3.2), machinists (−3.4), clerks (−2.0), operators (−0.6). Since Maisonneuve's population consisted primarily of workers, it is hardly surprising that there were so so many tenants.

Though a number of factors were involved in a family's decision whether or not to buy a home, the primary one was whether it could. That, in turn, was determined by the socio-economic structure. And as Terry Copp has shown, the socio-economic structure of the Montreal region between 1897 and 1920 did not make it possible for a factory worker to save the substantial amount of money needed to buy a house.[18]

Tenancy had political consequences. The only political right that tenants had at the municipal level was the right to vote in elections. To become a candidate it was necessary to own property worth a minimum value determined by law. Only property owners could vote on the ratification of bylaws, so only property owners made the decisions on large-scale public works, even though the bill would ultimately be paid by the tenants.

The census and the assessment roll offer little more than a statistical view of the social structure, and virtually nothing about the living conditions of the masses of workers who arrived in Maisonneuve in the early twentieth century. What life was like for workers in Montreal provides a window on Maisonneuve, given the large working-class composition of both cities.

In 1897, industrialist and philanthropist Herbert Brown Ames issued *The City Below the Hill*, a statistical study of an industrial, working-class area near the Lachine Canal in southwestern Montreal.[19] Using Ames's work as a starting point for his study of workers' living conditions in Montreal between the turn of the century and the onset of the Depression, Terry Copp concluded that most workers lived below the poverty line and that the situation did not improve much over the period.[20] To earn an adequate income, a worker needed a full-time job. But in a number of economic sectors — notably, dock work and construction — there was substantial seasonal unemployment that could last up to five months. To make ends meet, a working-class family had to depend on several incomes and send children out to work at a fairly early age.

The worker's inadequate income went hand-in-hand with substandard living conditions: he could not afford nutritious food or a satisfactory, well-ventilated dwelling. The whole environment in working-class neighbourhoods was a problem, and particularly serious was its effect on health. The death rate, especially of infants, in working-class areas of Montreal was very high. Sanitary conditions remained clearly unsatisfactory even though a variety of agencies began to make serious efforts at improvement in the early twentieth century.[21] These general conditions could have been similar to those in Maisonneuve, although the houses were recently built and this could have produced a significant difference.

Some death statistics are available for Maisonneuve. According to data published by the Provincial Board of Health, between 1908 and 1917 infant mortality accounted for about half the deaths in Maisonneuve — the proportion varied from 46.7 per cent to 57.8 per cent. Since birth statistics for non-Catholics were not provided until 1915, the infant mortality rate can be calculated only for the last three years of Maisonneuve's existence as a town. During 1915, 1916 and 1917, there was a substantial increase in the number of births and a drop in the number of deaths, so that the infant mortality rate fell from 251.3 per thousand in 1915 to 109.3 per thousand in 1916 and 101.0 per thousand in 1917. A few years later, Montreal statistics reported an infant mortality rate of 123.1 per thousand in Maisonneuve. This was comparable to the situation in Hochelaga and De Lorimier, but these wards were not nearly as murderous as old working-class areas like Sainte-Marie and Saint-Henri, where the infant mortality rate was over 200 per thousand.

There may be several factors involved in this drop in infant mortality. Montreal Water and Power began to supply filtered water in 1911, which was the same year public health advocates stepped up their campaigns. At the instigation of the director of Maisonneuve's Board of Health, Dr. Lussier, a laboratory was installed in the new town hall in 1912, and a branch of the Goutte de Lait (Milk Drop), which distributed milk to children, was established.

A typical worker's dwelling was the same in Maisonneuve as in the east end of Montreal. Houses were built in rows, attached to one another, with sunlight entering only through the front and back. They were long, narrow houses, with rooms linked by a long corridor. The typical house in Maisonneuve had either two storeys with three dwellings or three storeys with five dwellings.

Overcrowding does not appear to have been any worse than in other comparable neighbourhoods. Average family size varied during the period. With 261 families reported in the 1891 census, the average size was 4.7. In the 1901 census, with 752 families in a population of 3,958, it was 5.26. This increase in average family size seems to indicate that newcomers to Maisonneuve were young adults with a number of children. In 1911, average family size was again 5.2 people (3,590 families in a population of 18,684). Calculations carried out on the basis of the assessment roll for 1911 yield an average of 4.94 residents per head of household — a slightly lower figure than the average family size calculated from the census. All these figures are fairly close to the average family size of 4.9 people calculated in 1897 by H.B. Ames.[22]

Almost nothing is known about working conditions in Maisonneuve's factories nor about union organization. Not surprisingly, the town council boasted in its advertising that "the town is not inconvenienced by strikes," but is a promotional statement of this sort reliable?[23]

The establishment in 1910 of the Club Ouvrier of Maisonneuve, affili-

An example of working-class housing in Maisonneuve.

These two houses in Viauville were more comfortable.

Notre-Dame Street at Letourneux Street, looking east, November 18, 1912.

ated to the Parti Ouvrier, indicated a degree of militancy among the town's workers. Its members were recruited primarily in the specialized trades. The Club Ouvrier presented its position on a number of questions — streetcar tickets for workers, the wages of municipal employees, for example — to the town council and also intervened actively in local politics by participating in the 1915 election.[24]

A significant achievement of the Club Ouvrier was the establishment of placement offices financially supported by the town council.[25] This issue touches on one of industrial society's major problems — unemployment. The Montreal region was particularly susceptible to seasonal unemployment, particularly in the construction and transportation sectors, but there was also cyclical unemployment, which showed up during depressions. In early 1915, Maisonneuve's workers staged a raucous invasion of the town council chamber, shouting out their demands for jobs. (Unfortunately, available sources give no indication of the extent of the unemployment problem.)

Maisonneuve was a city of workers, and more specifically, of factory workers employed in the manufacturing sector. They lived near their places of employment, even though there were distinct residential and industrial zones within the town.

This group of workers was relatively young and included large numbers of young women working in factories and commercial enterprises. While women did not make up as large a proportion of the workforce as in the neighbouring city of Montreal, they nevertheless constituted more than a sixth of Maisonneuve's working population. Immigrants, a minority in the population as a whole, were clearly overrepresented in the workforce, which included large numbers of unskilled day-labourers.

Workers lived in all parts of the town, and the local bourgeoisie was not large enough to monopolize an area of its own. Sections of some streets, notably Pie-IX Boulevard, contained concentrations of bourgeois residents, but these clusters were not large enough to indicate a clear pattern of residential segregation. While each ward had concentrations of specific occupations, the main feature of residential distribution in Maisonneuve was diversity.

Though civic leaders tried to paint a picture of a town where workers owned their own homes, the truth was that this happened only rarely. Because so few workers were homeowners, they had little control over political life and thus over their environment.

Maisonneuve may have been a city of workers but it was not run by workers. It was dominated by a local bourgeoisie of developers, industrialists and merchants. This group had determined the direction of Maisonneuve's development, deciding that it should become the industrial suburb of Montreal. By 1910 the town had attained this status and the local bourgeoisie, aware of its power, now wanted to leave its mark by launching an ambitious program of beautification and public investment. They had made Maisonneuve the "Pittsburgh of Canada"; now they wanted to make it the "Garden of Montreal."

PART III

"THE GARDEN OF MONTREAL": DEVELOPMENT BY BEAUTIFICATION, 1910-1918

CHAPTER 7

THE BANNER OF PROGRESS

In about 1910 Maisonneuve entered a new stage in its history. While it continued to implement its industrial development policy, it also launched a vast beautification campaign intended as the capstone of Maisonneuve's spectacular material success. Substantial public investment funds were authorized for a group of majestic buildings and a spacious park.

Three major factors converged to produce this turn of events. First, the liberal ideology, characterized by a belief in progress, was being expressed with growing force in Quebec. Second, the prosperity of the early twentieth century produced a climate of euphoria. And finally, within Maisonneuve itself, a new generation of the local bourgeoisie was on the rise and wanted to show off its achievements.

Belle Epoque and Belief in Progress

The Quebec ideological scene was far from being monolithic. There were two major, radically different currents: the clerical-nationalist and the liberal.

The clerical-nationalist ideology was formulated primarily by the clergy, members of the liberal professions and intellectuals in newspapers and journals, religious sermons and patriotic speeches. It placed a high value on agriculture as both an economic activity and a way of life.

Fundamental to this ideology was the superiority of agriculture and the rural way of life over industry and urban life. The country represented simplicity, honesty and frugality; the city stood for wage slavery, physical degeneracy and moral decadence. This meant that government policies and government money should support farmers, with particular emphasis on adding more farmland by opening up Quebec's colonization zones. It also meant that the rural exodus had to be checked and urban growth kept within bounds. While the ideology did not oppose industrial development outright, it regarded industry as desirable only under certain conditions: industry should be subordinated to the interests of agriculture; industrialization should be decentralized; and industries that used raw materials produced by agriculture and provided winter employment for rural manpower should be emphasized.

A number of representative thinkers within the clerical-nationalist current were convinced of the truth of a second fundamental idea: that French Canadians had a natural predisposition for agriculture and that preserving this basic cultural trait was necessary to ensure their survival. In this view, there was only one possible definition of the French Canadian: he was Catholic and French and rural. Because it harboured moral degeneracy, the city posed a threat to religion and, since industry was dominated by Anglo-Saxons — Canadians or Americans — industrialization endangered the French language and culture. This correspondence between French Canadians and agriculture also led to the belief that Francophones were not cut out for managing industry or for manipulating capital and that Anglophones were much better suited to these jobs. The suggestion that French Canadians could really take control of the economy was a delusion. At most, French Canadians could hope to control — in addition to agriculture — small industries that were rooted in rural life.

The other major current — the liberal ideology — rejected this form of determinism. It was formulated by businessmen and political leaders who, without denying the importance of agriculture, believed that full economic development was possible in Quebec. This current was based on two ideas that were diametrically opposed to the fundamental ideas of the clerical-nationalist current. First, proponents of the liberal ideology believed that it was through industrialization that Quebec would achieve a sufficiently high level of economic development to provide work for all its citizens and to stop the massive exodus to the United States. They considered industry the engine of economic growth. Thus, the government's priority should be to encourage the establishment of industries and the entry of new capital. Where this capital came from was of little importance, and American investment — synonymous with prosperity and job creation — was to be welcomed with open arms. Humanity was on the march towards progress. If the agriculturalists tried to return to the past, they would only impede this progress and slow the increase in collective wealth that it would bring.

The second fundamental belief of the liberal current was that French Canadians had a role to play in Quebec's economic development. Starting in the mid-nineteenth century, a substantial number of French Canadian businessmen had succeeded in establishing their own companies and, while they were not a majority within the bourgeoisie, they were a significant minority. Thus, French Canadians did not have any more of a special calling for agriculture than other people. They too could be captains of industry, and their role in Quebec's economic development could be expanded.

To achieve this goal, all they needed were the tools. And in the early twentieth century, one tool considered extremely important was education. Many political leaders, headed by Premier Lomer Gouin, were convinced that education would be a determining element in advancing the French Canadian cause. Several institutions were established for the express purpose of training French Canadian experts and specialists to fill important positions in business. The Quebec government founded the Ecole des Hautes Etudes Commerciales (School of Higher Commercial Studies) in Montreal, technical schools in Montreal and Quebec City, and a number of other specialized schools. The French Canadian people would ensure their survival not by retreating into themselves but by being able to absorb aspects of North American culture without renouncing their own language or culture. To proponents of the liberal ideology, the successful French Canadian businessman thus became a model, an example for others to follow, and stories of these individual successes were a regular feature in mass-circulation newspapers.[1]

The French Canadian businessmen who ran the town of Maisonneuve and sat on the town council just before the First World War shared the views of the liberal current. They were themselves living proof that French Canadian businessmen could succeed and they now wanted to publicize their success. Of course, Maisonneuve's leaders had believed that industry was the most important engine of economic growth from the time the town was founded. Now, however, they had concrete results to show off, and they did so in public declarations and in advertisements published in newspapers and magazines.

"The most industrious town in the Province of Quebec" promised the "Capitalists, Industrialists, Builders, Workers and Young People of initiative who invest their capital, savings and labour there A Quick and Solid FORTUNE."[2] In 1912 Mayor Alexandre Michaud declared that "Maisonneuve has a brilliant future ahead of it. This is a prosperity unequalled in the history of the country. It is due to a policy of progress, to which the leaders of the municipality of Maisonneuve have always demonstrated their commitment."[3] This "policy of progress" clearly referred to the generous support given private enterprise by the town council. In these circumstances, "progress" meant that public institutions were placed at the service of private enterprise.

Progrès constants et ininterrompus

DE

MAISONNEUVE

¶ La ville la plus industrieuse de la Province de Quebec et dont le developpement considerable vaut à Messieurs les Capitalistes, Industriels, Constructeurs, Ouvriers et aux Jeunes Gens d'initiative qui y placeront leurs capitaux, leurs economies et leur travail

UNE FORTUNE
Rapide et Solide

"The most industrious town in the Province of Quebec" promises residents "A Quick and Solid FORTUNE."

These statements spoke admiringly of the massive industrialization of Maisonneuve:

> The following figures are a partial demonstration of the astonishing progress of Maisonneuve, which was unknown only a few years ago. Within half a dozen years, Maisonneuve has progressed so rapidly in its commercial development that it is today at the head of the list, eclipsing Montreal, Toronto and every other city and town in the Dominion in the per capita value of its output, with a total well over twenty-one million dollars. For this reason, Maisonneuve is now recognized as the most attractive manufacturing town in Canada, and manufacturers establish their major industries in Maisonneuve, the Pittsburg [sic] of Canada.[4]

Journalists consistently expressed the same view, and gave their articles such headlines as "The Progress of Maisonneuve" or "The Prosperity of Maisonneuve."

However, for North American businessmen in the early twentieth century who wished to be thought of as progressive, it was not enough to talk about big bucks. These businessmen were also interested in developing a pleasant living environment in an urban context. The concerns of what is referred to as "the progressive movement" in North America were felt in Maisonneuve, and they took shape in the ambitious plan to beautify the town.

The high-flown statements of Maisonneuve's publicists appear in a somewhat different light when they are regarded in the context of the euphoria that marked the early part of the twentieth century before the First World War. This was a period of rapid economic growth in both Canada and the United States. Production and population grew substantially, and immigrants came by the hundreds of thousands, dreaming of making their fortune in North America. The fortunes, however, were made by large capitalists on the immigrants' backs, and the period that has been called the "belle epoque" was a kind of golden age of capitalism. Large industrialists and financiers accumulated great wealth, built luxurious, ostentatious houses and spent their money extravagantly. The stories of their careers appeared in mass-circulation newspapers, like *La Presse* in Montreal, and became a form of entertainment for people who had neither wealth nor power.

Prosperity led to optimism, and leaders looked to the future with confidence. Canadian Prime Minister Wilfrid Laurier said that the twentieth century belonged to Canada, and his government financed two new transcontinental railways. There were occasional cyclical depressions but recovery was quick. With no end to prosperity in sight, it seemed that opportunities for growth were infinite and unlimited progress was inevitable. Of course, not everybody shared in this prosperity, but society's leaders did not appear to be much concerned with the inequities that surrounded them.[5]

The Local Bourgeoisie Asserts Itself

Armed with ambitious plans and suffused with a spirit of euphoria, a new and primarily French Canadian bourgeoisie asserted itself in Maisonnueve. By this time, the group of developers had grown. In the early years of the twentieth century, a second generation came along, breathing new life into land development in Maisonneuve and speeding up its pace. These new developers chose corporate forms of organization, with directors and shareholders. The new generation would become heavily involved in the crowning episode of land development in the town, the creation of Maisonneuve Park.

The Viauville Land Company acquired a large portion of the lands belonging to the Viau estate. The company's president was Senator William Mitchell, its vice-president, A.-P. Frigon, and its secretary, D.R. Murphy. Its shareholders included a number of well-known figures — Alexandre Michaud, mayor of Maisonneuve from 1909 to 1915; Oscar Dufresne, a Maisonneuve town councillor during the same period; L.-A. Lavallée, mayor of Montreal from 1912 to 1914; J.-B. Mayrand, brother-in-law of Sir Lomer Gouin (who was premier of Quebec from 1905 to 1920); Clément Robillard, E. D. Ouellette and Rodolphe Tourville, all members of the Quebec Legislative Assembly; and L.-J.-S. Morin, the town counsel for Maisonneuve

Oscar Dufresne, town councillor, 1909-1915.

and Alphonse Desjardins's son-in-law; as well as Rodolphe Lemieux, L.-P. Bérard, A. Tourville, J.-O. Marchand and Emilien Daoust.[6]

The Montreal East Land Company set out to develop the portion of the Bennett farm between Boyce Street and Maisonneuve's northern limits, after purchasing the the land from Marie Virolle, Mayor Michaud's wife. Dr. Hector Desloges was the president of the company, and its shareholders, in addition to Desloges, were Dr. Adelstand de Martigny; A.-A. Ranger; Armand Grenier, a lawyer; L. Saint-Jacques, a Saint-Hyacinthe lawyer; Victor Morin, a notary; E. Clavet of Maisonneuve; T. Laframboise, a merchant; and Mendoza Langlois, a Montreal real estate agent who acted as the developer in this enterprise and was particularly active in its promotion.[7] Mayor Michaud also played an important role. His wife was a party to the transactions involved and she retained possession of a number of lots.

The St. Lawrence Construction Company was incorporated in 1904. Its first president was F.S. Mackay, and he was succeeded by Joseph Ethier; its

Alexandre Michaud, town councillor from 1905–1909 and mayor from 1909–1915.

secretary was Henri Audette. It was heavily involved in the transactions surrounding Maisonneuve Park, as was the Société d'Administration Générale, which in 1913 sold land for the park in trust for Mendoza Langlois and James Morgan.[8]

The developers were not the only businessmen with an interest in Maisonneuve's future, and other groups also emerged during this period. One group included Maisonneuve factory owners, some of whom — especially in the shoe industry — had also chosen to live in Maisonneuve. Typical of this group was Oscar Dufresne, but there were others like him. Some industrialists wanted to participate in making the decisions that directly affected the future of the town and indirectly the future of their companies. They sought to benefit from Maisonneuve's prosperity and invested in real estate. Another group consisted of local merchants whose business was increasing as the town grew.

These three groups — developers, industrialists and local merchants —

along with members of the liberal professions formed a local bourgeoisie which lived in Maisonneuve and was actively involved in the town's economic development. It was an expanding social class which had considerable opportunity to enrich itself in the early twentieth century. This rising class was very well represented by the new political slate which came to power in 1909 and controlled the town council for six years. Two figures dominated the council during this period: Mayor Alexandre Michaud and the chairman of the finance committee, Oscar Dufresne.

After serving as a town councillor from 1905 to 1909, Alexandre Michaud was elected mayor by acclamation in 1909 and re-elected, again by acclamation, in 1911 and 1913. Born in Black River on January 27, 1868, Michaud became involved in the grain trade, founding his own export company. In 1907 — only two years after he entered the town political scene — he left this company to concentrate on real estate development, though he has also been credited as being the main organizer of an electric company, Dominion Light, Heat and Power.[9] Michaud's biographers portrayed him as a leading public figure. They praised him for his wisdom, his great administrative ability and his dynamism. In their view, he was the prototype of the progressive politician.[10]

Oscar Dufresne, born in Pointe du Lac near Trois-Rivières, was the son of Thomas Dufresne, one of the founders of the Pellerin & Dufresne shoe company, which later became Dufresne & Locke. Oscar Dufresne was manager of Dufresne & Locke when it established its factory in Maisonneuve at the turn of the century. The shoe company evidently provided him with a sizable fortune: he invested in real estate and built the most luxurious individual residence in Maisonneuve, the Chateau Dufresne. This rich industrialist represented West Ward on the town council between 1907 and 1915 and held the important position of finance committee chairman.

Two other councillors served without interruption for a number of years: Charles Belanger (1907-1915), a merchant, and Robert Fraser (1908-1915), superintendent of the Watson, Foster & Co. factory. J.-Ephrem Lemay served also on the council from 1911 to 1915. Thus, Maisonneuve's town council was a very stable one in the immediate prewar years, with only two seats changing hands, and the so-called "policy of progress" was pursued energetically and consistently as a result.

In 1910 the new team appointed Marius Dufresne, Oscar's brother, as town engineer. In this position, he was to play an important role in developing Maisonneuve's new projects.

CHAPTER 8

MAISONNEUVE'S POLITIQUE DE GRANDEUR

The public works carried out by the town of Maisonneuve before 1910 were essentially utilitarian. These works, which involved heavy, long-term investments for the town, were directed towards creating an urban infrastructure — sewers, water pipes, streets. The few public buildings were designed to meet the day-to-day requirements of a small municipality. However, with the rapid growth of the town and the substantial increase in its population, new public buildings were needed. In 1910, when the Michaud-Dufresne team took the reins of town government, the council's perspective on public buildings changed and, under a new town engineer, it adopted an ambitious beautification plan.

Since 1890 Maisonneuve's engineer had been J. Emile Vanier, who had been one of the first graduates of Montreal's Ecole Polytechnique and did engineering work for a number of suburban municipalities.[1] In Maisonneuve he drew up the town plan (adopted in 1891) and plans for the town's numerous public works, whose construction he then supervised.[2] However, he does not appear to have been in the good graces of the new administration that took office in 1909, and the council decided to have Vanier's plans checked by another engineer, Marius Dufresne, brother of Oscar.[3] A few months later, the council blamed Vanier for delays in the progress of public works, and Vanier himself suggested that some of his work be turned over to Dufresne. Soon afterwards, Dufresne was appointed town engineer.[4]

In Marius Dufresne's mind, plans were developing which would make Maisonneuve the focal point of the east end of Montreal Island — a huge park that would be the eastern counterpart of Mount Royal Park in the west, a magnificent boulevard spanning the island from north to south, and a group of majestic public buildings. The town council saw these projects as demonstrations of the dynamism of Maisonneuve and its leaders.[5]

New Trends in Urban Design

From 1910 public development plans in Maisonneuve were characterized by a preoccupation with esthetic concerns: Maisonneuve's leaders wanted to make things that were beautiful and grand, and a policy of creating a new environment now underlay the construction of streets, public buildings and parks. This new orientation did not spring full-grown from the minds of Maisonneuve's leaders but was part of a current of urban beautification that had spread all over North America.

In both North America and Europe, many planners, developers and civic leaders in the early twentieth century were concerned with improving the conditions of urban life and creating a more pleasant environment. Two urban planning movements provided them with many of their ideas. The first of these, the City Beautiful movement, originated in the United States. City Beautiful was an outgrowth of the Park and Boulevard movement, which in turn was inspired by the development of Central Park in New York by Frederick Law Olmsted in the 1850s. Central Park aroused considerable interest and was widely imitated, and Olmsted suggested that municipalities establish a network of parks linked by wide boulevards. Others took up the idea, and the Park and Boulevard movement which emphasized landscape design grew up in the 1870s. In this context, Montreal created Mount Royal Park in 1873 and invited Olmsted himself to design it.[6] In preparation for the 1893-1894 Chicago world's fair, a small city was built from scratch, and this gave rise to the City Beautiful movement, which adopted the landscape design ideas of its predecessor and added the notion of overall esthetic planning. The second movement, Garden City, was born in Britain in the early years of the twentieth century. Its goal was the creation of small towns surrounded by green belts.

Beautification plans inspired by these ideas were proposed in all parts of Europe and North America. The plans worked out for Canadian cities were sometimes expensive and grandiose.[7] Quebec, and more specifically Maisonneuve, also felt the influence of these concepts, for differences in language and culture were in no way an obstacle to the circulation of ideas. Through journals and conferences, architects and municipal leaders were aware of the latest developments in urban design. In Maisonneuve Marius Dufresne adopted American models for some of his buildings. In this sense, the Maisonneuve projects were as much the product of an era as a statement by a French Canadian bourgeoisie.

Marius Dufresne, town engineer, 1910-1918.

Grandiose Public Buildings

In its first twenty years of existence, the town of Maisonneuve built only one building worth mentioning, a combined town hall and fire station on Notre-Dame Street. Built in 1888 and enlarged substantially in 1897, it was designed to meet purely functional needs. It was on an appropriate scale for a small town and was modified as the town's requirements changed. In 1906-1907 a new fire station, a conventional building with no architectural pretensions, was built on Ontario Street.

And then Maisonneuve began construction of four public buildings in the space of five years. All these buildings — town hall, market, a public bath, and fire station — had definite esthetic pretensions. Work began with the new town hall, which was needed because the growth of the town and the increased services provided by its government had made the old location

Maisonneuve town hall (1912), on Ontario Street at the corner of Pie-IX Boulevard.

inadequate. The new building would be located on Ontario Street, between Pie-IX and Desjardins, and this move to the north was testimony to Maisonneuve's physical expansion. An amendment to the town charter, adopted in 1910, authorized the council "to borrow a sum not exceeding fifty thousand dollars for purchasing lands required for building a town hall, erecting the town hall, and furnishing the same."[8] The next year the council's borrowing power was extended: "The council is also authorized to expend an amount of twenty-five thousand dollars in all, to organize a municipal library, complete the town hall and the municipal bacteriological laboratory."[9]

In June 1910 the council bought ten lots from H. Watson and Watson, Foster and Co. at a total cost of $12,876.35.[10] The first contracts were granted in the summer and the work was carried out during 1910 and 1911.[11] Classically inspired, the building was on a scale to suit the aspirations of Maisonneuve's civic leaders. In 1915 a journalist described it in the following terms: "Maisonneuve has had its town hall since 1912. With an elegant Greek colonnade adorning its front, a superb candelabrum on each flank and a lawn growing around it, it stands stern and magnificent on Ontario Street. Heavy bronze doors introduce you to the interior of the building."[12]

Next came the market. Many public markets where farmers from the surrounding regions could come and sell their produce were established in the Montreal region around the turn of the century. The idea of building a market was raised in the Maisonneuve town council, which rejected it in 1899; the next year, however, the council formed a committee to study the question again.[13] A lack of financial resources was probably the reason why no action was taken on the proposal at that time. But in 1912 the council decided to build a market which would occupy a large area on the north side of Ontario Street opposite Morgan Boulevard, and obtained authorization from the Quebec Legislature which specified that "the council may erect and maintain a public market and purchase the land required for that purpose, but the amount to be expended therefore shall not exceed one hundred and fifty thousand dollars."[14]

The plans were approved in June 1912. The market took two years to build and was opened in September 1914. Once again, Maisonneuve did not scrimp. It constructed a majestic building with a massive portal, a central dome and four turrets, and equipped it with ultra-modern facilities. No more than a glance at the market reveals that the town went well beyond utilitarian concerns. Inside the market was a vast hall which could accommodate large meetings, and it would be east-end Montreal's favourite political meeting hall for many years.[15] The cost of building the market was $261,347.79.[16] In addition, the sculptor Alfred Laliberté was commissioned to create a monumental fountain in the market square; the fountain alone cost Maisonneuve's taxpayers more than $20,000.[17]

The proposal for a building containing a public bath and gymnasium was brought before the council in 1911, and a bylaw authorizing the town to borrow $30,000 was passed and then ratified by the Legislature.[18] However, construction of the building did not begin until three years later, in the summer of 1914.[19] It was built on Morgan Boulevard, near the market, at a total cost of $215,000 — considerably more than the initial estimate — and officially opened on May 17, 1916.[20] Its architecture was chosen by Marius Dufresne, and again harkened back to classical models. The overall lines of the building resemble those of Grand Central Station in New York, built between 1903 and 1913.

Finally, in 1914 the council decided to rebuild the no. 1 fire station at the corner of Letourneux and Notre-Dame streets, originally built in 1888. Again the Legislature granted its approval: "The council is authorized to borrow the amounts required for rebuilding the police and fire station at the

The public market building (1914) on Ontario Street facing Morgan Boulevard.

corner of Letourneux and Notre Dame Streets, and for purchasing fire engines and apparatus."[21] This building too was the work of Marius Dufresne. According to *Le Devoir* in 1914, "the building will be forty feet wide and a hundred feet long. Its style will be Egyptian."[22] Work on the fire station began in the summer of 1914 and ended in late 1915, at a total cost of $142,000.[23] As *La Patrie* noted, "it goes without saying that the building leaves absolutely nothing to be desired. All the vehicles are motorized and completely outfitted with modern equipment."[24] In this case, Dufresne was inspired largely by the plans for the Unity Temple built by Frank Lloyd Wright in Oak Park, Illinois, in 1906. Comparing either the architects' drawings or photographs of the buildings themselves, the similarity between the two buildings is striking — except that a tower had to be added to the Maisonneuve building for drying hoses. This more modern style of architecture differentiated the fire station from Maisonneuve's other public buildings.

Maisonneuve Park

The architecture of Maisonneuve's public buildings was not the only manifestation of this new direction. Civic leaders wanted to modify the whole urban environment by adding grandiose touches. Thus Maisonneuve Park was born.

Parks were not an issue during the early years of Maisonneuve's existence as a municipality, since large tracts of woodland and grassland were close at hand. The waterfront had not yet been encased in concrete frames and Maisonneuve residents had easy access to it. An amusement playground, Riverside Park, was built on the river just after the turn of the century and lasted until about 1908.

In 1902 the council decided to lease a large tract of land between Notre-Dame Street and the river from the Viau estate and turn it into Viau Park. The park included a pier providing access to the St. Lawrence and the Maisonneuve yacht club had its headquarters there. Trees were planted, and in 1906 the town began to develop the landscape on the basis of a plan drawn up by A. Beaugrand-Champagne. In 1911, however, the owners of the land decided to cancel the lease.[25]

In 1910 Maisonneuve was still very poorly equipped with parks. Vacant lots could not take the place of green spaces indefinitely, and the town council decided to acquire the land that would become Maisonneuve Park. There were two sides to the story of this project: the park as a public investment in the context of municipal development policy, and the park as a land speculation operation.

Maisonneuve Park would cover a large area — some 250 hectares in a vast rectangle bounded by Boyce Street (now Pierre-de-Coubertin Street) in the south, Pie-IX Boulevard in the west, Rosemount Boulevard in the north and the town limits in the east (see Map 2, page 18). This expanse was put together in stages, and the town council does not appear to have had such a large park in mind at the beginning. The Quebec Legislature authorized the creation of the park during its 1910 session.[26]

In September 1910 the council called for bids. There was only one, from Mendoza Langlois, who offered 137,816 square metres of land, part of the old Bennett farm. The town council accepted it and floated a $222,500 loan to pay for the land. Approval from Quebec City was obtained without difficulty.[27] A few weeks later, the town invited the Viauville Land Company to sell it an adjacent piece of land covering an area of 265,049 square metres, or almost double the area bought from Langlois. The unit price was the same and the town had to borrow $428,000 to pay for this tract. The transaction was completed in January 1911.[28]

By early 1911 Maisonneuve had a rectangular park covering an area of about sixty hectares, extending from Viau Street (the present Ray Murphy Street) north past Armand Street (Saint-Joseph Boulevard) and from the

The public bath (1916) on Morgan Boulevard.

town's eastern limits to William David Street. This is where matters remained for several months. But an ambitious plan, sponsored by Oscar Dufresne, took shape in 1912. Part of the plan was to enlarge the park still further to make it a gathering place for all the residents of the east end of Montreal Island. Consideration was also given to linking the park with Mount Royal via a large boulevard that would provide access to Lafontaine Park as well (shades of Frederick Law Olmsted and the Park and Boulevard movement).[29] In addition, the plan envisaged organizing profit-making activities, such as horse races and various forms of entertainment, in the park. The income from these activities would be used for paying the expenses incurred in establishing the park and for the benefit of Maisonneuve's residents. The town proposed that a commission separate from the municipality be established to administer this enterprise. The act establishing the

Maisonneuve Park Commission was approved on December 21, 1912. Its goals were explicitly stated in the preamble:

> Whereas it is urgent and in the public interest to aid the homes, hospitals, educational establishments, houses of refuge and charitable institutions which now or may hereafter give their services to the sick and poor of the municipality;
>
> Whereas the town of Maisonneuve has a park of considerable extent and whereas it should also in the public interest be embellished and organized like the parks in large European cities, in order to derive a revenue from it which would be wholly given over to the town and to the charitable works above mentioned....[30]

The commission consisted of three members appointed by the Maisonneuve town council for five-year terms. It had all the powers normally granted to a corporation, and these powers were to be used to beautify and administer Maisonneuve Park. It was authorized to make a wide variety of improvements to the park and could borrow up to a million dollars. The commission was also granted some authority over the distribution of the income from the park:

> The net receipts of the Commission, after deducting the interest and sinking fund of its consolidated debt, shall annually be divided and allotted as follows: one half to the city of Maisonneuve and one half to the homes, hospitals, educational establishments, houses of refuge and charitable institutions situated within the present limits of the city, according to the needs of such institutions whereof the commissioners shall be the sole judges.[31]

The bill did not pass without controversy in Maisonneuve. At a town council meeting, Alderman Germain and a number of taxpayers suggested that speculators, with the support of some council members, were behind the project.[32] Another speaker called the project a "scheme," and Oscar Dufresne retorted: "I take responsibility for the bill as it has been presented to the Legislature, and in the proper time and place I will be able to show that when the public becomes familiar with the Park bill, far from covering up a scheme, it will be to the full advantage of its originators."[33]

Alderman Germain called a public meeting to convince Maisonneuve's citizens to resist the bill. However, many supporters of the council came to the meeting and succeeded in having their position accepted. The president of the Club Ouvrier de Maisonneuve, among others, was on their side. A petition circulated by Germain gathered only one signature.[34]

No. 1 fire station (1915) at the corner of Letourneux and Notre-Dame streets.

Under the new legislation, the town acquired land for the park and sub-sequently transferred ownership of it to the commission. The commission did not begin to operate until late 1914, when the council appointed its first three members: Alderman Oscar Dufresne as chairman, large landowner James Morgan, and one of the principals of the newspaper *La Patrie*, L.-J. Tarte.[35]

Early in 1913 the town council began the task of enlarging the territory it had acquired in 1910. An amendment to Maisonneuve's charter author-ized it to "purchase by mutual agreement or by expropriation and to main-tain for ever as a public park the lands required to complete Maisonneuve Park."[36] This time, there was no limit to the price the municipality could pay.

Through a series of acquisitions between June 21, 1913, and February 1, 1916, the town quadrupled the area covered by the park in 1911. Even lands outside Maisonneuve's town limits, in Rosemount Ward in Montreal, were

Brochure de combat   Rodrigue Langlois

Scandale

du parc de

MAISONNEUVE

Ils ont fait Maisonneuve,..............
Contribuables, faites Maison   *nette*

This pamphlet exposed the speculation surrounding land purchases for Maisonneuve Park. Playing on the word Maisonneuve, it invited taxpayers to "clean house."

purchased. These purchases were the occasion for large-scale land speculation operations which led to the "Maisonneuve Park scandal" and were described in great detail by Rodrigue Langlois. It is difficult to determine exactly who profited from these operations, as the largest sellers were clearly intermediaries who acted as figureheads. The procedure of successively reselling the same property at intervals of a few days was systematically used. Most of Maisonneuve's large landowners appear to have profited at some stage of these operations.[37]

In 1911 and 1912 the developers who had been so successful in the southern part of Maisonneuve were having great difficulty selling their lots in the northern part of the town. Northern Maisonneuve was not as favourably situated in relation to Montreal's developed area and did not have good communications with downtown Montreal. It was far from the railways and streetcar lines and was not served by any major traffic artery. It became clear that many lots in this part of town would remain vacant for a number of years, and this impression was reinforced by the general difficulties of the real estate market in the period that began in 1913.

Thus, the purchase of lands for Maisonneuve Park served to stimulate the weak real estate market. This objective was clearly stated in 1915: "The council's goal was to develop the northern part of [Montreal's] sister city, making it possible for it to expand in a sustained manner and flourish as it has so far not been able to do, and at the same time to provide Montreal Island with a park truly worthy of the name, where crowds will gather constantly and provide Maisonneuve with a source of income."[38]

Above all, it would provide the developers with an opportunity to unload many of their less profitable lots — but not at bargain-basement prices. Through deals and the use of intermediaries, the price of the developers' lands rose rapidly. The profits the developers realized on these lands were much greater than if the lands had been sold to individuals.

The land purchases were financed through loans, and the interest on the loans could also be financed during the first ten years.[39] The total purchase price of Maisonneuve Park lands reached $6,445,615.[40] A report in March 1917 established that, if accumulated interest, the cost of issuing debentures, expenses already incurred and other costs were added to the purchase price, the total was as high as $7,758,787.11.[41]

Although the town council had hoped to realize a return on its investment in the form of income from operating the park, this never happened. The park commission was established in December 1914, and it had Marius Dufresne draw up a development plan. *La Patrie* described the commission's plans in the following terms:

> Two monumental gates, one at Pie-IX Boulevard and Sherbrooke Street and the other at 1st Avenue and Sherbrooke Street, will give access to [the park]. Apart from a magnificent racetrack more than a mile long, which will in itself be a source of considerable income for the town, the park will have amphitheatres with stone stands for hockey, baseball, lacrosse, etc., raceways for automobiles and horses, artificial lakes with elegant hotels built beside them, clubhouses with gazebos and arbours, cafes, etc. Then, on the educational side, the public will benefit from an arts centre with a museum and library and a botanical garden with an aquarium and a zoo. To relieve the hours of boredom there will be a cafe with music and, to satisfy more exotic tastes, a Japanese cafe with gardens decorated with enchanting waterfalls. In the middle of the central avenue a monument to [Sieur de] Maisonneuve will be built.[42]

Work was begun on some installations, and the town on two occasions agreed to advance $25,000 to the commission to provide work for the unemployed.[43] Unfortunately for the commission, it was established in the midst of the war and, lacking funds, it was condemned to inactivity. At a town council meeting, Mayor Levie Tremblay said: "When it was decided to establish the Park and this decision was implemented, there was no way of foreseeing the disastrous war that would ruin the world and plunge all endeavours such as the Park into complete immobility until the state of the financial markets improves."[44] Commissioners L.-J. Tarte and Oscar Dufresne agreed: "The upshot of all that has been said is that if the Commission has not yet achieved the goal for which it was established, it is because of the crisis from which we are now suffering. The Commissioners are guided by their wish to do their best, and say: who knows? If we are patient and wait a few more years, this vast piece of land may serve one day as the site of a world's fair."[45]

Other reasons for the lack of progress were given as well: the manpower shortage, which superseded the unemployment that had prevailed in the early part of the war, and the city of Montreal's refusal to open up Sherbrooke Street, which restricted access to the park.[46] The commission's inertia was also attributed to the repeated absences of one of its members, James Morgan, who was reported to "spend most of his time in Bermuda."[47]

The grandiose plan to develop Maisonneuve Park may have been premature or too ambitious, and a combination of circumstances made it impossible to complete. As a public investment, it did not have the anticipated impact on the value of nearby lands, but it did come along at a good time for the developers and speculators, and revived a declining real estate market.

Maisonneuve Park would eventually become what the town's civic leaders intended it to be — a place for cultural and athletic activities — but it would be developed in stages over sixty years. The land purchased by the town of Maisonneuve would be the site of the municipal golf course, built during the 1920s and more recently converted into a park; the Botanical Gardens, established during the 1930s; the Centre Maisonneuve sports facilities and the Maurice Richard Arena; and finally the sports complex built for the 1976 Olympic Games.

The Large Boulevards

All that, however, was a long way in the future. Back in Maisonneuve in the Michaud-Dufresne era, there was one more element in the town council's urban development plan: the creation of large boulevards.

The most important of these, Pie-IX Boulevard, already had a special character. It was wider than Maisonneuve's other streets (a hundred feet instead of sixty-six) and a number of members of the local bourgeoisie had chosen to live on Pie-IX Boulevard. As early as 1907, the council decided to make it Maisonneuve's communications link with Rosemount, its neighbour to the north.[48] In tune with currently fashionable ideas in urban design, engineer Marius Dufresne dreamed of making it a large tree-lined boulevard with a grassy island in the middle. The project soon extended beyond Maisonneuve and planners envisioned a boulevard connecting a series of municipalities from the south end of Montreal Island to the north end and even beyond, with a bridge providing a link to the north bank of Rivière des Prairies.

The boulevard would have to go through Saint-Michel and Montreal North, two small municipalities that were in no position to implement such an ambitious plan. But this would be no problem — Maisonneuve would take charge of the project! It would expropriate the necessary land and carry out the work in the two municipalities and bill them for the cost. The Quebec Legislature approved the project in 1912 and ratified the official plan drawn up by Marius Dufresne.[49] According to the plan, the sidewalks would be ten feet wide and there would be "two traffic lanes twenty-seven feet wide and a grassy island twenty-six feet wide in the centre."[50] Construction on the southern part of the boulevard, in Maisonneuve, was started first. Construction of the northern section, in Saint-Michel and Montreal North, was begun in 1915 and was already well advanced by the end of the year.[51]

Maisonneuve also assigned a special function to its magnificently situated east-west artery, Sherbrooke Street. The town council decided to widen it, hoping that some residents would build beautiful estates along the street, as the Dufresne brothers did. However, the development of this part of Maisonneuve was limited by Montreal's refusal to open Sherbrooke Street through Hochelaga.[52] A third boulevard, Morgan Boulevard, was developed with a grassy island in the middle, opening a vista onto two of the public buildings — the market and the bath. James Morgan and Alexandre Michaud donated lands for the widening of Morgan Boulevard.[53]

The opening up of these large boulevards provided the town with an opportunity to establish zoning regulations governing construction. Thus, the following regulations were established for Pie-IX Boulevard:

> In future, no factory, mill or works whatever shall be built on boulevard Pius IX from the river St. Lawrence, to the Rivière des Prairies, except between Notre Dame street and the St. Lawrence river, and from Ontario street to the railway tracks of the Canadian Pacific Railway, and Canadian Northern Railway. The establishment of wood and coal yards and the construction of ice-houses, are also prohibited. Dwelling houses, shops and stores which may be built there shall be at a uniform distance of twelve feet from the homologated line of the said boulevard, be at least two stories in height, and be built either in brick or stone or in wood covered with stone or brick.
>
> Staircases in front of the above mentioned buildings or structures are prohibited.[54]

Regulation of this sort was later extended to other Maisonneuve streets. Since zoning was a very new procedure at the time, Maisonneuve placed

A vista opens from Morgan Boulevard onto two of Maisonneuve's public buildings: the public bath on the right and the public market.

itself in the vanguard of urban design. It is worth noting in this context that, elsewhere in North America, zoning often had the effect of establishing residential segregation based on wealth.

Zoning also indicated a desire to harmonize private buildings with the new public developments. The trend-setters in this area were the Dufresne brothers, who not only blithely spent public money but also built a luxurious residence of their own. Located at the corner of Sherbrooke Street and Pie-IX Boulevard, adjacent to the Maisonneuve Park lands, Chateau Dufresne was based architecturally on no less a model than the Petit Trianon at Versailles. In the private sphere, the chateau was as much an expression of dreams of grandeur as Maisonneuve's public buildings; it was also one of the castles and large houses that businessmen all over North America were building in this era. There were even American companies that specialized

Château Dufresne.

in selling decorative items for such houses by catalogue, furnishing the Dufresne brothers with many ideas for embellishing the interior of their chateau.

These were the most visible elements of the urban development policy implemented after 1910. Late in 1915 *La Patrie* published a special section entitled "The New Maisonneuve" which described the changes that Maisonneuve had undergone in the years before the war. In five years, the town's face had been changed significantly. Maisonneuve's civic leaders were proud of these changes and did not hesitate to use them for advertising purposes. The *La Patrie* reporter wrote:

The prodigious development of Maisonneuve can best be seen in its public buildings. Its town hall, its market, its public place with its splendid

In this advertisement for "Maisonneuve Day" (May 27, 1917), aimed at making "the public in general and manufacturers in particular aware of this progressive town's immense resources from the industrial and commercial point of view and as a financial investment," the new public buildings are used to help project an image of the town.

fountain, its gymnasium and bath, its fire station and its boulevards have transformed the face of the town and truly made it a new Maisonneuve.... Come in and read, preserved for tomorrow on a plaque fastened to the wall, the names of the aldermen who provided their town with this superb endowment.[55]

The reputation of Maisonneuve's ruling group was confirmed in 1912 with the appointment of Mayor Michaud to the Metropolitan Parks Commission, established that same year by the provincial government.[56] And in 1917, on the occasion of a celebration in Maisonneuve, the provincial minister Jérémie Decary also spoke in praise of what had been done: "I have seen beautiful things, good things, solid things in Maisonneuve.... I am proud and happy that you decided to do something artistic. You decided, as did your fathers, to build to stay here. What you have built is beautiful and solid."[57]

In 1917 Maisonneuve published an advertisement describing the town as both the "Pittsburgh of Canada" and the "Garden of Montreal." These two

MAISONNEUVE

JARDIN DE MONTREAL

Maisonneuve possède dans son grand boulevard de l'Avenue Pie X, qui part du Saint-Laurent et s'étend jusqu'à la rivière des Prairies la plus belle artère de toute l'Ile de Montréal. Ses édifices publics comme on peut le constater par la vignette ci-dessus, sont les plus beaux que nous ayons sur toute l'Ile et constituent à eux seuls le plus beau monument érigé à l'initiative de ses gouvernants.

A new definition of the town: "Maisonneuve, garden of Montreal."

apparently contradictory expressions are an apt summary of the concerns of the real estate developers who were the town's real founders.

To make a profit on their lands, they had to stimulate development and populate the town. They did this initially by attracting industries and then, as concern for quality increasingly took hold in North America, they sought to attract still more residents by beautifying Maisonneuve.

Beautification, however, could have been achieved on a much more modest scale. Maisonneuve's pursuit of magnificence can only be explained as the work of parvenus. The French Canadian businessmen who carried out this politique de grandeur were self-made men showing off their newly acquired wealth. Their cultural vision was highly limited, involving little more than importing foreign — and especially American — models.

The politique de grandeur was also a statement by a social class — the bourgeoisie, and specifically the French Canadian bourgeoisie, whose numbers had swelled in the rapid economic growth of the period. It wanted to lay claim to its place in the sun and let the world know of its achievements. It was not ruralist or agriculturalist: it believed in progress and sought prosperity. And, like the bourgeoisie elsewhere in North America during the belle epoque, it spent money with abandon in the overly optimistic belief that prosperity would last forever.

Working-class residents of Maisonneuve, who made up a large majority of the population, were not consulted about the politique de grandeur and had no voice in it. They, however, would have to pay the bill.

CHAPTER 9

THE END OF MAISONNEUVE

Maisonneuve's beautiful facade was barely finished when it began to crack. The belle epoque came to an abrupt end with the outbreak of the First World War in 1914. In prosperous times, it was easy to get people to support a politique de grandeur but, with the onset of a leaner period, many of these people had second thoughts. In 1915 the situation in Maisonneuve began to change radically. The Michaud-Dufresne group was beaten in that year's election. With the end of growth, the town had begun to feel the effects of the war. Maisonneuve's financial situation deteriorated, and rumours of impending annexation to Montreal increased year by year. In 1918 these rumours became a reality.

The War and the End of Growth

Discontent with the town council had been festering for some time, and in late November 1914 a group of 137 citizens established the Parti de la Reforme Municipale (Municipal Reform Party) to defeat the incumbent administration.[1] The party's chief organizer was A. Meert, secretary of the Club Ouvrier de Maisonneuve, and its mayoral candidate was Levie Tremblay, a wood merchant and school commissioner who had sat on the council from 1911 to 1913.[2] It also ran candidates for the other council seats.

The ruling group reacted vigorously to the rise of this opposition party. On November 4, Councillor Oscar Dufresne had announced his intention to retire from municipal politics, but his colleagues, led by Mayor Alexandre Michaud, offered him the mayoral candidacy in an effort to get him to change his mind.[3] Dufresne refused and Michaud again ran for mayor. Meanwhile, four councillors had already announced their decision to run for re-election.[4] The struggle between the two groups was a lively one and, less than a month before the election, the council made a major strategic move. On the grounds that Maisonneuve's impending annexation to Montreal was being rumoured, it asked the provincial government to delay the election from February 1 to April 1 so that a useless election would be avoided if annexation did in fact take place. Reacting to this manoeuvre, the opposition came out strongly against annexation, and on January 20 the council withdrew its proposal.[5] The election twelve days later was a thorough repudiation of the ruling group, and the Reform party was swept into power.[6]

The first problem the new administration had to deal with was the plight of the unemployed, who made their presence felt by coming in force to town council meetings in April and May of 1915. Following the lead of Montreal Mayor Médéric Martin, who had made a similar pledge the year before, Mayor Tremblay promised jobs to the unemployed through municipal public works, but not all the councillors were pleased with his demagogic attitude. The unemployed criticized the contractor who had obtained the town paving contract for employing labourers who did not live in Maisonneuve. They also demanded an end to the use of steam shovels so that more workers would be employed. The council promised to act on their demands but, when it was slow in keeping its promise, the unemployed expressed their dissatisfaction by again showing up en masse at a council meeting. The frightened councillors had the police eject the intruders.[7] These tensions appear to have been resolved soon afterwards, no doubt because the Canadian economy became adjusted to war production after a few unsettled months.

But the new town council still had to bear the legacy of its predecessor. Some of the major projects of the Michaud-Dufresne regime were still uncompleted. The prestige surrounding these projects still properly belonged to the old council. And while the new council was inclined to claim that prestige for itself, the context was no longer the same, for the war marked the end of Maisonneuve's two decades of expansion. Even before the war, in 1913, the real estate market had entered a difficult period, so that one of the major components of Maisonneuve's success — real estate development — slowed down. The early part of the war brought hard times to a number of industrial firms, and production came to a near-standstill. As war contracts came in, these companies appear to have been able gradually to start up again but still not to expand their facilities. The only firm that may have recovered more quickly was Canadian Vickers whose factories produced armaments.

The absence of industrial expansion, the constraints of the war and the enlistment of thousands of men in the armed forces all helped dampen urban growth. There were few resources available to build new houses, and the entry of new industries also slowed down. The town council did grant tax exemptions and bond guarantees to some new companies in 1917, but the

Quebec Legislature cancelled these benefits a few months later when Maisonneuve was annexed to Montreal. And, most seriously of all, Maisonneuve's town government faced a very difficult financial situation resulting from the large investments undertaken in the preceding years.

The Town's Debt

The story of Maisonneuve's wartime financial situation actually begins a number of years before the war. Like all other new municipalities, Maisonneuve financed its major public works through long-term borrowing. Starting in 1909, its debt grew at a phenomenal rate, partly because of the needs that arose as masses of new residents arrived in Maisonneuve and partly because of the Michaud-Dufresne administration's ambitious and costly projects.

The town of Maisonneuve floated forty-five bond issues in its thirty-five years of existence, a little more than two-thirds of them in the last nine years, between 1909 and 1918 (Table 9-1). When the town borrowed money, certain formalities had to be observed. First the town council had to adopt the borrowing plan as a bylaw, and then the town's property owners had to ratify it by a double majority. As of 1898, the bylaw also had to be approved by Quebec's Lieutenant-Governor in Council. In addition, there was a limit to the municipality's borrowing capacity, established as a percentage of total assessed value of taxable real property. This ceiling was initially fixed at 15 per cent in 1883, raised to 20 per cent in 1893, and then raised again to 25 per cent in 1897.[8]

Loan bylaws did not always pass without difficulty, since there were sometimes divergent interests among the town's property owners. On the one hand, large developers saw public works as essential to their real estate operations; on the other, small homeowners feared the tax increases that new expenditures might bring. Within each of these groups, individuals might support or oppose a projected loan on the basis of the proximity of their own lands to the public works. Two proposals — a $400,000 loan in 1907 and a $600,000 loan in 1908 (reduced to $500,000 before it was accepted) — involved much larger sums than Maisonneuve was accustomed to and, while both were ultimately approved, they faced strong opposition even within the town council.[9]

The chairman of the finance committee at the time was Alexandre Michaud. He appears to have learned some lessons from the experience for, when his "équipe du progrès" came to power in 1909, the town council adopted a new strategy. The public works planned by the Michaud group were on a larger scale than before and required going above the 25 per cent ceiling. Going directly to the Legislature, the council obtained amendments to Maisonneuve's charter, authorizing it to carry out the proposed

Table 9-1
**Town of Maisonneuve
Bond Issues, 1887-1917**

Amount ($)	Rate (%)	Term (years)	Date of Issue	Date of Maturity
10,000.00	5	25	1887	1912
10,000.00	5	25	1888	1913
15,000.00	4.5	20	1890	1910
40,000.00	5	25	1891	1916
45,000.00	5	50	1894	1944
80,000.00	5	50	1896	1946
112,000.00	5	50	1896	1946
150,000.00	4.5	50	1899	1949
254,000.00	4.5	40	1900	1940
100,000.00	4.5	40	1901	1941
80,000.00	4.5	40	1902	1942
100,000.00	4.5	40	1903	1943
175,000.00	4.5	40	1905	1945
400,000.00	4.5	40	1906	1946
500,000.00	4.5	40	1909	1949
200,000.00	4.5	40	1909	1949
200,000.00	4.5	40	1909	1949
500,000.00	4.5	40	1909	1949
50,000.00	4.5	40	1909	1949
54,000.00	4.5	40	1909	1949
222,500.00	4.5	40	1910	1950
428,000.00	4.5	40	1910	1950
64,890.00	4.5	40	1911	1951
500,000.00	4.5	40	1911	1951
79,000.00	4.5	40	1911	1951
750,000.00	4.5	40	1912	1952
229,000.00	4.5	40	1912	1952
30,000.00	4.5	40	1912	1952
700,000.00	5	40	1912	1952
700,000.00	5	40	1912	1952
450,166.66	5	40	1913	1953
508,080.00	5	40	1913	1953
176,686.67	5	40	1913	1953
550,420.00	5	40	1914	1954
150,000.00	5	40	1914	1954
2,000,000.00	5	40	1914	1954
1,000,000.00	5	40	1914	1954

Table 9-1 (cont'd)

Amount ($)	Rate (%)	Term (years)	Date of Issue	Date of Maturity
800,000.00	6	3	1915	1918
1,000,000.00	6	3	1915	1918
2,500,000.00	5.5	15	1915	1930
500,000.00	6	3	1915	1918
355,000.00	6	10	1915	1925
600,000.00	5.5	20	1916	1936
355,000.00	5.5	3	1916	1919
700,000.00	5.5	20	1917	1937
355,000.00	5.5	3	1917	1920

Sources: Archives of the City of Montreal, file 1068-71; minutes of the Maisonneuve town council.

public works and to borrow without having to go through the formality of ratification by the property owners. Only approval by the Lieutenant-Governor in Council would now be required.[10]

From 1909 all Maisonneuve's borrowing was carried out under this new system, and the town's level of indebtedness increased rapidly. In the five years between 1909 and 1913, it grew from $2,875,000 to $7,712,000, an increase of 168 per cent. Fortunately, however, property assessment grew at a comparable rate, so that the ratio of debt to total assessed property value remained between 26 and 28 per cent.[11]

After 1913 the situation deteriorated. Maisonneuve floated large bond issues, and by 1917 debt represented 58.5 per cent of total assessed property value. The huge purchases for Maisonneuve Park, totalling $7,370,000 by 1917, were clearly responsible for this imbalance. But even if park purchases are eliminated from the calculation, the ratio of debt to total assessed property value was still 35.3 per cent. The real burden of Maisonneuve's debt increased even more as the growth of its revenues and assessment slowed during the war, reaching the point in 1916 and 1917 where Maisonneuve had to resort to long-term borrowing to pay the interest on its existing debt (which normally would have been paid out of the municipality's current revenues).

This was the culmination of a situation that had begun to develop in the years immediately preceding the war, when debt servicing occupied an increasingly large place in the annual budget. In 1912 it represented 53 per cent of current expenses, and four years later this figure had grown to 62.7 per cent. To make these payments, the municipality depended on two major sources of revenue, both based on property assessment: property tax, which provided 57 per cent of town revenues in 1912, and cost-sharing payments for sewers and sidewalks, which accounted for another 28 per cent. Business taxes and licences of all kinds represented less than 10 per cent of Maisonneuve's revenues.

Property assessment was based not only on land but also on "the value of the buildings, workshops and machinery thereon erected, and that of all other improvements made thereon."[12] In other words, vacant lots were assessed at a much lower level than built-up lands. Since the owners of large vacant lands were taxed on the basis of special conditions and industrial firms benefited from tax exemptions and limited assessments, the burden of municipal taxation, and thus of the town's investments, fell on the residential sector, on small property owners who owned houses and were quick to transfer the cost to their tenants in the form of rent increases.

It was in this context that the question of annexation to Montreal began to be discussed. Initially, the developers had derived great benefit from the existence of a separate municipality: they could establish the rules of the game more easily than in a large city and thus attract industry and stimulate urban development. But when it came to public investment, a suburban municipality was at a disadvantage. It was not always well enough organized to complete large public works, thus it tumbled into debt at a rapid rate. As a result, the cost of subsequent loans rose and the tax burden was increased and, when this happened, annexation became an attractive option. If the town were annexed, the huge debt would be distributed over the whole population of the big city, borrowing power would be greater, and the quality and quantity of public works would be guaranteed.

Annexation plans were debated frequently throughout Maisonneuve's history. Once the municipality had got its start, annexation seemed advantageous to some of its large landowners on one condition — that Montreal agree in advance to spend a specific amount on capital improvements. However, Montreal occasionally balked at this condition, and the Maisonneuve town council was able to find the human and material resources needed to carry out public works on its own. Meanwhile, population increases kept vindicating the council's optimism and providing a little more money for the town coffers.

The war brought this process to a halt, as the real estate market collapsed and construction came to a standstill. The heavy basic investments of the past few years could only be financed if new residents continued to arrive. When the municipality didn't obtain the additional revenues it needed, its financial situation deteriorated rapidly.

At first, the council took economy measures, reducing expenditures and staff and closing services such as the Goutte de Lait. It also had to ask the Quebec government for help, since its revenues were not enough to meet current administrative expenses. In 1916 Maisonneuve was "authorized to borrow an amount not exceeding six hundred thousand dollars, for a term of not more than twenty years, to pay the expenses of administration and the interest to become due during the year 1916."[13] If there was a balance left after these payments had been made, it could be used for capital improvements to Maisonneuve's street network. A ban was also placed on any further borrowing by the council (except to pay the interest on the Maisonneuve Park debt), and the council had to levy a special tax to cover the interest on the $600,000 loan and the repayment of the loan. A few months later, the Legislature authorized a $700,000 loan to pay administrative expenses and interest due in 1917.[14]

Annexation

To some people, annexation appeared to be the solution to all of Maisonneuve's problems. Notable among the supporters of annexation were members of the Association des Citoyens de Maisonneuve (Maisonneuve Citizens' Association), which came to the fore late in 1915.[15] The leaders of the association were the same people who had backed Alexandre Michaud and his supporters in the 1915 election and included former mayor Hubert Desjardins. In an effort to attain its goal, the association even went to the Legislature, and this move earned it a severe reprimand from the town council.[16] The Club Ouvrier, meanwhile, opposed annexation and demanded that the matter be decided by all of Maisonneuve's voters in a referendum.[17] Montreal reacted rather coolly to the idea of annexing Maisonneuve. Mayor Médéric Martin was firmly opposed to annexation, at least for the moment, because of Maisonneuve's huge debt.[18] Ultimately, the provincial government did not authorize the annexation of Maisonneuve, but it did merge Maisonneuve's school commission with Montreal's.[19]

The Association des Citoyens took up the issue again late in 1916 and decided to run a full slate of candidates in the 1917 election, with Hubert Desjardins as its mayoral candidate.[20] Desjardins would no longer support annexation if Maisonneuve could solve its financial difficulties by itself. In any case, he proposed that the people be consulted on the matter. Desjardins's opponents accused him of changing his position from one day to the next, but in vain.[21] Although Levie Tremblay was re-elected mayor, the association took all the other council seats.[22]

Maisonneuve's financial situation did not improve. In the spring of 1917, the municipality could not pay $500,000 it owed the Christian Brothers.[23] The council even decided to close Maisonneuve's playgrounds as an economy measure.[24] It still felt generous enough to offer tax exemptions and bond guarantees for companies establishing plants in Maisonneuve, thus arousing the ire of Montreal. But the end was near. Maisonneuve's creditors were uneasy about the town's poor financial situation, and some went directly to Premier Lomer Gouin. *Le Devoir* reported early in 1918:

> A delegation of holders of Maisonneuve municipal bonds came before Sir Lomer Gouin yesterday. Speaking for the group, lawyer Aimé Geof-frion said that Maisonneuve could not pay its debts in the amount of $17 million, and if no one came to its assistance it would be quite simply bankrupt. Mr. Aimé Geoffrion showed that if Maisonneuve were aban-doned to its sad fate, it would have unfortunate financial repercussions not only for Quebec but for all of Canada, since Maisonneuve is an important town and a recognized industrial centre. In conclusion, Mr. Geoffrion explained to Sir Lomer that, in his view, the best solution to the problem would be the annexation of Maisonneuve to Montreal. Mr. Gouin promised the delegation that he would consider the matter seriously.[25]

It is unclear how large a role this initiative played in the final decision, but it was very likely considerable. The annexation of Maisonneuve to Montreal was discussed in the Private Bills Committee on February 5 and 6, 1918. Montreal's representatives were still less than enthusiastic: Mayor Martin, supported by the city's counsellor, Mr. Laurendeau, was firmly opposed to annexation.[26] Martin would agree to annexation only if a 4 per cent tax were imposed on Maisonneuve's residents, and Maisonneuve's representatives objected vigorously to this condition. The provincial government finally decided the issue, and the act annexing Maisonneuve to Montreal was approved on February 9, 1918:

> The following territory is annexed to the city of Montreal, namely, the city of Maisonneuve, with its territorial limits as defined by its charter, which shall be annexed to and form part of Mercier Ward, which shall hereafter be known as Mercier-Maisonneuve Ward.
>   The assets and liabilities of the city of Maisonneuve hereby annexed shall form part of the assets and liabilities of the city of Montreal.[27]

The act provided for a tax of 2.5 per cent of the value of taxable property, to be levied on Maisonneuve property owners for a period of fifteen years. In addition, all tax exemptions, guarantees and cash subsidies granted by the Maisonneuve town council after January 1, 1917, were cancelled "unless approved by the administrative commission" of the city of Montreal. Finally, the act provided that "the debts of the city of Maisonneuve shall not have the effect of diminishing the borrowing powers possessed by the city of Montreal."

Little is known about the dealings that surrounded the annexation of Maisonneuve. Médéric Martin tried to arouse interest in what he maintained was the scandal of the former suburban municipality's administration and the acquisition of Maisonneuve Park. But the affair quickly died down. Martin, meanwhile, was appointed to Quebec's Legislative Council.[28] And so the independent existence of Maisonneuve, which had lasted almost thirty-five years, came to an end.

CONCLUSION

At least two conclusions can be drawn from the story of Maisonneuve. The first is that there is a form of capital called land capital, which is separate from banking, industrial and commercial capital but closely linked with them, and which performs a specialized function: managing and developing space. Land capital, represented mainly by the developer, plays a key role in urban growth, and municipal authorities follow its lead. The second conclusion is that within the group of developers, French Canadian businessmen have occupied a significant place. In Maisonneuve their position was a dominant one.

Some writers on Quebec tend to present a limited view of investment in land and real estate development, regarding it as the expression of a conservative mentality that shuns risk-taking and seeks security. In this view, investment in the land sector is only a sophisticated form of hoarding and can be placed in the same category as the purchase of government bonds.

While this view is not wholly false, it corresponds to only part of the real situation. It does not stand up well to an examination of the case of Maisonneuve, for the most fundamental characteristic of land capital in Maisonneuve is precisely its dynamism. Motivated by the profit that would reward their effort, the developers engaged in authentic capitalist exploitation of their landed property. They sought to organize development more effectively through concentration of ownership. The Viau family, with its aspirations to found a parish and a town on its property, represented this phenomenon in its purest form. And when the developers are looked at as a group, they do not fit the image of a set of cautious coupon-clippers. The developers created their own town, controlled its town council and used all the means at their disposal to ensure its growth. Were they aiming for security — or for high profits?

The developers took very real risks. Their success depended not only on their own dynamism but also on general economic conditions. In these terms, Maisonneuve clearly represents a success story. The developers' activities and the rapid economic growth of the early twentieth century stimulated the development of the southern part of the town. But the northern part of Maisonneuve, with its less advantageous location, remained empty, and just when its time appeared to have come, the recession began. The developers, and especially the second generation that had established itself in Maisonneuve a few years earlier, ran a considerable risk of failure. Through the Maisonneuve Park project, they transformed risk of failure into substantial profits.

Thus, Maisonneuve's developers were successful all along the line. But not all developers in the Montreal area were so fortunate. Newspaper advertisements in the years preceding the First World War reveal that a large number of urban development projects on Montreal Island were conceived in this period, some of them at considerable distances from downtown Montreal. For decades some of these towns existed only on paper. Thus, if Maisonneuve was a success story, there was failure elsewhere, and real estate investment involved elements of risk that should not be underestimated. In addition, land development required long-term investment, distributed over several decades. A revealing instance is the case of Alphonse Desjardins, who started buying land in Maisonneuve in 1874 and was still actively involved in development in the town when he died almost forty years later. And even after his death, members of his family continued his work.

In the years before the First World War, the urban function with the greatest allure was industry. If a town's growth were to be placed on a solid footing, steps had to be taken to attract industrial capital. Maisonneuve established an authentic industrial policy, as did a number of other municipalities. Implementing this policy involved two major steps: a sustained advertising campaign that proclaimed the town's advantages to industrialists and financial inducements — tax exemptions, cash grants, limitations on property assessment or tax liability, bond guarantees. The ultimate goal of this generosity was to populate the town and increase the surplus value of its land. Companies would themselves buy large tracts of land and, even more important, they would attract thousands of new residents. In both these processes, there would be a profit for the developers.

But for real estate development to be profitable, an industrial policy was not enough. Public investment was required as well, a problem that was expedited by the presence of developers on the town council. In addition, there was an association between land capital and industrial capital in the form of close links between the developers and some of Maisonneuve's new manufacturers. Merchants, for whom population growth could only be beneficial, joined this coalition to form a local bourgeoisie which dominated municipal institutions. This group was exemplified by the team of Alexandre Michaud and Oscar Dufresne and the councillors who supported them.

The most dynamic developers in Maisonneuve — Alphonse Desjardins, Charles-Théodore Viau, Isaïe Préfontaine — were French Canadians. How can their success in this field be explained?

A preliminary answer to this question can be found in the origins of landed property. Initially, rural land was granted to Francophones, who passed it down from generation to generation. When this land was ripe for urbanization, ethnic solidarity would operate in favour of French Canadian developers. This, however, is only a partial explanation. The nature of this sector of the economy also has to be looked at. The land sector did not depend on external markets as much as the commercial sector or on foreign technology as much as the industrial. To a much greater extent than these other sectors, it was based on an information network that operated inside Quebec. Success in the land sector required knowledge of local conditions and a close relationship with municipal authorities. These factors probably made the land sector easier for French Canadians to penetrate, in contrast with the difficulty they experienced in trying to break into commerce and industry. In real estate operations, they found a home for their dynamism and a way to reap large profits.

Of course, the land sector did not operate in isolation, and its growth was closely linked to commerce and industry. Land capital was often associated with other sectors of capital. After his land purchases, Alphonse Desjardins invested in finance and industry. Charles-Théodore Viau was able to depend on a solid industrial base when he decided to invest in urban development, as was Oscar Dufresne. And the intervention of commercial capital in land development is illustrated by the Letourneux family and Mayor Alexandre Michaud, all part of a complex network of relationships. In any case, it appears that in Maisonneuve, landed property was an important economic foundation for the French Canadian bourgeoisie. It provided them not only with substantial profits but also with considerable power.

With this foundation supporting it, the French Canadian bourgeoisie developed an ideology that was highly favourable to economic growth, industrialization and urbanization. It tried to get workers to share this ideology, and the words "progress" and "prosperity" were the mainstays of official speeches and articles in the press. When the town council invited workers in its advertisements to come to Maisonneuve to make "a quick and solid fortune," it was expressing the liberal ideology, the ideology of free enterprise and equal opportunity for all. In this respect, French Canadian capitalists in Maisonneuve behaved just like capitalists everywhere in North America.

The developers' actions and a favourable economic climate led to the emergence of a new city: a working-class, industrial town which civic leaders wanted to surround with an aura of grandeur. In 1883 Maisonneuve was a semi-rural zone on the periphery of the urbanized area of Montreal Island; thirty years later it had become Montreal's leading industrial suburb. This transformation took place in three stages.

Hardly more than a village at the beginning, Maisonneuve slowly became urbanized in its first dozen years. Circumstances did not lend themselves to rapid growth and, with Montreal relatively far away, a systematic extension of Maisonneuve's urban fabric was not yet possible. This waiting period, however, provided an opportunity for land developers and civic leaders to establish an infrastructure on which future growth would be based. Municipal institutions had to be created, a series of bylaws had to be passed, and, even more important, utilities had to be organized. The arrival of the electric streetcar, making it possible for the metropolitan centre to expand towards the suburbs at a faster rate, had a particularly significant impact.

Thus, Maisonneuve was in an advantageous position when the economic recovery began in 1896. Now the town had to seize the opportunity and look for industrial capital to foster economic growth. The policy of subsidies and tax concessions undertaken by Maisonneuve's civic leaders was a fruitful one. However, the establishment of factories in Maisonneuve was not the only goal of this policy. Even more important, it was aimed at getting employees of these factories to come live in Maisonneuve. These efforts led to rapid population growth and the extension of Maisonneuve's populated area which, in turn, brought increased demand for services. More and more money had to be invested to build streets and sewers and provide public transportation. The private monopolies that operated the major utilities took advantage of this situation to solidify their control and demand more from Maisonneuve's civic leaders, who had little power to resist them.

Between 1896 and 1910, Maisonneuve gradually became a major industrial centre. In 1910 a third stage began, characterized by a *politique de grandeur*. Maisonneuve's rapid progress went to the heads of its civic leaders, especially the Michaud-Dufresne team. These leaders wanted to make their town a model city, a monument to the glory of the rising bourgeoisie. In this period, large public buildings and great boulevards were constructed, streets were paved in the most up-to-date fashion and, most spectacularly, the grandiose Maisonneuve Park project was undertaken. This policy was very expensive and made the municipality's debt burden much heavier than it had been before.

If municipal financing was not an unmanageable problem in a time of growth and prosperity, the situation was very different in a period of recession. Such a period began in 1913, but even more serious negative effects were felt when Canada entered the war in the autumn of 1914. The real estate market collapsed, residential construction came to a virtual halt, and companies cut back production. The population growth needed to provide the increased revenues to finance the town's debt was cut off. Early in 1915 Maisonneuve entered a critical period and faced grave financial problems: on two occasions, it had to borrow to pay the interest on previous loans. Maisonneuve was no longer in a position to bear the cost of its politique de grandeur, and annexation became a necessity. The town's bondholders favoured annexation to protect their investment, and the developers were no longer opposed to it: having made their profits and put the town in debt, they hoped to distribute the cost of the operation over the whole population of Montreal.

In the thirty-five years of Maisonneuve's existence, a new community was formed. What were its social and economic characteristics?

First of all, Maisonneuve was an industrial town. Unlike many of Quebec's urban centres, however, it was not a company town. On the basis of volume of production, size of facilities or number of employees, Maisonneuve had several major enterprises. The shoe industry and its suppliers were prominent, but not to the exclusion of other industries. It was primarily because of the proximity of Montreal that Maisonneuve's industrialization was so extensive and diversified, since the suburbs participated in the industrial function of the metropolis. It is also noteworthy that few new companies were created in Maisonneuve. Rather, its industrialization took the form of companies moving their facilities from the central city to the periphery.

Maisonneuve was also a working-class town. While it had a local bourgeoisie made up of industrialists, merchants and members of the liberal professions, the great mass of its residents were workers. Among these, factory workers were the dominant group, and they included a large number of unskilled labourers. Shoe manufacturing was the largest industry in terms of numbers of workers employed.

Maisonneuve was also a city of tenants. Only one head of household in ten owned his own home, a consequence of Maisonneuve's occupational structure. Low-paid workers were hardly in a position to aspire to home ownership, and labourers and shoe-factory workers had to be satisfied with inferior dwellings. The fact that these workers were tenants also meant that they were shut out of active participation in municipal politics, except for the right to vote on election day. Only property owners had full political rights, and they alone could play a part in making important decisions. Thus, this city of tenants, where tenants essentially paid the cost of urban development (or at least paid more than their share, since industrial corporations and large landowners who held vacant lots enjoyed special tax privileges), was dominated by property owners. In their day-to-day life, Maisonneuve's workers could see the effects of the domination that was a condition of their existence.

Finally, Maisonneuve was a city of newcomers. Its population grew rapidly and most of its residents came from outside the town. In fact, at the turn of the century, natural increase accounted for only one-fifth of Maisonneuve's population growth. Though immigrants came to Maisonneuve, 85 per cent of its population consisted of French Canadians from Montreal or from the rural areas of Quebec.

Are there any conclusions about Quebec society as a whole that can be drawn from the history of Maisonneuve between 1883 and 1918? Of course, Maisonneuve was an integral part of Quebec, so that studying this part contributes to a better understanding of the whole. But to what extent is it possible to generalize from the phenomena observed in Maisonneuve?

First, the story of Maisonneuve has something important to say about the process of urban development, and especially the particular form represented by the creation of a new town. Concerted action by land capital and industrial capital, policies of "boosterism" undertaken by the municipal council and the role of utilities are all elements that can be found in varying degrees in most other municipalities. Maisonneuve certainly provides a model whose relevance can be checked in studying the history of other Quebec towns.

Second, the story of Maisonneuve provides information about the industrialization of Quebec. Early in the twentieth century, manufacturing production became even more concentrated in the Montreal region than it had been before. Through the case of Maisonneuve, the scope of the expansion of productive capacity and the rapidity of the changes that took place at this time can be seen. We also noted that Maisonneuve was industrialized by companies that had already been in business for some time and moved their installations. This phenomenon, which could also be observed in other suburban municipalities, sheds a different light on the debate about the pace of industrialization in Quebec. It is increasingly being recognized that the economic growth of the 1896-1914 period took off from an industrial base established earlier, and that this existing industrial base was much more solid than was previously believed. In addition, it is being perceived that the industrialization of Quebec at the turn of the century cannot be explained only by the rise of natural resource processing in peripheral regions. In this respect, the history of Montreal and its metropolitan area has to be placed in a wider context and regarded as central to the history of Quebec.

Finally, there is an area in which studying the case of Maisonneuve leads to a better understanding of Quebec society — the role and position of land capital in economic activity. We have been able to observe the dynamism with which land capital operated, its integration into the capitalist economy, and its fundamental role in urban development. A serious questioning of traditional interpretations of this subject is called for, and a new hypothesis can be proposed. While land capital can become conservative, it is not conservative by nature. Rather, it is a risk-taking activity, a potential source of high profits, and the basis of considerable political power. For the French Canadian bourgeoisie, it represents one of the bases of capital accumulation, and hence one of the factors contributing to its political and ideological domination of Quebec. The validity of this new interpretation, however, can only be tested by studying other Quebec towns.

APPENDIX

Industrial Enterprises Operating in Maisonneuve

Company	Arrival in Maisonneuve	Grant	Tax Exemption	Limit on Assessment or Taxes
Food products				
St. Lawrence Sugar Refining Co.	1887		✓	✓
Viau et Frère	1907		✓	
Geo. N. Pichet	1900		✓	
National Licorice Co.	1907		✓	
(J.A. Richard & Co.)*				
(Dionne Sausage Factory)				
(Bernier & Gadbois)				
Iron and steel products				
N. Commire Fils & Cie	1897	✓		
Warden King & Son	1904			✓
United Shoe Machinery Co. of Canada	1911		✓	
(Neverslip Manufacturing Co.)				
(Woodhall Nail Factory)				
(A.B. Stove Co.)				

Industrial Enterprises Operating in Maisonneuve (Cont'd)

Company	Arrival in Maisonneuve	Grant	Tax Exemp- tion	Limit on Assessment or Taxes
Wood and construction materials				
Hubert Prévost	n.a.		✓	
Hamel et Bleau[a]	n.a.		✓	
J.P. Abel Fortin & Cie	1907			
Montreal Last Co.	1909		✓	
Dominion Die Co.	1911		✓	
United Last Co.	1914			
Montreal Terra Cotta Lumber Co.[b]	1888		✓	
(Amédée Allard)				
(Corbeil et Frères)				
(Montreal Box Toe)				
(Meunier & Fils)				
(Maisonneuve Cast Stone Works)				
(Artificial Stone Factory) ·				
(A. Bremner Ltd.)				
Shoes				
Laniel & Co. (& Jos. Laurin)[c]	1898	✓		✓
Kingsbury Footwear Co.	1900	✓		✓
Dufresne & Locke[d]	1900	✓	✓	✓
Geo A. Slater	1900	✓		✓
Royal Shoe Co.[e]	1901	✓		✓
McDermott Shoe Co.	1909		✓	
Poliquin & Gagnon	1909		✓	
Dupont & Frère	1910		✓	
James Muir Co.	1913		✓	
(J.P. Côté)				
Textiles				
Canadian Spool Cotton Co.	1909		✓	

Industrial Enterprises Operating in Maisonneuve (Cont'd)

Company	Arrival in Maisonneuve	Grant	Tax Exemption	Limit on Assessment or Taxes
Paper and printing				
Watson Foster & Co.	1897	✔	✔	
King Paper Box Co. Ltd.	1908		✔	
Chemical products				
L'Air Liquide	1911		✔	
J.W. Jamieson Co.	1912		✔	
Non-ferrous metals				
Acme Can Works[f]	1901	✔		✔
Gilmour Brass Works	1907			✔
Gagnon Brass Works	1896			✔
Other industries				
Canadian Vickers Ltd.	1910		✔	
Hadd Cigar Factory	1915			
Oxford Motor Car[g]	1914		✔	
Dominion Ice Co.	1898		✔	
United Soap Co.	1909			
J.T. Robertson & Co.	1914			

* No information available for bracketed companies.
[a] Bankrupt in 1901.
[b] Moved out of Maisonneuve in 1911.
[c] Acquired by Rideau Shoe in 1908; factory destroyed by fire in 1913.
[d] Originally Pellerin & Dufresne.
[e] Acquired by Dufresne & Locke in 1904.
[f] Acquired by American Can Co. in 1908.
[g] In business only until 1915 or 1916.

Sources: *La ville de Maisonneuve, P.Q. Canada, 1911. Le principal faubourg industriel de Montréal;* Archives of the City of Montreal (Maisonneuve, file 959, minutes of the council and assessment roll 1911-12); *La Patrie,* June 26, 1909; *Montreal Illustrated; Montreal, Old and New; Le Canada,* July 28, 1906.

NOTES

Abbreviations Used

ACM Archives of the City of Montreal
ACMM Archives of the City of Montreal, Maisonneuve
MMTC Minutes of Maisonneuve Town Council
RHAF *Revue d'Histoire de l'Amérique Française*
SQ   *Statutes of Quebec*

Chapter 1: The Birth of Maisonneuve

[1.] See Raoul Blanchard's remarkable discussion of water transport questions in *L'Ouest du Canada français: Montréal et sa région* (Montreal: Beauchemin, 1953), pp. 233-52. See also Pierre Brouillard, "Le développement du port de Montréal" (MA thesis [history], University of Quebec at Montreal, 1976).

[2.] Jean Hamelin and Yves Roby, *Histoire économique du Québec 1851-1896* (Montreal: Fides, 1969), pp. 104-9 and appendix 13.

[3.] *Montreal in 1856* (Montreal: John Lovell, 1856), pp. 36-50; G.J.J. Tulchinsky, *The River Barons: Montreal Businessmen and the Growth of Industry and Transportation 1837-1853* (Toronto: University of Toronto Press, 1977), pp. 220-28.

[4.] Hamelin and Roby, *Histoire économique*, pp. 278-80.

[5.] Hamelin and Roby, *Histoire économique*, pp. 261-78; Blanchard, *Ouest du Canada français*, pp. 271-75; D. Suzanne Cross, "The Neglected Majority: The Changing Role of Women in Nineteenth-Century Montreal," in *Histoire*

Sociale/Social History IV, no. 12 (November 1973), pp. 203-33. T.W. Acheson, "The Social Origins of Canadian Industrialism: A Study in the Structure of Entrepreneurship" (PhD thesis, University of Toronto, 1971), pp. 117-19; Eve Martel, "L'industrie à Montréal en 1871" (MA thesis [history], University of Quebec at Montreal, 1976); Paul-André Linteau, Jean-Paul Bernard and Jean-Claude Robert, "L'industrialisation de Montréal au 19e siècle" (Paper delivered at the conference of the Institut d'Histoire de l'Amérique Francaise, Montreal, October 1978).

6. Jean-Paul Martin, "Villes et régions du Québec au XIXe siècle: Approche géographique" (Doctorat de troisième cycle thesis [geography], Louis-Pasteur University, Strasbourg).

7. Jean De Bonville, *Jean-Baptiste Gagnepetit: Les travailleurs montréalais à la fin du 19e siècle* (Montreal: L'Aurore, 1975); Fernand Harvey, *Révolution industrielle et travailleurs* (Montreal: Boréal Express, 1978).

8. Paul-André Linteau, "Quelques réflexions autour de la bourgeoisie québécoise 1850-1914," RHAF 30, no. 1 (June 1976): 55-56.

9. Henry W. Hopkins, *Atlas of the City and Island of Montreal Including the Counties of Jacques Cartier and Hochelaga: From Actual Surveys, Based upon the Cadastral Plans Deposited in the Office of the Department of Crown Lands* (n.p.: Provincial Surveying and Pub. Co., 1879). The maps dealing with Maisonneuve are on pages 75 and 103.

10. On this subject see Kenneth T. Jackson, "Metropolitan Government versus Political Autonomy: Politics on the Crabgrass Frontier," in *Cities in American History*, edited by Kenneth T. Jackson and Stanley K. Schultz (New York: Alfred A. Knopf, 1972), pp. 442-62; Kenneth T. Jackson, "Urban Deconcentration in the Nineteenth Century: A Statistical Inquiry," in *The New Urban History*, edited by L.F. Schnore (Princeton, N.J.: Princeton University Press, 1975), pp. 110-42.

11. "An Act to incorporate the Town of Hochelaga," SQ, 46 Vict. (1883), chap. 82.

12. Minutes of the Hochelaga town council, August 24, 1883.

13. *La Patrie*, September 4, 1883.

14. Bylaw no. 39, ACM, Hochelaga file.

15. *La Patrie*, December 22, 1883.

16. *Journals of the Legislative Assembly of Quebec*, February 1, 1883, p. 49; minutes of the council of the village of Hochelaga, December 29, 1882; *Journals of the Legislative Assembly of Quebec*, February 16, 1883, p. 94. Although bills pre-

sented to the Quebec Legislature are preserved in the library of the Legislature, those for the years 1867-1883 are missing, thus there is little information on this petition.

17. *SQ*, 46 Vict. (1883), chap. 82, pp. 422-23.

18. *La Presse*, July 29, 1905, p. 19.

19. *La Patrie*, June 26, 1909.

20. ACM, Hochelaga file.

21. *Quebec Official Gazette*, 1883, pp. 2090-91.

22. Hormidas Magnan wrote in 1925: "The town of Maisonneuve was created on December 27, 1883 under the name of Hochelaga, by virtue of the Act 46 Vict. chap. 62, approved on March 30, 1883. The town of Hochelaga took the name of Maisonneuve by virtue of the Act 61 Vict. chap. 67 on January 15, 1898" (*Dictionnaire historique et géographique des paroisses, missions et municipalités de la province de Québec* [Arthabaska: Imprimerie d'Arthabaska, 1925], pp. 727-28). This is an error. The town was clearly given the name Maisonneuve in 1883 even though it was governed under the old charter of Hochelaga. In 1898 the charter was revised completely for the first time. Magnan's error was repeated in a number of publications issued by the city of Montreal and in Ludger Beauregard, *Toponymie de la région métropolitaine de Montréal* (Quebec: Department of Lands and Forests, 1968), p. 105.

23. Blanchard, *Ouest du Canada français*, p. 180.

24. Ibid., p. 173.

25. Ibid., pp. 176-78.

26. "Proclamation," December 27, 1883, *Quebec Official Gazette*, 1883, p. 2091.

27. Use of the terms north, east, south and west can lead to confusion. As commonly used in Montreal, these terms indicate particular parts of the city or the island that do not correspond exactly to the cardinal points of the compass. The direction referred to as north in Montreal is really west-northwest, east is really north-northeast, and so on. Since Maisonneuve place names were based on common Montreal usage, this usage is followed consistently throughout this book.

28. Blanchard, *Ouest du Canada français*, pp. 190-202.

Chapter 2: The Developers

1. Francois Lamarche, *Pour une analyse marxiste de la question urbaine* (Quebec: Conseil des Oeuvres et du Bien-être de Québec, 1972), p. 74. Lamarche calls this form of capital "capital immobilier" (real estate development capital), giving the word "immobilier" a very precise meaning that does not include the historical dimension. We will come back to this question further on. The term "capital foncier" (land capital) appears to this writer to be closer to the mark.

2. Alain Lipietz, *Le tribut foncier urbain* (Paris: Maspero, 1974), p. 31.

3. This schema is influenced by the works of Lamarche and Lipietz mentioned above as well as the author's own reflections based on his research into land ownership in Quebec.

4. Paul-André Linteau and Jean-Claude Robert, "Land ownership and society in Montreal: An hypothesis," in *The Canadian City: Essays in Urban History*, edited by Gilbert Stelter and Alan Artibise (Toronto: McClelland and Stewart, 1977).

5. Jacques Lautman, "La spéculation, facteur d'ordre ou de désordre économique," *Revue française de sociologie* 10 (1969); p. 625; quoted in Lamarche, *Pour une analyse marxiste*, p. 94.

6. Lipietz, *Tribut foncier urbain*, p. 58.

7. Maurice Halbwachs, *Les expropriations et le prix des terrains à Paris (1860-1900)* (Paris: Publications de la société nouvelle de librairie et d'édition E. Cornely, 1909), p. 377.

8. For Alphonse Desjardins, see *Le Devoir*, June 5, 1912, p. 6; H.J. Morgan, *Canadian Men and Women of the Time* (Toronto, 1912), p. 320; J.C. Lamothe, *Histoire de la corporation de la cité de Montréal* (Montreal: Montreal Printing & Publishing Co., 1903), p. 315-17; *Montreal Star*, March 25, 1885, p. 4; Léon Trepanier, "Figures de maires: Alphonse Desjardins," *Les cahiers des dix* 23 (1958), pp. 261-83. This writer also used information obtained during interviews with Edouard Desjardins and information contained in the Maisonneuve archives.

9. *Montreal Illustrated* (Montreal: Consolidated Illustrating Co., 1894), p. 99; *La Patrie*, June 26, 1909; *La Presse*, May 6, 1899, p. 16.

10. ACMM, file 959-5.

11. *La Presse*, September 3, 1910, p. 12.

12. Morgan, *Canadian Men and Women*, p. 915.

[13] Ibid., pp. 821-22.

[14] MMTC, December 9, 1914; MMTC, July 18, 1917; MMTC, August 29, 1917.

[15] See C.N. Dorion, *Evolution de la législation générale et spéciale concernant les corporations municipales de la province de Québec: Partie d'un mémoire présenté à la Commission Tremblay par l'Union des municipalités de la province de Québec*, 3 vols. (Quebec, 1954), part 2, chap. 4; "La communauté urbaine: une formule d'organisation et de gestion des agglomérations," *Quebec Yearbook 1971* (Quebec: Editeur Officiel du Québec, 1971), pp. 1-40.

[16] The general provisions of the Municipal Code and the Cities and Towns Act were valid for Maisonneuve, but there were also other pieces of legislation—the town charters—that applied to Maisonneuve alone and granted it additional powers. The following were Maisonneuve's charters: *SQ*, 46 Vict. (1883), chap. 82; *SQ*, 51-52 Vict. (1888), chap. 89; *SQ*, 56 Vict. (1893), chap. 57; *SQ*, 60 Vict. (1897), chap. 65; *SQ*, 61 Vict. (1898), chap. 57; *SQ*, 63 Vict. (1900), chap. 53; *SQ*, 9 Ed. VII (1909), chap. 89; *SQ*, 1 Geo. V (1910), chap. 52; *SQ*, 1 Geo. V (2nd session—1911), chap. 64; *SQ*, 2 Geo. V (1912), chap. 62; *SQ*, 3 Geo. V (1912), chap. 58; *SQ*, 4 Geo. V (1914), chap. 78; *SQ*, 6 Geo. V (1916), chap. 47; *SQ*, 7 Geo. V (1916), chap. 64.

[17] *SQ*, 9 Ed. VII (1909), chap. 89.

[18] The required papers were signed before the notary Gustave Ecrement. See Ecrement Record, nos. 222, 252, 262, 277, 424, 523 and 642, and MMTC, 1892 to 1899 *passim*.

[19] "Acte de donation de rues par Alphonse Desjardins & al.," Record of N.D. Préfontaine, notary, no. 61, November 25, 1884.

[20] MMTC, August 9, 1889; August 21, 1889; September 9, 1889; September 19, 1889; September 23, 1889; October 2, 1889; and October 26, 1889.

[21] *La Patrie*, June 26, 1909.

[22] *Le diocèse de Montréal à la fin du dix-neuvième siècle* (Montreal: Eusèbe Sénécal et Cie, 1900), p. 406.

[23] Ronald Rudin, "The Development of Four Quebec Towns 1840-1914: A Study of Urban and Economic Growth in Quebec" (PhD thesis [history], York University, Toronto, 1977).

[24] Alan F.J. Artibise, *Winnipeg: A Social History of Urban Growth, 1874-1914* (Montreal: McGill-Queen's University Press, 1975); Alan F.J. Artibise, "Boosterism and the Development of Prairie Cities 1867-1913," in *Town and City: Aspects of Western Canadian Urban Development* (Regina: Canadian Plains Research Center, 1981), pp. 209-35.

[25.] ACMM, files 1-1-6 and 13.

[26.] *La Presse*, June 20, 1906, p. 1; *La Presse*, July 27, 1906, p. 3; *La Presse*, July 28, 1906, p. 13.

[27.] *La Presse*, October 28, 1904, p. 8; *La Presse*, March 18, 1905, p. 24.

[28.] "Let us first acknowledge that, understood in a certain sense, the price of land is a vague concept, and may not exist at all. For it to be possible to speak of the price of all the lots that are currently in existence in Paris, would it not be necessary for all those lots to be sold at least once in the same year? However, it is generally imagined that the prices for which particular lots are sold can be applied to lots of similar location, shape and area that are not sold. Nothing is less certain.... It is entirely possible that if a lot that was not sold had been substituted for the one that was, it would have fetched the same price. But if both lots had been sold at the same time—rather than one in place of the other—and if the sale of lots had become a more general phenomenon, then prices could have been very different, not only because of the increased supply, but also, and more significantly, because of the new and different cast of mind that would have developed among buyers and sellers when they were faced with a market that was widened in this way." (Halbwachs, *Les expropriations*, pp. 364-65)

[29.] Halbwachs, *Les expropriations*, pp. 369-76.

[30.] I consulted all the relevant documents in the Montreal registration office. As most of these summarize earlier transactions, I will refer the interested reader to the one that gives the best overall view of the situation: "Acte de partage entre Alphonse Desjardins, Zaïde Paré et J.J.A. Desjardins, s.j.," Registration office of Hochelaga and Jacques-Cartier counties, register B, vol. 5, no. 64791, November 16, 1896.

[31.] "Acte de société entre M.M. Trudel, Desjardins & autres," record of M. Garand, notary, no. 8830.

[32.] Charles Edward Goad, *Atlas of the City of Montreal and Vicinity in Four Volumes: From Official Plans & Special Surveys, Showing Cadastral Numbers, Buildings & Lots* (Montreal: Chas. E. Goad Inc., 1912-14).

[33.] Alphonse Desjardins to the mayor and councillors of Maisonneuve, April 3, 1887, ACMM, file 78-B.

[34.] Registration office of Hochelaga and Jacques-Cartier counties, register D, vol. 9, p. 265, no. 18196, July 18, 1885.

[35.] Registration office of Hochelaga and Jacques-Cartier counties, register D, vol. 41, no. 64808, December 11, 1896.

[36.] Registration office of Hochelaga and Jacques-Cartier counties, register D, vol. 51, no. 80426, August 8, 1899.

[37.] Registration office of Hochelaga and Jacques-Cartier counties, register D, vol. 64, no. 98590, December 15, 1902.

[38.] *La Presse*, June 15, 1907, p. 22.

[39.] MMTC, August 23, 1905.

[40.] Rodrigue Langlois, *Scandale du parc Maisonneuve* (n.p., n.d.) pp. 15-17, 42-49.

[41.] This is an estimate made by the author from the will of C.-T. Viau, Registration office of Hochelaga and Jacques-Cartier counties, register A, vol. 5, p. 27, no. 77520, July 27, 1893.

[42.] Registration office of Hochelaga and Jacques-Cartier counties, register D, vol. 10, p. 715, no. 20204, July 12, 1886.

[43.] "Mr Viau owns a splendid farm of some 700 acres at Maisonneuve and Longue Pointe, where he keeps the finest blooded stock, including 40 cows, whose milk is received daily at the factory for use in the manufacture of the justly celebrated biscuits." (*Montreal Illustrated*, Montreal: Consolidated Illustrating Co., 1894, p. 99)

[44.] ACMM, file 1-1-3.

[45.] ACMM, file 1-1-6.

[46.] *La Presse*, May 6, 1899.

[47.] ACMM, file 1-1-6.

[48.] MMTC, February 8, 1899.

[49.] ACMM, file 1-1-13.

[50.] Except for the Viau estate's holdings in Longue-Pointe, which are beyond the scope of this study.

[51.] Goad, *Atlas of the City of Montreal* (1914).

[52.] Langlois, *Scandale*, p. 9; *Le Devoir*, May 13, 1911, p. 5.

Chapter 3: Organizing the Town

[1.] MMTC, *passim*; *La Patrie*, June 26, 1909.

[2.] MMTC, November 15, 1889.

[3.] MMTC, November 25, 1889; MMTC, December 8, 1889; MMTC, December 23, 1889.

4. MMTC, September 23, 1889.

5. See C.N. Dorion, *Evolution de la législation générale et spéciale concernant les corporations municipales de la province de Québec: Partie d'un mémoire présenté à la Commission Tremblay par l'Union des municipalités de la province de Québec*, 3 vols. (Quebec, 1954), *passim*.

6. Charles N. Glaab and A. Theodore Brown, *A History of Urban America* (New York: Macmillan, 1967), p. 182.

7. Ibid., p. 183.

8. Glaab and Brown, *Urban America*, pp. 183-87; Blake McKelvey, *The Urbanization of America 1860-1915* (New Brunswick, N.J.: Rutgers University Press, 1963), pp. 82-84.

9. ACMM, file 78-D.

10. MMTC, May 27, 1889; MMTC, June 5, 1889; MMTC, August 9, 1889; ACMM, file 78-A.

11. ACMM, files 78-A and 78-N.

12. MMTC, November 10, 1890.

13. Bylaws of the town of Maisonneuve, I, pp. 74-87.

14. MMTC, June 5, 1891; MMTC, September 30, 1891; Bylaws of the town of Maisonneuve, I, pp. 94-95.

15. F. Clifford Smith, *L'aqueduc de Montréal: Son historique pour la période comprise entre l'année 1800 et l'année 1912* (Montreal, 1913), pp. 56-57; "Extract from Minutes of Meeting of Shareholders of the Montreal Water and Power Company held at Company's Office in Montreal, on the 30th day of June, 1892," ACMM, file 78-1-11.

16. MMTC, December 16, 1892; "Déclarations, réquisitions et protêt par la ville de Maisonneuve à la Montreal Water & Power Co.," Ecrement Record, no. 238, March 15, 1893; MMTC, April 10, 1893; MMTC, May 3, 1893; MMTC, May 17, 1893.

17. MMTC, June 8, 1898; MMTC, June 15, 1898; MMTC, August 10, 1898; "Agreement between the Town of Maisonneuve and the M.W.&P. Co.," Ecrement Record, no. 596, August 18, 1898.

18. Glaab and Brown, *Urban America*, pp. 147-54; S.B. Warner, "Streetcar Suburbs: The Consequences," in *The City in American Life: A Historical Anthology*, edited by Paul Kramer and Frederick L. Holborn (New York: Capricorn, 1970), p. 278; McKelvey, *Urbanization of America*, pp. 76-77; Glen E. Holt, "The Changing Perception of Urban Pathology: An Essay on the Development of

Mass Transit in the United States," in *Cities in American History*, edited by Kenneth T. Jackson and Stanley K. Schultz (New York: Alfred A. Knopf, 1972), pp. 324-43.

[19.] See the works cited in the previous note.

[20.] "A Brief History of the Montreal Street Railway Company from 1861 to 1910," in *Annual Report of the Montreal Street Railway Company for the Fiscal Year Ended 30th September 1910*, pp. 25-42; John Irwin Cooper, *Montreal: A Brief History* (Montreal: McGill-Queen's University Press, 1969), pp. 104-5.

[21.] E. Lusher, manager, to J.-J. Beauchamp, December 14, 1885, ACMM, file 98-1-1.

[22.] H.A. Everett, managing director, to the mayor of Maisonneuve, August 3, 1892, ACMM, file 98-1-1.

[23.] MMTC, May 3, 1893; MMTC, May 9, 1893; MMTC, May 17, 1893; E. Lusher to M.-G. Ecrement, May 12, 1893, ACMM, file 98-1-1.

[24.] ACMM, file 98-1-1.

[25.] John H. Dales, *Hydroelectricity and Industrial Development: Quebec, 1898-1940* (Cambridge, Mass.: Harvard University Press, 1957), pp. 13-21.

[26.] Dales, *Hydroelectricity and Industrial Development*, pp. 102-4; Cooper, *Montreal*, pp. 108-10; Clarence Hogue, André Bolduc and Daniel Larouche, *Québec: Un siècle d'électricité* (Montreal: Libre Expression, 1979), pp. 15-70.

[27.] MMTC, September 2, 1885; MMTC, January 7, 1886; MMTC, September 7, 1888.

[28.] MMTC, October 7, October 12, October 15, October 21, November 4, November 11, 1891.

[29.] MMTC, January 22, 1892.

[30.] MMTC, September 22, 1892; MMTC, July 5, 1893; MMTC, September 13, 1893; MMTC, February 21, 1894; MMTC, April 18, 1894; MMTC, September 19, 1894; MMTC, October 29, 1895; MMTC, November 20, 1895.

[31.] M.-G. Ecrement to Gabriel Marchand, June 26, 1899, ACMM, file 83-1.

[32.] MMTC, January 7, 1885.

[33.] MMTC, October 1, 1884.

[34.] MMTC, August 26, 1887; ACMM, file 959-35.

[35.] MMTC, May 2, 1888; ACMM, file 959-1.

[36.] MMTC, April 28, 1890; "Règlement divisant la Ville de Maisonneuve en quartiers et en arrondissements de votation," Bylaw no. 31, April 28, 1890.

37. Decree of Mgr Edouard-Charles Fabre, archbishop of Montreal, August 20, 1888, Archives of the Chancery of the Archdiocese of Montreal; *Le diocèse de Montréal a la fin du dix-neuvième siècle* (Montreal: Eusèbe Sénécal et Cie, 1900), p. 393.

Chapter 4: Industrial Development

1. W.T. Easterbrook and Hugh G.J. Aitken, *Canadian Economic History* (Toronto: Macmillan, 1967); Paul-André Linteau, René Durocher and Jean-Claude Robert, *Quebec: A History 1867-1929*, translated by Robert Chodos (Toronto: James Lorimer and Co., 1983), chapters 18 through 24.

2. "Messrs Stone and Company wrote to the council that they intended to build an electrical equipment factory in Outremont; they asked what concessions the town would provide. In reply, the council told them that they would do better to approach the town of Maisonneuve." (*Le Devoir*, June 5, 1913, p. 5)

3. For the harbour of Montreal, see Pierre Brouillard, "Le développement du port de Montréal, 1850-1896" (MA thesis [history], University of Quebec at Montreal, 1977); and Paul-André Linteau, "Le développement du port de Montréal au début du 20e siècle," Canadian Historical Association, *Historical Papers* (1972), pp. 181-205. The most important printed source on the port is the series of annual reports published in English and French by the Montreal Harbour Commission and reprinted in part in the federal Sessional Papers.

4. MMTC, July 18, 1894; MMTC, April 22, 1895; MMTC, June 5, 1895; MMTC, August 10, 1896.

5. J. Israël Tarte to George Hadrill, secretary of the Board of Trade, cited in Montreal Board of Trade, *Council Report*, 1898, pp. 7-9.

6. George Hadrill to J. Israël Tarte, cited in Montreal Board of Trade, *Council Report* 1898, pp. 7-9.

7. *Bulletin de la Chambre de commerce du district de Montréal*, I, December 1, 1899, p. 95.

8. Montreal Harbour Commissioners, *Annual Report* 1891, doc. 10a, appendix 17, Canada, *Sessional Papers* 25, no. 8 (1892) 174; *Idem, Annual Report* 1896, doc. 11e, appendix 2, *Sessional Papers* 31, no. 9 (1897) p. 85.

9. Montreal Harbour Commissioners, *Annual Report* 1894, doc. 11c, appendix 2, *Sessional Papers* 28, no. 8 (1895), p. 73; *Idem, Annual Report* 1896, doc. 11e, appendix 2, *Sessional Papers* 31, no. 9 (1897), p. 92.

10. Canada, Department of Public Works, *Reports, Sessional Papers*, 1900-1908, *passim*.

11. Montreal Harbour Commissioners, *Annual Reports*, 1911-1914, *passim*.

12. Linteau, "Développement du port de Montréal," p. 198.

13. MMTC, October 13, 1896; October 15, 1896.

14. MMTC, July 6, 1910; MMTC, December 6, 1911.

15. MMTC, April 15, 1896; MMTC, May 1, 1896; ACMM, file 959-25.

16. *Montréal et le congrès eucharistique* (Montreal, 1910), pp. 54-55.

17. *La ville de Maisonneuve, P.Q., Canada, 1911: Le principal faubourg industriel de Montréal* (Montreal: Commercial Magazine Co. Ltd., 1911).

18. There is a large collection of correspondence on this subject in the archives. See ACMM, file 959-53.

19. *La chambre de commerce du district de Montréal*, 1911-12, pp. 40-41.

20. *Le Devoir*, May 26, 1917, p. 9.

21. *La ville de Maisonneuve*, p. 11; *La chambre de commerce du district de Montréal*, 1911-12, p. 40.

22. *Le Devoir*, July 8, 1911; *Le Devoir*, January 17, 1911.

23. *Le Devoir*, November 16, 1912; *Le Devoir*, May 26, 1917.

24. See Albert Faucher, *Québec en Amérique au XIXe siècle: Essai sur les caractères économiques de la Laurentie* (Montreal: Fides, 1973), chap. 3.

25. *Revised Statutes of Quebec*, 1888, article 4404.

26. Ibid., article 4406.

27. Ibid., articles 4642, 4559.

28. Ibid., article 4642.

29. *Revised Statutes of Quebec*, 1909, article 5929.

30. Ibid., article 5930.

31. *SQ*, 56 Vict. (1893), chap. 57, article 4.

32. *SQ*, 60 Vict. (1897), chap. 65, article 8.

33. *SQ*, 63 Vict. (1900), chap. 53, article 20.

34. Ibid., article 13.

35. MMTC, November 25, 1903; "Conventions entre la Ville de Maisonneuve et Warden King & Son," Ecrement Record, no. 1153, June 30, 1904.

36. MMTC, October 30, 1901.

37. MMTC, November 6, 1901; November 13, 1901.

38. MMTC, May 25, 1905; June 7, 1905; September 27, 1905.

39. See ACMM, file 959, and MMTC.

40. MMTC, *passim*; ACMM, files 959-9 to 959-18.

41. MMTC, April 23, 1905: August 9, 1905; August 16, 1905.

42. Interview with Dr. Edouard Desjardins, June 28, 1973.

43. MMTC, May 8, 1912; May 29, 1912; June 19, 1912.

44. In Quebec as a whole, the value of industrial output increased by 122 per cent between 1900 and 1910, and the number of workers rose by 42 per cent.

45. *Le Devoir*, December 16, 1912.

46. Information about companies comes from the following sources: *La ville de Maisonneuve*; ACMM, file 959, MMTC, and the 1911-1912 assessment roll; *La Patrie*, June 26, 1909; *Montreal Illustrated* (Montreal: Consolidated Illustrating Co., 1894); Lorenzo Prince, *Montreal, Old and New* (Montreal: International Press Syndicate, 1915); *Le Canada*, July 28, 1906.

47. Howland E. Watson, "La sixième industrie du Canada," *Le Devoir*, November 21, 1911; Nap. Tellier, "L'industrie de la chaussure," *Le Devoir*, December 5, 1911.

48. Interview with Dr. Edouard Desjardins, July 1973; Romeo Bastien, "Monographie de la tuilerie 'Montreal Terra Cotta Limited'" (licence thesis [commercial science], Ecole des Hautes Etudes Commerciales, Montreal), in *Thèses* (Montreal: HEC, 1947), supplement, pp. 1-82.

49. Joanne Burgess, "L'industrie de la chaussure à Montréal: 1840-1870—le passage de l'artisanat à la fabrique," *RHAF* 31, no. 2 (September 1977), pp. 187-210.

50. ACMM, file 959-14; *La Patrie*, June 26, 1909.

51. *La Patrie*, June 26, 1909.

52. ACMM, file 959-15; *La Patrie*, June 26, 1909; *Montréal fin de siècle: Histoire de la métropole du Canada au dix-neuvième siècle* (Montreal: Gazette Printing Company, 1899), pp. 123-24; Prince, *Montreal, Old and New*, p. 393; assessment roll, 1911-1912.

53. ACMM, file 959-17; *La Patrie*, June 26, 1909; *La ville de Maisonneuve*, p. 19.

54. *La ville de Maisonneuve*, p. 17.

55. Herbert Brown Ames, *The City Below the Hill* (1897; Toronto: University of Toronto Press, 1972), p. 19; *Montreal Illustrated*, 1894, p. 122.

56. MMTC, March 9,1896; March 17, 1896.

57. Watson Foster & Co. to the mayor and council of the Town of Maisonneuve, March 11, 1896, ACMM, file 959-7.

58. MMTC, March 21, 1896; Ecrement Record, no. 451.

59. Watson Foster Co. Ltd. to M.-G. Ecrement, September 9, 1898, ACMM, file 959-7.

60. *Le Canada*, July 28, 1906.

61. *La Patrie*, June 26, 1909.

62. Montreal Harbour Commissioners, *Annual Report* 1912, doc. 21, appendix 16, *Sessional Papers* 48 (1914), pp. 295-96; F.W. Cowie, *Transportation Problems in Canada and Montreal Harbour* (London: Institution of Civil Engineers, 1915), pp. 26-29; MMTC, August 3, 1910; MMTC, January 25, 1911; MMTC, January 20, 1915; "Agreement for exemption of taxes between the City of Maisonneuve and Canadian Vickers Limited," Ecrement Record, no. 3610, January 28, 1915.

Chapter 5: The Power of the Utility Monopolies

1. Ecrement Record, no. 531.

2. See correspondence for the following dates in ACMM, file 98-8-2: December 10, 1898; December 16, 1898; January 9, 1899; October 21, 1899; October 24, 1899; November 13, 1899; November 20, 1899; December 6, 1899; December 8, 1899; January 24, 1900; March 23, 1900; March 27, 1900; February 5, 1902; April 11, 1902; October 10, 1902; November 12, 1902.

3. John Irwin Cooper, *Montreal: A Brief History* (Montreal: McGill-Queen's University Press, 1969), pp. 105-6.

4. Ecrement Record, no. 1121.

5. "A Brief History of the Montreal Street Railway Company from 1861 to 1910," in *Annual Report of the Montreal Street Railway Company for the Fiscal Year Ended 30th September 1910, passim.*

6. ACMM, file 98-6.

7. L.-J.-S. Morin to L.-J. Forget, December 7, 1903, ACMM, file 98-17-1.

8. W.G. Ross to M.-G. Ecrement, March 18, 1904, ACMM, file 98-17-1.

9. W.G. Ross to M.-G. Ecrement, April 25, 1904, ACMM, file 98-17-1.

10. M.-G. Ecrement to the Montreal Street Railway, May 7, 1904, ACMM, file 98-17-1.

11. W.G. Ross to M.-G. Ecrement, June 2, 1904, ACMM, file 98-17-1.

12. W.G. Ross to L.-J.-S. Morin, July 12, 1904, ACMM, file 98-17-1.

13. W.G. Ross to the mayor and councillors of the town of Maisonneuve, September 7, 1904, ACMM, file 98-17-1.

14. *La Presse*, October 11, 1904, p. 4.

15. *La Presse*, October 10, 1904, p. 12.

16. *La Presse*, October 11, 1904, p. 4.

17. *La Presse*, October 11, 1904; *La Presse*, October 13, 1904; *La Presse*, October 29, 1904; MMTC, October 12, 1904.

18. *La Presse*, October 28, 1904, p. 14.

19. *La Presse*, March 1, 1905, p. 2; *La Presse*, March 6, 1905, p. 1.

20. ACMM, file 326-2-20.

21. MMTC, November 23, 1904.

22. ACMM, file 98-18.

23. MMTC, January 18, 1905; *La Presse*, January 19, 1905, p. 15; MMTC, February 20, 1905; Ecrement Record, no. 1271.

24. *La Presse*, March 10, 1905, p. 4.

25. *La Presse*, February 15, 1905, p. 4; *La Presse*, February 27, 1905, p. 4; *La Presse*, March 28, 1905.

26. *La Presse*, February 28, 1905, p. 1; *La Presse*, March 1, 1905, p. 2; *La Presse*, March 3, 1905, pp. 1, 7; *La Presse*, March 6, 1905, pp. 1, 9; *La Presse*, March 7, 1905, p. 1; *La Presse*, March 8, 1905, pp. 1, 7.

27. *La Presse*, March 10, 1905, p. 8.

28. *La Presse*, March 21, 1905, pp. 1, 11.

29. *La Presse*, May 26, 1905, p. 1.

30. *La Presse*, October 28, 1904, p. 8; *La Presse*, March 18, 1905, p. 24.

31. "Brief History of the Montreal Street Railway," p. 34.

32. ACMM, file 495-37; MMTC, October 6, 1897; MMTC, October 15, 1897;

John H. Dales, *Hydroelectricity and Industrial Development: Quebec, 1898-1940* (Cambridge, Mass.: Harvard University Press, 1957), pp. 102-4.

33. Dales, *Hydroelectricity and Industrial Development*, p. 102.

34. "Contrat d'éclairage électrique," Ecrement Record, no. 539.

35. MMTC, November 29, 1899.

36. "Contrat," Ecrement Record, no. 685.

37. Dales, *Hydroelectricity and Industrial Development*, pp. 104-6; W.A. Duff, *The Montreal Electrical Handbook* (Montreal: American Institute of Electrical Engineers, 1904), pp. 58-59; Clarence Hogue, André Bolduc and Daniel Larouche, *Québec: Un siècle d'électricité* (Montreal: Libre Expression, 1979), pp. 63-70.

38. ACMM, file 495-6, November 22 to December 13, 1905; MMTC, November 29, 1905; MMTC, December 6, 1905.

39. ACMM, file 495-20; MMTC, April 16, 1902; MMTC, October 16, 1907; MMTC, September 8, 1909; MMTC, November 3, 1909.

40. L.-J.-S. Morin to M.-G. Ecrement, January 31, 1912; ACMM, file 495-23-3.

41. *SQ*, 9 Ed. VII (1909), chap. 111; *SQ*, 1 Geo. V (1910), chap. 78.

42. Ecrement Record, no. 2139, November 8, 1909.

43. ACMM, file 495-22-6.

44. *La Presse*, April 26, 1910, p. 10.

45. *La Presse*, December 2, 1909, p. 8; L.-J.-S. Morin letter, October 1, 1910, ACMM, file 495-23-2.

46. *La Presse*, January 19, 1910, p. 1.

47. "Contrat entre la ville de Maisonneuve et la Dominion Light, Heat & Power Co.," Ecrement Record, no. 2384, November 28, 1910; MMTC, October 5, 1910; MMTC, October 12, 1910; *La Presse*, October 13, 1910, p. 1.

48. *La Presse*, October 20, 1910, p. 16; *Le Devoir*, July 14, 1911, p. 2.

49. MMTC, January 17, 1912; *Le Devoir*, January 18, 1912, p. 8.

50. L.-J.-S. Morin to M.-G. Ecrement, January 31, 1912; ACMM, file 495-23-3.

51. L.-J.-S. Morin to M.-G. Ecrement, January 31, 1912; ACMM, file 495-23-3; "Contrats, transactions et compromis," Ecrement Record, nos. 2717 and 2718, February 6, 1912.

52. According to John H. Dales, Dominion Light, Heat and Power became part of the conglomerate in 1908; this is impossible since Dominion Light, Heat and

Power did not exist at that time. The date of the takeover appears to have been about 1912 or 1913. See Dales, *Hydroelectricity and Industrial Development*, pp. 112, 247; ACMM, file 495-33; Hogue et al., *Quebec: Un siècle d'électricité*, p. 81.

53. MMTC, November 26, 1902; "Conventions, compromis et transport entre la Ville de Maisonneuve et M.W.&P. Co.," Ecrement Record, no. 933, December 31, 1902.

54. ACMM, file 78-15.

55. *La Presse*, April 18, 1904.

56. *La Presse*, April 27, 1904, p. 11; *La Patrie*, April 27, 1904, p. 3.

57. A. Carvell, secretary, to E. Guay, n.d., ACMM, file 78-15.

58. A. Carvell, secretary, to M.-G. Ecrement, ACMM, file 78-15.

59. MMTC, June 22, 1904.

60. Extract from the minutes of the meeting of the executive committee of the Quebec Provincial Board of Health held on January 7, 1907, ACMM, file 78-15.

61. ACMM, file 78-15.

Chapter 6: A Working-Class Town

1. *Le Devoir*, October 19, 1911, p. 2.

2. M.-G. Ecrement to A.-J. De Bray, October 4, 1912, ACMM, file 40-7.

3. MMTC, December 6, 1911.

4. It is certainly conceivable that there were deficiencies in the federal census. In a rapidly growing town it is possible that new residents would be missed. It is hard to believe, however, that 7,351 people could be "forgotten." The situation becomes clearer when the 1911-1912 assessment roll, which was officially confirmed in the autumn of 1911 and therefore complied in the preceding months, is examined in fine detail. One column of the assessment roll specifies the number of "residents" for each property owner or tenant. There is a figure in this column even when the property owner or tenant is a business. Kingsbury Footwear has 500 "residents," the sugar refinery, 436. The School Commission is listed as having 1,800 "residents," probably the number of children of school age in the town. There are also a large number of merchants and shopkeepers listed as heads of a household in two separate places; these "bigamists" are listed once at their homes and again at their business addresses. Double counting seems to be at work in all these cases. If they are eliminated from the

calculation, a total of 19,024 "residents" is obtained, or 340 more than the fig-ure reported by the federal census-takers. This is a negligible difference, and the results of the census can be accepted even if their accuracy is not necessarily absolute.

This criticism of the 1911-1912 assessment roll throws the population figures of the town assessors for other years into doubt as well. But if these figures can-not be accepted as they stand, they can still be taken as an indication of Mai-sonneuve's rate of growth. The *Lovell's Directory* estimates were very vague; from 1902 on they were based on the municipality's figure of the preceding year.

5. These figures are taken from the annual report of the Quebec Provincial Board of Health; see Paul-André Linteau, "Histoire de la ville de Maisonneuve (1883-1918)" (PhD thesis [history], University of Montreal, 1975), pp. 130-32.

6. Everett C. Hughes, *French Canada in Transition* (1943; Chicago: University of Chicago Press, Phoenix Books, 1963), pp. 40-83.

7. Emile Benoist, *Monographies économiques* (Montreal: Le Devoir, 1925), pp. 135-36; Robert Rumilly makes the same affirmation in his *Histoire de Montréal* (Montreal: Fides, 1972), 3, p. 398.

8. A.R. Pinsonneault, *Atlas of the Island and City of Montreal and Ile Bizard: A Compilation of the Most Recent Cadastral Plans from the Book of Reference* (n.p.: Atlas Publishing Co., [1907]). Pinsonneault's inclusion of the Ontario Street fire station and the Viau biscuit factory led me to conclude that 1907 was the date of the atlas.

9. Charles Edward Goad, *Atlas of the City of Montreal and Vicinity in Four Volumes: From Official Plans & Special Surveys, Showing Cadastral Numbers, Buildings & Lots* (Montreal: Chas. E. Goad Inc., 1912-1914), vol. 4 (1914).

10. Marie Lavigne and Jennifer Stoddart, "Analyse du travail féminin à Montréal entre les deux guerres" (MA thesis [history], University of Quebec at Montreal, 1973), p. 225.

11. Ibid., p. 228.

12. Ibid., *passim*.

13. Paul-André Linteau and Jean-Claude Robert, "Land Ownership and Society in Montreal: An Hypothesis," in *The Canadian City: Essays in Urban History*, edited by Gilbert Stelter and Alan F.J. Artibise (Toronto: McClelland and Stewart, 1977), p. 27.

14. Terry Copp, *The Anatomy of Poverty: The Condition of the Working Class in Montreal 1897-1929* (Toronto: McClelland and Stewart, 1974), p. 70.

15. John Irwin Cooper, *Montreal: A Brief History* (Montreal: McGill-Queen's University Press, 1969), p. 101.

16. *La ville de Maisonneuve, P.Q., Canada, 1911: Le principal faubourg industriel de Montréal* (Montreal: Commercial Magazine Co. Ltd., 1911), p. 11.

17. *Le Devoir*, May 26, 1917, p. 9.

18. Copp, *The Anatomy of Poverty, passim.*

19. Herbert Brown Ames, *The City Below the Hill* (1897; Toronto: University of Toronto Press, 1972).

20. Copp, *The Anatomy of Poverty.*

21. Claudine Pierre-Deschênes, "La tuberculose au Québec au début du XXe siècle: problème social et réponse réformiste" (MA thesis [history], University of Quebec at Montreal, 1980).

22. Ames, *The City Below the Hill*, p. 24.

23. *La chambre de commerce du district de Montréal*, 1911-12, pp. 40-41.

24. MMTC, 1911-17, *passim.*

25. MMTC, December 3, 1913.

Chapter 7: The Banner of Progress

1. For the Quebec ideological scene in the early twentieth century, see Paul-André Linteau, René Durocher and Jean-Claude Robert, *Quebec: A History 1867-1929*, translated by Robert Chodos (Toronto: James Lorimer and Co., 1983), pp. 528-40; R.R. Heintzman, "The Struggle for Life: The French Daily Press of Montreal and the Problems of Economic Growth in the Age of Laurier, 1896-1911" (PhD thesis [history], York University, Toronto, 1977).

2. *Montréal et le congrès eucharistique* (Montreal, 1910), pp. 54-55.

3. *Le Devoir*, October 3, 1912, p. 5.

4. *Le Devoir*, November 16, 1912.

5. Terry Copp, *The Anatomy of Poverty: The Condition of the Working Class in Montreal 1897-1929* (Toronto: McClelland and Stewart, 1974).

6. Rodrigue Langlois, *Scandale du parc Maisonneuve* (n.p., n.d.) pp. 2, 73.

7. *La Presse*, September 13, 1907, p. 5.

8. Langlois, *Scandale, passim; Canada Gazette*, July 30, 1904, p. 219.

9. Lorenzo Prince, *Montreal, Old and New* (Montreal: International Press Syndicate, 1915), p. 389.

10. Prince, *Montreal, Old and New*; William Henry Atherton, *Montreal, 1535-1914* (Montreal: S.J. Clarke, 1914), vol 2, pp. 140-44; "Monsieur Alexandre Michaud, maire de Maisonneuve. Le grand financier. Le sage administrateur. L'homme public," *La Presse*, September 3, 1910, p. 19.

Chapter 8: Maisonneuve's Politique de Grandeur

1. MMTC, September 8,1890; October 15, 1890; *La Presse*, March 16, 1910, p. 12.

2. MMTC, November 11, 1909.

3. MMTC, August 11, 1909.

4. MMTC, June 1, 1910; MMTC, June 8, 1910; J.E. Vanier to the Maisonneuve town council, June 22, 1910, ACMM, file 691.

5. *Le Devoir*, May 26, 1918, p. 9.

6. Frederick Law Olmsted, *Report on Mount Royal Park* (New York, 1874); Jean-Claude Marsan, *Montreal in Evolution* (Montreal: McGill-Queens's University Press, 1981), pp. 299-301.

7. Charles N. Glaab and A. Theodore Brown, *A History of Urban America* (New York: Macmillan, 1967), pp. 254-56, 259-62, 289-90; Paul Rutherford, "Tomorrow's Metropolis: The Urban Reform Movement in Canada, 1880-1920," Canadian Historical Association, *Historical Papers* (1971), pp. 208-11; W. Van Nus, "The Fate of City Beautiful Thought in Canada, 1893-1930," in *The Canadian City: Essays in Urban History*, edited by Gilbert Stelter and Alan F.J. Artibise (Toronto: McClelland and Stewart, 1977), pp. 162-85; Alan Artibise and Gilbert Stelter, eds., *The Usable Urban Past: Planning and Politics in the Modern Canadian City* (Toronto: Macmillan, 1979).

8. SQ, 1 Geo. V (1910), chap. 52, article 4.

9. SQ, 1 Geo. V (2nd session—1911), chap. 64, article 13.

10. Ecrement Record, nos. 2288, 2289; MMTC, June 1, 1910; MMTC, June 8, 1910; MMTC, June 15, 1910.

11. MMTC, 1910-11, *passim*.

12. *La Patrie*, December 4, 1915, p. 10.

13. MMTC, December 6, 1899; MMTC, December 5, 1900.

14. SQ, 2 Geo. V (1912), chap. 62, article 4.

15. MMTC, June 19, 1912; MMTC, April 30, 1913; MMTC, September 10, 1913;

MMTC, October 22, 1913; MMTC, December 3, 1913; MMTC, January 28, 1914; MMTC, February 4, 1914; MMTC, February 18, 1914; MMTC, April 1, 1914; *Le Devoir*, March 14, 1912, p. 8; *Le Devoir*, August 20, 1914, p. 2; *Le Devoir*, October 3, 1914, p. 6; *La Patrie*, December 4, 1915, p. 10.

16. ACMM, file 487-1-23.

17. *Le Devoir*, December 2, 1915, p. 2; *La Patrie*, December 4, 1915, p. 10.

18. MMTC, September 13, 1911; *SQ*, 2 Geo. V (1912), chap. 62, article 5.

19. MMTC, August 19, 1914.

20. *Le Devoir*, May 18, 1916, p. 7.

21. *SQ*, 4 Geo. V (1914), chap. 78, article 1.

22. *Le Devoir*, June 18, 1914, p. 9.

23. MMTC, July 29, 1914; MMTC, December 29, 1915; *Le Devoir*, October 21, 1915, p. 2.

24. *La Patrie*, December 4, 1915, p. 10.

25. MMTC, *passim*; "Résiliation de bail entre la Ville de Maisonneuve et J.L. Clément & Cie," Ecrement Record, no. 2512, June 23, 1911; *La Patrie*, June 26, 1909.

26. *SQ*, 1 Geo. V (1910), chap. 52, article 5.

27. MMTC, September 2, 1910; MMTC, September 28, 1910; Rodrigue Langlois, *Scandale du parc Maisonneuve* (n.p., n.d.), pp. 7-8; "Vente à la Ville de Maisonneuve par Mendoza Langlois," Ecrement Record, no. 2340, September 29, 1910.

28. MMTC, November 2, 1910; MMTC, November 30, 1910; MMTC, December 7, 1910; Langlois, *Scandale*, pp. 9-10; "Vente à la Ville de Maisonneuve par Viauville Land Co.," Ecrement Record, no. 2407, January 4, 1911.

29. *Le Devoir*, January 21, 1914, p. 6.

30. *SQ*, 3 Geo. V (1912), chap. 59.

31. Ibid.

32. *Le Devoir*, November 28, 1912, p. 2.

33. Ibid.

34. *La Presse*, November 29, 1912, pp. 1-2; *La Patrie*, November 29, 1912, pp. 1-2.

35. MMTC, December 9, 1914; *La Patrie*, December 4, 1915, p. 10.

[36.] *SQ*, 3 Geo. V (1912), chap. 58, article 11.

[37.] Langlois, *Scandale, passim.*

[38.] *La Patrie*, December 4, 1915.

[39.] *SQ*, 2 Geo. V (1912), chap. 62, article 8.

[40.] Langlois, *Scandale*, p. 76.

[41.] *Le Devoir*, March 15, 1917, p. 6.

[42.] *La Patrie*, December 4, 1915, p. 10.

[43.] MMTC, November 3, 1915; MMTC, April 19, 1916; *Le Devoir*, April 20, 1916, p. 4.

[44.] *Le Devoir*, July 19, 1917, p. 2.

[45.] *Le Devoir*, March 8, 1917, p. 3.

[46.] *Le Devoir*, February 22, 1917, p. 4.

[47.] *Le Devoir*, July 19, 1917, p. 2.

[48.] MMTC, April 17, 1907.

[49.] *SQ*, 3 Geo. V (1912), chap. 58.

[50.] *La Patrie*, December 4, 1915, p. 10.

[51.] *La Patrie*, December 4, 1915, p. 10; MMTC, 1914-15, *passim.*

[52.] *Le Devoir*, October 2, 1913, p. 6.

[53.] Ecrement Record, no. 3451, September 30, 1914; MMTC, July 29, 1914; MMTC, October 7, 1914.

[54.] *SQ*, 3 Geo. V (1912), chap. 58, article 5.

[55.] *La Patrie*, December 4, 1915, p. 10.

[56.] MMTC, August 28, 1912. For the Metropolitan Parks Commission, see Terry Copp, *The Anatomy of Poverty: The Condition of the Working Class in Montreal 1897-1929* (Toronto: McClelland and Stewart, 1974).

[57.] *Le Devoir*, May 28, 1917, p. 2.

Chapter 9: The End of Maisonneuve

[1.] *Le Devoir*, November 24, 1914, p. 8.

[2.] *Le Devoir*, January 13, 1915, p. 5; *Le Devoir*, February 1, 1915, p. 5.

[3.] *Le Devoir*, November 5, 1914, p. 2; *Le Devoir*, December 3, 1914, p. 4.

4. *Le Devoir*, November 25, 1914; MMTC, January 7, 1915.

5. *Le Devoir*, January 13, 1915, p. 5; *Le Devoir*, January 21, 1915, p. 3.

6. *Le Devoir*, February 2, 1915, p. 6.

7. *Le Devoir*, May 6, 1915, p. 6.

8. Charters of the town of Maisonneuve, *passim*.

9. MMTC, January 9, 1907; MMTC, January 30, 1907; MMTC, March 20, 1907; MMTC, March 27, 1907; MMTC, August 5, 1908; MMTC, August 19, 1908; MMTC, September 11, 1908; *La Presse*, January 22, 1907, pp. 1, 9; *La Presse*, January 29, 1907, p. 11; *La Patrie*, July 14, 1908, p. 11; *La Patrie*, August 11, 1908, p. 11; *La Patrie*, August 18, 1908, p. 1.

10. *SQ*, 9 Ed. VII (1909), chap. 89, article 14, and subsequent acts dealing with Maisonneuve.

11. ACMM, files 784 and 1068-71.

12. *SQ*, 51-52 Vict. (1888), chap. 89, article 11.

13. *SQ*, 6 Geo. V (1916), chap. 47.

14. *SQ*, 7 Geo. V (1916), chap. 64.

15. *Le Devoir*, December 13, 1915, p. 2.

16. *Le Devoir*, December 16, 1915, p. 2.

17. *Le Devoir*, December 30, 1915, p. 2; *Le Devoir*, January 20, 1916, p. 2.

18. *Le Devoir*, December 12, 1915, p. 2; *Le Devoir*, March 1, 1916, p. 2.

19. *Le Devoir*, March 1, 1916, p. 6.

20. *Le Devoir*, December 2, 1916, p. 5; *Le Devoir*, January 9, 1916, p. 3.

21. *Le Devoir*, January 25, 1917, p. 2.

22. *Le Devoir*, February 2, 1917, p. 6.

23. *Le Devoir*, May 3, 1917, p. 2; *Le Devoir*, May 10, 1917, p. 2.

24. *Le Devoir*, June 30, 1917, p. 12.

25. *Le Devoir*, January 12, 1918, p. 3.

26. *Le Devoir*, February 6, 1918, pp. 2-3; *La Presse*, February 6, 1918.

27. "An Act to amend the charter of the city of Montreal," *SQ*, 8 Geo. V (1918), chap. 84.

28. Langlois, *Scandale*, *passim*.

BIBLIOGRAPHY

I. Sources

A: Manuscript Sources

1. Archives of the Town of Maisonneuve, 1884-1918

These archives constitute the main documentary foundation for a study of Maisonneuve. They are deposited in the Archives of the City of Montreal, while Maisonneuve's contracts are deposited in the Archives of the Finance Department of the City of Montreal. The series that were of greatest use to me were:

— Minutes of town council meetings (15 volumes).

— Bylaws (1 volume and 2 boxes).

— Files (62 boxes). This is the richest series, consisting of documentary files, organized by subject and containing the town's correspondence, plans, reports, newspaper clippings and various other documents.

— Assessment rolls (26 volumes). The assessment roll, drawn up yearly, provides information on property (location, name of owner and assessed value) and on heads of household (homeowner or tenant, address, occupation, number or residents in the dwelling and the assessed value of the rent).

The Maisonneuve archives also contain other documentary series which were of little use for my study: the files of the engineer J. Emile Vanier (5 boxes) and the account books: cash-book (11 volumes) and ledger (8 volumes).

The Archives of the City of Montreal also have a documentary file devoted to Maisonneuve (file 3035.23).

2. *Archives of the Village and Town of Hochelaga*

These archives are deposited in the Archives of the City of Montreal. I consulted the minutes of the Hochelaga municipal council and the file on annexation.

3. *Notarial Records*

These records are deposited at the Palais de Justice (court house) in Montreal.
— Record of the notary Marie-Gustave Ecrement, 1888-1915. Ecrement was secretary-treasurer of the town of Maisonneuve from 1889 until 1915, and almost all of Maisonneuve's contracts and other notarized documents are in his record.
— Records of other notaries. I looked at documents in the records of the following notaries: A. Perodeau, J.A. Cameron, O. Morin, F.-J. Durand, N.-D. Préfontaine.

4. *Registration Office of Hochelaga and Jacques-Cartier Counties (Registration Office of Montreal)*

I consulted the numerous documents concerning land ownership within the territory of Maisonneuve between 1874 and 1918.

5. *Archives of the Chancery of the Archdiocese of Montreal*

I consulted the decrees erecting parishes in Maisonneuve.

B: Printed Sources

1. *Newspapers*

Le Devoir. Examined systematically for the years 1911-1918.

L'Etendard. Examined for the year 1883.

The Herald. Examined for the year 1905.

The Montreal Star. Examined for the years 1904-1905.

La Patrie. Examined systematically for the years 1883-1884, 1904-1905, 1915 and 1917-1918 and sporadically for other years.

La Presse. Examined systematically for the years 1904-1910, 1915 and 1917-1918, and sporadically for other years.

2. *Other Periodicals*

Bulletin de la Chambre de commerce du district de Montréal, 1889-1914.

Gazette municipale de Montréal, 1904-1911.

3. Maps and Atlases

Canada. Department of National Defence. Mapping and Charting Establishment. *Outremont* (scale 1:25,000), map no. 31 H/12a, edition 3, 1967.

Goad, Charles Edward. *Atlas of the City of Montreal from Special Surveys and Official Plans, Showing All Buildings and Names of Owners.* 2 vols. Montreal, 1881-1890.

————— . *Atlas of the City of Montreal and Vicinity in Four Volumes: From Official Plans & Special Surveys, Showing Cadastral Numbers, Buildings & Lots.* 4 vols. Montreal: Chas. E. Goad Inc., 1912-1914.

Hopkins, Henry W. *Atlas of the City and Island of Montreal Including the Counties of Jacques Cartier and Hochelaga: From Actual Surveys, Based upon the Cadastral Plans Deposited in the Office of the Department of Crown Lands.* Provincial Surveying and Pub. Co., 1879. 107 pp.

Pinsonneault, A.R. *Atlas of the Island and City of Montreal and Ile Bizard: A Compilation of the Most Recent Cadastral Plans from the Book of Reference.* Atlas Publishing Co., (1907).

4. Government Publications

Canada. *Canada Gazette,* 1883-1918.

Canada. *Census of Canada,* 1881, 1891, 1901 and 1911.

Canada. Department of Public Works. *Report.* Published in the Sessional Papers of Canada, 1897-1908.

Canada. Department of Trade and Commerce. Census and Statistics Office. *Postal Census of Manufactures 1916.* Ottawa: King's Printer, 1917.

Canada. Harbour Commissioners of Montreal. *Annual Report.* Published in the Sessional Papers of Canada, 1890-1918.

Canada. *List of the Shareholders in the Chartered Banks of the Dominion as on the 31st December....* Published in the Sessional Papers of Canada, 1869-1899.

Canada. Port Warden at Montreal. *Report.* Published in the Sessional Papers of Canada, 1896-1918.

Canada. *Statutes of Canada,* 1883-1918.

Quebec. Board of Health of the Province of Quebec. *Annual Report.* Published in the Sessional Papers of Quebec, 1895-1917.

Quebec. *Journals of the Legislative Assembly of the Province of Quebec,* 1883 and 1899.

Quebec. *Municipal Statistics or Municipal Returns for the Year Ending 31st December....* Published in the Sessional Papers of Quebec, 1893-1917.

Quebec. *Quebec Official Gazette*, 1883-1918.

Quebec. *Revised Statutes of Quebec*, 1888-1909.

Quebec. *Statutes of Quebec*, 1883-1918.

5. Miscellaneous Publications

Ames, Herbert Brown. *The City Below the Hill*. Introduction by P.F.W. Rutherford. 1897. Toronto: University of Toronto Press, 1972. xviii + 116 pp.

Cowie, F.W. *Transportation Problem in Canada and Montreal Harbour*. London: Institution of Civil Engineers, 1915. 117 pp.

Duff, W.A. *The Montreal Electrical Hand-book*. Montreal: American Institute of Electrical Engineers, 1904. 204 pp.

Dugré, Alexandre. *Les avantages de l'agriculture*. Montreal: Ecole Sociale Populaire, 1916. 32 pp.

Field, Fred W. *Capital Investments in Canada*. Montreal and Toronto: Monetary Times of Canada, 1911. 244 pp. Chapter 7, "Municipal Borrowings in London," pp. 74-81.

Langlois, Rodrigue. *Scandale du parc Maisonneuve*. N.p., n.d. 79 pp.

La ville de Maisonneuve, P.Q., Canada, 1911: Le principal faubourg industriel de Montréal. Montreal: Commercial Magazine Co. Ltd., 1911. 38 pp.

Le diocèse de Montréal à la fin du dix-neuvième siècle. Montreal: Eusèbe Sénécal et Cie, 1900. 800 pp.

Montreal Board of Trade. *Council Report*. Annual, 1896-1914.

Montreal Directory. Montreal: John Lovell. Annual, 1883-1918.

Montréal et le congrès eucharistique. Montreal, 1910.

Montréal fin de siècle: Histoire de la métropole du Canada au dix-neuvième siècle. Montreal: Gazette Printing Company, 1899. 216 pp.

Montreal Harbour Commissioners. *Annual Report*, 1896-1918.

Montreal Illustrated, 1894. Montreal: Consolidated Illustrating Co., 1894. 367 pp.

Montreal in 1856. Montreal: John Lovell, 1856. 51 pp.

Montreal Street Railway Company, *Annual Report for the Fiscal Year Ended....*, 1904-1915.

Morgan, H.J. *Canadian Men and Women of the Time*. Toronto, 1912.

Olmsted, Frederick Law. *Report on Mount Royal Park*. New York, 1874.

Prince, Lorenzo. *Montreal, Old and New*. Montreal: International Press Syndicate, 1915. 509 pp.

Saint-Pierre, T. *Histoire du commerce canadien-français de Montréal*. Montreal, 1894. 136 pp.

Smith, F. Clifford. *L'aqueduc de Montréal: Son historique pour la période comprise entre l'année 1800 et l'année 1912*. Montreal, 1913. 57 pp.

Terril, F.W. *A Chronology of Montreal and of Canada*. Montreal: Lovell, 1893. 501 pp.

C: Oral Sources

Interviews with Dr. Edouard Desjardins conducted in June and July 1973.

II. Studies

A: Bibliographies and Reference Works

Angers, François-Albert, and Parenteau, R. *Statistiques manufacturières du Québec*. Montreal: Ecole des Hautes Etudes Commerciales, 1966. 166 pp.

Artibise, Alan F.J. and Stelter, Gilbert A. *Canada's Urban Past: A Bibliography to 1980 and Guide to Canadian Urban Studies*. Vancouver: University of British Columbia Press, 1981. 396 pp.

Beaulieu, André; Hamelin, Jean; and Bernier, Benoît. *Guide d'histoire du Canada*. Quebec: Presses de l'Université Laval, 1969. 540 pp.

Beaulieu, André, and Morley, William F.E. *Histoires locales et régionales canadiennes des origines à 1950. II. La province de Québec*. Toronto: University of Toronto Press, 1971. 408 pp.

Durocher, René, and Linteau, Paul-André. *Histoire du Québec: Bibliographie sélective (1867-1970)*. Montreal: Boréal Express, 1970. 189 pp.

Lessard, Marc-André, ed. "Bibliographie des villes du Québec." *Recherches sociographiques* 9, no. 2 (Jan.-Aug. 1968), pp. 143-209.

Linteau, Paul-André, and Thivierge, Jean. *Montréal au 19e siècle: Bibliographie*. Montreal: Groupe de Recherche sur la Société Montréalaise au 19e Siècle, 1972. 79 pp.

Magnan, Hormidas. *Dictionnaire historique et géographique des paroisses, missions et municipalités de la province de Québec.* Arthabaska, Quebec: Imprimerie d'Arthabaska, 1925. 738 pp.

Roy, Antoine. "Bibliographie des monographies et histoires de paroisses." In *Rapport de l'Archiviste de la province de Québec,* 1937-38, pp. 254-364.

Urquhart, M.C., and Buckley, K.A.H. *Historical Statistics of Canada.* Toronto: Macmillan, 1965. 672 pp.

B: Methodological and Comparative Studies

Artibise, Alan F.J. "Boosterism and the Development of Prairie Cities 1867-1913." In *Town and City: Aspects of Western Canadian Urban Development.* Regina: Canadian Plains Research Center, 1981, pp. 209-35.

————. *Winnipeg: A Social History of Urban Growth, 1874-1914.* Montreal: McGill-Queen's University Press, 1975. 382 pp.

Bastié, Jean. *La croissance de la banlieue parisienne.* Paris: Presses Universitaires de France, 1964. 624 pp.

Beaujeu-Garnier, Jacqueline, and Chabot, Georges. *Traité de géographie urbaine.* Paris: Armand Colin, 1963. 493 pp.

Callow, A.B., ed. *American Urban History: An Interpretive Reader with Commentaries.* New York: Oxford University Press, 1969. 674 pp.

Dyos, H.J., ed. *The Study of Urban History.* London: Edward Arnold, 1968.

Frisch, Michael H. "L'histoire urbaine américaine: reflexions sur les tendances récentes." *Annales. Economies. Sociétés. Civilisations* 25, no. 4 (July-Aug. 1970), pp. 880-96.

George, Peter J., and Oksanen, Ernest H. "Recent developments in the quantification of Canadian economic history." *Social History* 4 (November 1969), pp. 79-95.

George, Pierre. *Population et peuplement.* Paris: Presses Universitaires de France, 1969. 212 pp.

Glaab, Charles N., and Brown, A. Theodore. *A History of Urban America.* New York: Macmillan, 1967. 328 pp.

Goheen, Peter G. "The American City: Some Problems of Historical Interpretation." Paper delivered to the Historical Urbanization in North America Conference, York University, January 1973. Mimeographed. 30 pp.

————. *Victorian Toronto 1850 to 1900: Pattern and Process of Growth.* Chicago: University of Chicago, Department of Geography, 1970. 278 pp.

Halbwachs, Maurice. *Les expropriations et le prix des terrains à Paris (1860-1900)*. Paris: Publications de la société nouvelle de librairie et d'édition E. Cornely, 1909.

Handlin, Oscar, and Burchard, John, eds. *The Historian and the City*. Cambridge, Mass.: MIT Press, 1963. 299 pp.

Hauser, P.M., and Schnore, Leo F., eds. *The Study of Urbanization*. New York: John Wiley, 1965. 554 pp.

Hayward, Robert J. "Sources for Urban Historical Research: Insurance Plans and Land Uses Atlases." *Urban History Review/Revue d'histoire urbaine* 1 (May 1973), pp. 2-9.

Hirsch, Werner Z. *Urban Economic Analysis*. New York: McGraw-Hill, 1973. 450 pp.

International Labour Office. *International Standard Classification of Occupations*. Geneva, 1969. 355 pp.

Jackson, Kenneth T., and Schultz, Stanley K., eds. *Cities in American History*. New York: Alfred A. Knopf, 1972. 508 pp.

Katz, Michael. "The People of a Canadian City: 1851-1852." *Canadian Historical Review* 53, no. 4 (December 1972), pp. 402—26.

Kramer, Paul, and Holborn, Frederick L., eds. *The City in American Life: A Historical Anthology*. New York: Capricorn, 1970. 384 pp.

Lamarche, François. *Pour une analyse marxiste de la question urbaine*. Quebec: Conseil des Oeuvres et du Bien-être de Québec, 1972. 251 pp.

Ledrut, Raymond. *Sociologie urbaine*. Paris: Presses Universitaires de France, 1968. 222 pp.

Lipietz, Alain. *Le tribut foncier urbain*. Paris: Maspero, 1974. 290 pp.

McKelvey, Blake. *The Urbanization of America 1860-1915*. New Brunswick, N.J.: Rutgers University Press, 1963. 370 pp.

Mouchez, Philippe. *Démographie*. Paris: Presses Universitaires de France, 1968. 262 pp.

Mumford, Lewis. *The City in History*. New York: Harcourt, Brace and World, 1961. 657 pp.

Pressat, Roland. *Démographie sociale*. Paris: Presses Universitaires de France, 1971. 168 pp.

Rostow, Walt W. *Stages of Economic Growth: A Non-Communist Manifesto*. Cambridge: Cambridge University Press, 1960. 178 pp.

Saul, S.B. *The Myth of the Great Depression, 1873-1896*. London: Macmillan, 1969. 63 pp.

Schnore, Leo F., ed. *The New Urban History: Quantitative Explorations by American Historians*. Princeton, N.J.: Princeton University Press, 1975. 284 pp.

Stave, Bruce M. "Interview: Urban History in Canada; A Conversation with Alan F.J. Artibise." *Urban History Review/Revue d'histoire urbaine* 8, no. 3 (February 1980), pp. 110-43.

————. "A Conversation with Gilbert A. Stelter: Urban History in Canada." *Journal of Urban History* 6, no. 4 (August 1980), pp. 77-210.

Stelter, Gilbert A. "The Historian's Approach to Canada's Urban Past." *Histoire sociale/ Social History* 7, no. 13 (May 1974), pp. 5-22.

Thernstrom, Stephan, and Sennett, Richard, eds. *Nineteenth-Century Cities: Essays in the New Urban History*. New Haven: Yale University Press, 1969. 430 pp.

C: Quebec: Economic, Social and Ideological History

Acheson, T.W. "The Social Origins of Canadian Industrialism: A Study in the Structure of Entrepreneurship." PhD thesis, University of Toronto, 1971. pp. 114-86.

Angers, François-Albert. "Naissance de la pensée économique au Canada français." *Revue d'histoire de l'Amérique française* 15, no. 2 (September 1961), pp. 204-29.

Bernier, Jacques. "La condition des travailleurs, 1851-1896." In *Les travailleurs québécois, 1851-1896*, edited by Jean Hamelin, pp. 31-60. Montreal: Presses de l'Université du Québec, 1973.

Bertram, G.W. "Economic Growth in Canadian Industry, 1870-1915: The Staple Model." In *Approaches to Canadian Economic History*, edited by W.T. Easterbrook and M.H. Watkins, pp. 74-98. Toronto: McClelland and Stewart, 1967.

Brunet, Michel. "Trois dominantes de la pensée canadienne-française: l'agriculturalisme, l'anti-étatisme et le messianisme." In *La présence anglaise et les Canadiens*, pp. 113-66. Montreal: Beauchemin, 1964.

Côté, Real. "L'évolution de l'industrie de la chaussure en cuir, au Canada." Licence thesis (commercial science), Ecole des Hautes Etudes Commerciales, Montreal. In *Thèses*, 3, pp. 144-234. Montreal: HEC, 1952.

Creighton, Donald G. *British North America at Confederation*. Ottawa, 1939. 104 pp.

Dales, John H. *Hydroelectricity and Industrial Development: Quebec, 1898-1940*. Cambridge, Mass.: Harvard University Press, 1957. 269 pp.

Dandurand, Pierre. "Analyse de l'idéologie d'un journal nationaliste canadien-français: Le Devoir, 1911-1956." MA thesis (sociology), University of Montreal, 1961.

Desrosiers, Richard. *Le travailleur québécois et le syndicalisme*. Montreal: Presses de l'Université du Québec, 1973. 156 pp.

Easterbrook W.T., and Aitken, Hugh G.J. *Canadian Economic History*. Toronto: Macmillan, 1967. 606 pp.

Faucher, Albert. *Québec en Amérique au XIXe siècle: Essai sur les caractères économiques de la Laurentie*. Montreal: Fides, 1973. 247 pp.

————, and Lamontagne, Maurice. "Histoire de l'industrialisation." In *Le retard du Québec et l'infériorité économique des Canadiens français*, edited by René Durocher and Paul-André Linteau, pp. 25-42. Montreal: Boréal Express, 1971.

Hamelin, Jean, ed. *Les travailleurs québécois, 1851-1896*. Montreal: Presses de l'Université du Québec, 1973. 221 pp.

————, Larocque, Paul, and Rouillard, Jacques. *Répertoire des grèves dans la province de Québec au XIXe siècle*. Montreal: Presses de l'Ecole des Hautes Etudes Commerciales, 1970. 168 pp.

————, and Roby, Yves. *Histoire économique du Québec 1851-1896*. Montreal: Fides, 1969. 436 pp.

Harvey, Fernand. "Nouvelles perspectives sur l'histoire sociale du Québec." *Revue d'histoire de l'Amerique française* 24, no. 4 (March 1971), pp. 567-81.

————. *Révolution industrielle et travailleurs: Une enquête sur les rapports entre le capital et le travail au Québec à la fin du XIXe siècle*. Montreal: Boréal Express, 1978. 347 pp.

Heintzman, R.R. "The Struggle for Life: The French Daily Press of Montreal and the Problems of Economic Growth in the Age of Laurier, 1896-1911." PhD thesis (history), York University, Toronto, 1977.

Henripin, Jacques, and Péron, Yves. "The Demographic Transition of the Province of Quebec." In *Population and Social Change*, edited by D.V. Glass and Roger Revelle, pp. 213-31. London: Edward Arnold, 1972.

Hogue, Clarence; Bolduc, André; and Larouche, Daniel. *Québec: Un siècle d'électricité*. Montreal: Libre Expression, 1979. 405 pp.

Hughes, Everett C. *French Canada in Transition*. 1943. Chicago: University of Chicago Press, Phoenix Books, 1963. 227 pp.

Letarte, Jacques. *Atlas d'histoire économique et sociale du Québec, 1851-1901*. Montreal: Fides, 1971. 44 maps.

Levitt, Joseph. *Henri Bourassa and the Golden Calf: The Social Program of the Nationalists of Quebec (1900-1914)*. Ottawa: Editions de l'Université d'Ottawa, 1969. 178 pp.

Linteau, Paul-André. "La pensée économique et sociale de Georges Pelletier, 1910-1929." MA thesis (history), University of Montreal, 1969. 197 pp.

————; Durocher, René; and Robert, Jean-Claude. *Quebec: A History 1867-1929*. Translated by Robert Chodos. Toronto: James Lorimer and Co., 1983. 602 pp.

Parenteau, Roland. "Les idées économiques et sociales de Bourassa." In *La pensée de Henri Bourassa*, pp. 166-79. Montreal: L'Action Nationale, 1954.

Raynauld, André. *Croissance et structure économiques de la province de Québec*. Quebec: Department of Industry and Commerce, 1961. 657 pp.

Ryan, William. *The Clergy and Economic Growth in Quebec (1896-1914)*. Quebec: Presses de l'Université Laval, 1966. 348 pp.

Saint-Pierre, Arthur. *L'organisation ouvrière dans la Province de Québec*. Montreal: Ecole Sociale Populaire, 1913.

Wade, Mason. *The French Canadians 1760-1967*. 2 vols. Rev. ed. Toronto: Macmillan of Canada, 1968.

D: Aspects of Urbanization in Quebec

Artibise, Alan F.J., and Stelter, Gilbert, eds. *The Usable Urban Past: Planning and Politics in the Modern Canadian City*. Toronto: Macmillan, 1979. 383 pp.

Dorion, C.N. *Evolution de la législation générale et spéciale concernant les corporations municipales de la province de Québec: Partie d'un mémoire présenté à la Commission Tremblay par l'Union des municipalités de la province de Québec*. 3 vols. Quebec, 1954. Part 2, chapter 4.

Drolet, Antonio. *La ville de Québec: histoire municipale. III: De l'incorporation a la Confédération (1833- 1867)*. Quebec: Société historique de Québec, 1967. 144 pp.

Fortin, Gerald. "Le Québec: une ville à inventer." *Recherches sociographiques* 9, nos. 1-2 (Jan.-Aug. 1968), pp. 11-21.

"La communauté urbaine: une formule d'organisation et de gestion des agglomérations." *Quebec Yearbook 1971*, pp. 1-40. Quebec: Editeur Officiel du Québec, 1971.

Linteau, Paul-André. "L'histoire urbaine au Québec: bilan et tendances." *Revue d'histoire urbaine/ Urban History Review* 1 (February 1972), pp. 7-10.

Martin, Jean-Paul. "Le développement du réseau urbain québécois, 1830-1910." Paper delivered to the Historical Urbanization in North America Conference, York University, January 1973. Mimeographed.

————. "Villes et régions du Québec au XIXe siècle: Approche géographique." Doctorat de troisième cycle thesis (geography), Louis-Pasteur University, Strasbourg.

Robert, Jean-Claude. "L'activité économique de Barthélémy Joliette et la fondation du village d'Industrie (Joliette) 1822-1850." MA thesis (history), University of Montreal, 1971. 183 pp.

————. "Un seigneur entrepreneur, Barthélémy Joliette et la fondation du village d'Industrie (Joliette), 1822-1850." *Revue d'histoire de l'Amérique française* 26, no. 3 (December 1972), pp. 375-95.

Rudin, Ronald. "The Development of Four Quebec Towns 1840-1914: A Study of Urban and Economic Growth in Quebec." PhD thesis (history), York University, Toronto, 1977.

————. "Land Ownership and Urban Growth: The Experience of Two Quebec Towns, 1840-1914." *Urban History Review/Revue d'histoire urbaine* 8, no. 2 (October 1979), pp. 23-46.

Rutherford, Paul. "Tomorrow's Metropolis: The Urban Reform Movement in Canada, 1880-1920." In Canadian Historical Association, *Historical Papers* (1971), pp. 203-24. Ottawa, 1972.

Stelter, Gilbert, and Artibise, Alan F.J., eds. *The Canadian City: Essays in Urban History.* Toronto: McClelland and Stewart, 1977. 454 pp.

Stone, L.O. *Urban Development in Canada: An Introduction to the Demographic Aspects.* Ottawa: Dominion Bureau of Statistics, 1967. 293 pp.

Trotier, Louis. "Caractères de l'organisation urbaine de la province de Québec." *Revue de géographie de Montréal* 18, no. 2 (1964), pp. 279-85.

E: Montreal: General Works

Atherton, William Henry. *Montreal, 1535-1914.* 3 vols. Montreal: S.J. Clarke, 1914.

Beauregard, Ludger. *Montréal: Guide d'excursions/Field Guide.* Montreal: Presses de l'Université de Montréal, 1972. 197 pp.

Blanchard, Raoul. *L'Ouest du Canada français: Montréal et sa région.* Montreal: Beauchemin, 1953. 399 pp.

Cooper, John Irwin. *Montreal: A Brief History*. Montreal: McGill-Queen's University Press, 1969. 217 pp.

Culliton, John, ed. *Leacock's Montreal*. Toronto: McClelland and Stewart, 1963. 322 pp.

Dechêne, Louise. "La croissance de Montréal au XVIIIe siècle." *Revue d'histoire de l'Amérique française* 27, no. 2 (September 1973), pp. 163-79.

————. *Habitants et marchands de Montréal au XVIIe siècle*. Paris and Montreal: Plon, 1974. 588 pp.

Déry, Jacques. *Tableaux schématiques de l'évolution des municipalités de la région de Montréal*. Montreal: Bureau de Recherches Economiques, 1970. 38 pp.

Jenkins, Kathleen. *Montreal: Island City of the St. Lawrence*. Garden City, N.Y.: Doubleday & Co., 1966. 559 pp.

Lamothe, J.-C. *Histoire de la corporation de la cité de Montréal*. Montreal: Montreal Printing & Publishing Co., 1903. 860 pp.

Marsan, Jean-Claude. *Montreal in Evolution: Historical Analysis of Montreal's Architecture and Urban Environment*. Montreal: McGill-Queen's University Press, 1981, 423 pp.

Montréal économique. Montreal: Fides/Ecole des Hautes Etudes Commerciales, 1943. 430 pp.

Robert, Jean-Claude. "Montréal 1821-1871: Aspects de l'urbanisation." Doctorat de troisième cycle thesis, Ecole des Hautes Etudes en Sciences Sociales, Paris, 1977. 491 pp.

Roberts, Leslie. *Montreal: From Mission Colony to World City*. Toronto: Macmillan, 1969. 356 pp.

Rumilly, Robert. *Histoire de Montréal*. Montreal: Fides, 1972. Vol. 3. 527 pp.

Tulchinsky, G.J.J. *The River Barons: Montreal Businessmen and the Growth of Industry and Transportation 1837-1853*. Toronto: University of Toronto Press, 1977. 310 pp.

F: Montreal: Specialized Studies

"A Brief History of the Montreal Street Railway Company from 1861 to 1910." In *Annual Report of the Montreal Street Railway Company for the Fiscal Year Ended 30th September 1910*, pp. 25-42.

Atherton, William Henry. *History of the Harbour Front of Montreal since its Discovery by Jacques Cartier in 1535*. Montreal: Ligue du progrès civique, 1935. 16 pp.

Bastien, Roméo. "Monographie de la tuilerie 'Montreal Terra Cotta Limited'." Licence thesis (commercial science), Ecole des Hautes Etudes Commerciales, Montreal. In *Théses*, supplement, pp. 1-82. Montreal: HEC, 1947.

Beauregard, Ludger. *Toponymie de la région métropolitaine de Montréal*. Quebec: Department of Lands and Forests, 1968. 225 pp.

Benoist, Emile. *Monographies économiques*. Montreal: Le Devoir, 1925. 272 pp.

Bernard, Jean-Paul; Linteau, Paul-André; and Robert, Jean-Claude. "Les tablettes statistiques de Jacques Viger (1825)." In Groupe de recherche sur la société montréalaise au 19e siècle, *Rapport 1972-1973*. Montreal: University of Quebec at Montreal, 1973. 22 pp.

Bourassa, Guy. "The Political Elite of Montreal: From Aristocracy to Democracy." In *Politics and Government of Urban Canada: Selected Readings*, edited by Lionel D. Feldman and Michael D. Golderick, pp. 124-34. Toronto: Methuen, 1976.

Brouillard, Pierre. "Le développement du port de Montréal." MA thesis (history), University of Quebec at Montreal, 1976.

Burgess, Joanne. "L'industrie de la chaussure à Montréal: 1840-1870 — le passage de l'artisanat à la fabrique." *Revue d'histoire de l'Amérique française* 31, no. 2 (September 1977), pp. 187-210.

Copp, Terry. *The Anatomy of Poverty: The Condition of the Working Class in Montreal 1897-1929*. Toronto: McClelland and Stewart, 1974. 192 pp.

Cross, D. Suzanne. "The Irish in Montreal, 1867-1896." MA thesis, McGill University, Montreal, 1969.

————. "The Neglected Majority: The Changing Role of Women in Ninteenth-Century Montreal," *Histoire sociale/Social History* VI, 12 (November 1973), pp. 202-33.

De Bonville, Jean. *Jean-Baptiste Gagnepetit: Les travailleurs montréalais à la fin du 19e siècle*. Montreal: L'Aurore, 1975. 253 pp.

Gauthier, P. "Montréal et ses quartiers municipaux." *Bulletin des recherches historiques* 67, no. 4 (Oct.-Nov. 1961), pp. 115-35.

Henripin, Jacques. "L'inégalité sociale devant la mort: la mortinatalité et la mortalité infantile à Montréal." *Recherches sociographiques* 2, no. 1 (Jan.-Mar. 1961), pp. 3-33.

Lajeunesse, J.M. *Histoire du transport en commun à Montréal/History of Public Transportation in Montreal*. Montreal: Publications Apollon, 1973. 159 pp.

Lavigne, Marie, and Stoddart, Jennifer. "Analyse du travail féminin à Montréal entre les deux guerres." MA thesis (history), University of Quebec at Montreal, 1973. 265 pp.

Linteau, Paul-André. "Le développement du port de Montréal au début du 20e siècle." In Canadian Historical Association, *Historical Papers* (1972), pp. 181-205.

————. "Histoire de la ville de Maisonneuve (1883-1918)." PhD thesis (history), University of Montreal, 1975. 427 pp.

————. "Quelques reflexions autour de la bourgeoisie québécoise 1850-1914." *Revue d'histoire de l'Amérique française* 30, no. 1 (June 1976), pp. 55-56.

————. "Town Planning in Maisonneuve." *Canadian Collector* 13, no. 1 (Jan.-Feb. 1978), pp. 82-85.

————; Bernard, Jean-Paul; and Robert, Jean-Claude. "L'industrialisation de Montréal au 19e siècle." Paper delivered at the conference of the Institut d'Histoire de l'Amérique Française, Montreal, October 1978.

————, and Robert, Jean-Claude. "Land Ownership and Society in Montreal: An Hypothesis." In *The Canadian City: Essays in Urban History*, edited by Gilbert Stelter and Alan F.J. Artibise, pp. 17-36. Toronto: McClelland and Stewart, 1977.

————, and Robert, Jean-Claude. "Les divisions territoriales à Montréal au 19e siècle." In Groupe de recherche sur la société montréalaise au 19e siècle, *Rapport 1972-1973*. Montreal: University of Quebec at Montreal, 1973. 32 pp.

Martel, Eve. "L'industrie à Montréal en 1871." MA thesis (history), University of Quebec at Montreal, 1976. 107 pp.

Masters, D.C. "Toronto vs Montreal: The Struggle for Financial Hegemony 1860-1875." *Canadian Historical Review* 21, no. 1 (March 1941), pp. 133-46.

Pierre-Deschênes, Claudine. "La tuberculose au Québec au debut du XXe siècle: problème social et réponse réformiste." MA thesis (history), University of Quebec at Montreal, 1980.

Russel, D.J. "H.B. Ames as Municipal Reformer." MA thesis (history), McGill University, 1971.

Séguin, Georges F. *Toponymie*. Montreal: Service d'urbanisme (City Planning Department), 1966. 149 pp.

Tombs, L.C. *National Problems of Canada: The Port of Montreal*. Toronto: Macmillan, 1926. 178 pp.

Trepanier, Léon. "Figures de maires: Alphonse Desjardins." *Les cahiers des dix* 23 (1958), pp. 261-83.

Versailles, Yvan. "Développement industriel de Montreal-Est." Thesis, Ecole des Hautes Etudes Commerciales. In *Thèses* 8, pp. 179-242. Montreal: HEC, 1938.

INDEX